A VERGIL Workbook

—Second Edition—

Teacher's Manual

Latin Literature Workbook Series

A Series Edited by LeaAnn A. Osburn and Donald E. Sprague

A Horace Workbook (2005)
A Horace Workbook Teacher's Manual (2006)
An Ovid Workbook (2006)
An Ovid Workbook Teacher's Manual (2007)
A Catullus Workbook (2006)
A Catullus Workbook Teacher's Manual (2007)
A Cicero Workbook (2006)
A Cicero Workbook Teacher's Manual (2007)
A Vergil Workbook 2nd Edition (2012)
A Vergil Workbook 2nd Edition Teacher's Manual (2012)
A Caesar Workbook (2012)
A Caesar Workbook Teacher's Manual (2012)

A VERGIL Workbook

—Second Edition—
Teacher's Manual

Katherine Bradley
& Barbara Weiden Boyd

Bolchazy-Carducci Publishers, Inc.
Mundelein, Illinois USA

Series Editors: LeaAnn A. Osburn and Donald E. Sprague
Volume General Editor: Donald E. Sprague
Volume Contributing Editor: Laurel De Vries
Design & Layout: Adam Phillip Velez

A Vergil Workbook Teacher's Manual
Second Edition

Katherine Bradley and Barbara Weiden Boyd

AP is a registered trademark of the College Entrance Examination Board, which was not involved in the production of, and does not endorse, this product.

© 2012 Bolchazy-Carducci Publishers, Inc.
All rights reserved.

Bolchazy-Carducci Publishers, Inc.
1570 Baskin Road
Mundelein, Illinois 60060
www.bolchazy.com

Printed in the United States of America
2012
by Publishers' Graphics

ISBN 978-0-86516-775-9

CONTENTS

Foreword vii

Preface to the Student Workbook ix

Preface to the Teacher's Manual xv

Selections from the *Aeneid* with Exercises and Answers 1

   Lesson 1: Book 1.1–33 2

   Lesson 2: Book 1.34–80 10

   Lesson 3: Book 1.81–131 18

   Lesson 4: Book 1.132–179 26

   Lesson 5: Book 1.180–209 34

   Lesson 6: Book 1.418–440 42

   Lesson 7: Book 1.494–538 48

   Lesson 8: Book 1.539–578 54

   Lesson 9: Book 2.40–56 62

   Lesson 10: Book 2.201–249 68

   Lesson 11: Book 2.268–297 76

   Lesson 12: Book 2.559–620 82

   Lesson 13: Book 4.160–218 94

   Lesson 14: Book 4.259–299 104

   Lesson 15: Book 4.300–361 112

   Lesson 16: Book 4.659–705 122

   Lesson 17: Book 6.295–332 130

   Lesson 18: Book 6.384–425 138

- Lesson 19: Book 6.450–476 146
- Lesson 20: Book 6.847–899 152

Sight Passages with Exercises, Multiple Choice
Questions, and Answers 161
- Exercise in Sight Reading and Sight Passage #1 162
- Exercise in Sight Reading and Sight Passage #2 166
- Exercise in Sight Reading and Sight Passage #3 170
- Sight Passage #4 174
- Sight Passage #5 176
- Sight Passage #6 178
- Sight Passage #7 182
- Sight Passage #8 184
- Sight Passage #9 186
- Sight Passage #10 188
- Sight Passage #11 190
- Sight Passage #12 192

Vocabulary 195

FOREWORD

All Latin teachers want their students to read ancient authors in the original. Yet to study the authentic Latin of an ancient Roman author is a complex task. It requires comprehension of the text and its grammatical underpinnings; an understanding of the world events and the culture in which the work of literature was produced; an ability to recognize the figures of speech the author uses and to grasp the impact they have on the text; sensitivity to the way sound effects, including meter if a passage is poetry, interact with the meaning of the text; and the ability to probe whatever thoughts and ideas the author may be expressing. To be successful in this multifaceted task, students need not only a comprehensive textbook but also exercises of different kinds, with which to practice their newly developing literary and critical skills.

Students often need extensive drill and practice material—something not available in the traditional Latin author textbook—to help them master the grammar and syntax of the Latin text as well as the literary skills that the text demands of its readers. Teachers, too, no matter how many questions they ask in class to help their students analyze the syntax and the literary qualities of the text, often need and want more questions to be available. Realizing this need on the part of both students and teachers, Bolchazy-Carducci Publishers developed a series of workbooks to accompany Advanced Placement author textbooks. Initially, the series comprised five workbooks, one for each Advanced Placement author at the time: Catullus, Cicero, Horace, Ovid, and Vergil. A team of authors—one, a university scholar with special expertise in the Latin literary text and the other, a high school Advanced Placement Latin teacher—wrote each workbook.

Upon the announcement of a major revision of the AP Latin Curriculum beginning with the 2012–2013 school year, Bolchazy-Carducci commissioned the revision of *A Vergil Workbook* and the development of the new *A Caesar Workbook*. These workbooks contain the Latin text as delineated on the Advanced Placement Syllabus.

All the texts in the series provide exercises that drill grammar, syntax, and figures of speech. In addition, multiple choice questions that focus on the student's comprehension of the passage and on items of literary analysis are included. The workbooks also feature scansion practice, essays to write, and other short analysis questions in each section. By reading and answering these types of questions, students will gain experience with the types of questions that are used in upper level Latin classes on the college level as well as on the Advanced Placement Examinations. Students at the college level will also benefit from the additional practice offered in the workbooks.

These workbooks contain neither textual notes nor vocabulary on the page with the text nor on the facing page. The absence of these traditional features of textbooks will allow students, after reading the Latin passage in the textbook, to practice in the workbook what they have learned and to assess how much they have mastered already and what needs more study. The workbooks do, however, contain a Latin to English Vocabulary at the back of the book.

We are confident that this series of workbooks has a unique role to play in fostering students' understanding of authentic Latin text and will be a significant addition to the Advanced Placement and college materials that already exist.

LeaAnn A. Osburn and
Donald E. Sprague
Series Editors

PREFACE TO THE STUDENT WORKBOOK

This is a revision of the second in the series of workbooks on Advanced Placement (AP) Latin authors published by Bolchazy-Carducci Publishers. As collaborators on this project, we have greatly enjoyed the privilege of working on an author and a poem so dear to our minds and hearts. Our long friendship has indeed been founded on a shared dedication to the study and reading of Latin literature, and Vergil's *Aeneid* holds a unique place for both of us as a source of personal and professional inspiration. This common bond was reinforced in summer 2002, when one of us directed and the other participated in a workshop on Vergil for AP Latin teachers, offered through the Taft Education Center but held in Rome, the city that, like Vergil himself, witnessed Augustus's ascent to supreme power, and that, again like Vergil, continues to be shaped profoundly by that historical event. Since then, we have spent many hours discussing how best to help students attain the same love for Vergil that we enjoy, and we have been guided accordingly in our design of this workbook. It is a privilege to share the results of our labors with readers new to Vergil.

This workbook is designed to provide Latin students with exercises to accompany and support their reading of the selections from the *Aeneid* that form the basis of the AP Vergil syllabus. It is not, however, purely an AP workbook: we hope that its audience will include both AP Latin students and others who, in any classroom context whatsoever, have reason to find exercises in close reading to be of use. Likewise, this workbook can be used in tandem both with textbooks designed specifically with AP students' needs in mind and with textbooks that encompass a wider readership, including those commonly used on the college level. The Latin text used throughout this workbook is based on R. A. B. Mynors's Oxford text (1969; reprinted with corrections 1972), but incorporates the same cosmetic alterations found in Barbara Weiden Boyd, *Vergil's Aeneid: Selected Readings from Books 1, 2, 4, and 6* (Bolchazy-Carducci Publishers, 2012): the initial letters of words beginning a new sentence are printed in the upper case; and third-declension accusative plural nouns and adjectives ending in -is are here printed as ending in -es. The vocabulary list found at the end of this workbook is also taken from *Vergil's Aeneid: Selected Readings from Books 1, 2, 4, and 6* by Barbara Weiden Boyd (Bolchazy-Carducci Publishers, 2012).

The selections from the *Aeneid* included in this book have been divided into twenty units, or chapters. These divisions are not meant to hold great interpretive significance, nor do they necessarily conform to the divisions found in most textbooks. Rather, our goal has been to provide a lesson of appropriate length and complexity to accompany weekly assignments when spread out over an academic year of approximately thirty weeks. While we hope that this structure will add to the workbook's usefulness in the average Latin classroom, we recognize that few Vergil classes are "average" and that every teacher is likely to have a slightly different pace and set of priorities, as well as a unique group of students to work with, in any given year. The allotment of time suggested for answering some of the questions, therefore, is meant simply as a rough guideline; teachers and students alike should modify these suggestions in accordance with their unique needs and pace. Indeed, we encourage all users of this book to adapt it freely to their own needs and classroom settings, and to see it as a source of inspiration for their own creative innovations rather than as a prescriptive taskmaster.

In each lesson, we provide most or all of the following types of questions:

I. Comprehension Questions
II. Multiple Choice Questions
III. Translation Exercises
IV. Essay Questions
V. Scansion Exercises
VI. Short Answer Questions

Under the last of these headings can be found a variety of question types, including:

VIa. Translation and Analysis Questions
VIb. Questions on Literary Style
VIc. Identification Questions Covering Names, Places, and Historical and Mythical Characters and Events
VId. Questions on Grammar and Syntax

Some of these question types (II–IV in particular) are based closely on the types of questions found on the AP Latin Examination. All of these question types provide practice and review of the skills required to succeed on the Vergil portion of the AP Latin examination, as well as in other classroom contexts with other tests of proficiency. Our combined experience of many years with the AP Latin program nonetheless makes it clear to us that, while the AP Latin exam provides a thorough and reliable means to assess a variety of skills and types of knowledge, it does not presume to ask every possible type of question or to assess every measurable aspect of Latin reading comprehension. We have therefore provided many questions in this workbook that we are confident will make students better readers of Vergil, and that are at least sometimes meant to provoke thought in ways not easy to quantify through standardized tests. For an authoritative explanation of the format of the AP Latin Examinations teachers and students alike are urged to consult the publications of the College Entrance Examination Board, available through its website (apcentral.collegeboard.com). These publications also include examples of some of the examinations administered in recent years and a variety of supplemental materials to support the Advanced Placement experience.

I. Comprehension Questions

These questions ask, in an order that follows the sequence of the passage under review, about a wide variety of topics discoverable from close reading of the text. Some incorporate analysis of grammar and/or syntax, or draw attention to Vergil's diction; others require translation, interpretation, and analysis; and others invite the reader to express his or her personal reaction to a given event or scene. Many of these questions could be used as the basis for a more lengthy essay question should a teacher wish to do so; but as they stand, most of these questions can be used for homework or in-class assignments, to be completed by students working either individually or in small groups.

II. Multiple Choice Questions

Some of these questions ask about the same features as do the multiple choice questions on the Advanced Placement Examination: translation or interpretation, grammar, lexical details, allusions and references, meter, and figures of speech. Others, focusing primarily on comprehension and translation skills, require a higher degree of precision about grammar and syntax than is normally tested on the AP Latin Examination; and some are intended for quicker completion, especially in those cases when the student is required to choose the correct response from two rather than four options. The AP Latin Examination usually contains fifty multiple choice questions to be answered in an hour.

Because students generally find the multiple choice section of the AP exam to be challenging, we believe that they can profit from the extensive practice with multiple choice questions provided here. In addition, a special feature of this workbook is a set of multiple choice questions for twelve "sight" passages found at back of the book.

III. Translation Exercises

These exercises test the translation skills of students who have been reading the selections included here in a Latin course. Some of the passages tested here are of approximately the same length as those found on the AP Examination; others are longer or shorter. Even when not explicitly directed to do so, students should aim to provide a translation that is as literal as possible. For this reason, they should not change active verbs to passive voice or vice versa, or alter verb tenses. In translating the historical present, students may use either the English present tense for Latin present or consistently convert to past tense in English. Students should stay as close as possible to the range of standard definitions of words and should not impose from the context a sense that the word does not have.

IV. Essay Questions

Most of the essay questions in this workbook call for the in-depth literary analysis of a passage or entire selection. They are best undertaken either alongside the preparation and translation of the passages to which they pertain or after students have already discussed the passage or selection in class. Some essay questions also draw on students' familiarity with the content of a given book as a whole, that is, including those sections not read in Latin; when such questions appear, students should be encouraged to demonstrate their broader interpretive and analytical skills. These questions are intended to offer students practice with general comprehension essays, and invite students to synthesize their knowledge of the parts of the *Aeneid* read in English together with the Latin selections on the syllabus. This second edition also provides three essays that require students to synthesize their analysis of two different passages from the *Aeneid*.

Practice with these kinds of essays will build students' analytical skills by giving them practice in:

- supporting their essay with relevant details and evidence drawn from throughout a passage
- documenting the points in their essay with accurate citation of the Latin
- explaining (where appropriate) how the use of language and/or stylistic features contributes to analysis of the passage.

The AP Latin exam essays always pair two passages for discussion and analysis; these pairs consist of one of the following combinations: one passage from Vergil and one from Caesar, two passages from Caesar, or two passages from Vergil. All the essay questions in this workbook will help students prepare for essays that are based in whole or in part on Vergil. However, with the exception of three essays that require students to discuss two passages from Vergil, the essays in the workbook are not identical in format to the current AP Latin exam essay.

Wherever possible and appropriate, strong essay answers should

- address the question exactly as it is asked, especially if more than one task is entailed;
- analyze, not merely describe, the passage(s) or selection(s) being tested;
- address the passage(s) or selection(s) as a whole;
- and support claims and arguments with evidence drawn from the Latin text. In other words, when answering essay questions covering a specific passage or selection of lines, students should copy the relevant Latin words or cite the appropriate line numbers AND translate or paraphrase closely enough so that their comprehension of the Latin text is evident.

V. Scansion Exercises

Once they have learned dactylic hexameter, students can practice scansion with any excerpt from Vergil, whether or not they have translated it. Following the format of the Advanced Placement Examination, we do not provide macrons/long marks in the Latin text. We also include in these exercises some lines of unusual metrical difficulty, so that teachers may have the opportunity if they wish it to draw attention to Vergil's expressive use of metrical effects.

VIa. Translation and Analysis Questions

This question type appears only occasionally and is a logical extension of the Translation Exercises (see above, III). Students are first asked to translate, and in doing so should follow the guidelines for translation offered above in III. They are then asked to demonstrate how this translation can be used to support the analysis and interpretation of the passage under consideration.

VIb. Questions on Literary Style

The terms "figure of speech" and "rhetorical device" are used in this workbook to refer to figurative uses of language in general, whether they involve nonstandard senses of words (sometimes called tropes or figures of thought) or arrangements of words (sometimes called rhetorical figures or figures of speech). We use these terms in the broad sense in order to encompass not only all the literary devices for which students will be held responsible on the Advanced Placement Examination, but also devices that do not appear on the current list of figures of speech to be tested on the Advanced Placement Examination. Because we envision an audience for this workbook that includes not only students preparing for the AP Latin Examination but others who wish to appreciate the poetry of the *Aeneid* to the fullest, we encourage readers to learn as much as possible about the techniques of Latin poetry by acquainting themselves with literary devices besides those on the current AP list.

VIc. Identification Questions Covering Names, Places, and Historical and Mythical Characters and Events

The narrative richness of the *Aeneid* is enhanced throughout the poem by Vergil's use of proper names and epithets to designate characters, places, and events known from classical myth and/or ancient history and geography. While the current AP Latin Examination does not include questions that test students' specific knowledge of these names and epithets, we believe it is important to reward those students who observe such details by emphasizing this central aspect of Vergil's poetic diction. These names and epithets are often essential, furthermore, both to success in the reading process and to an appreciation of Vergil's artistry. Teachers may use these exercises if they wish as an opportunity to introduce cultural materials into their classes to enrich the context in which the *Aeneid* is studied. These questions can serve as helpful preparation for the short answer questions regularly found on the AP exam.

VId. Questions on Grammar and Syntax

Sound knowledge of Latin grammar and syntax is fundamental to strong comprehension and translation skills. Therefore, although grammar and syntax per se are tested only on the multiple choice section of the AP Examination, and there only to a limited degree, we have included here occasional exercises aimed at keeping students' philological abilities as keen as possible.

Sight Passage Exercises and Sight Passages

The Advanced Placement Latin Examination requires a student to read Latin passages at sight, to comprehend what the passage is communicating, and to answer questions about the passage. The multiple choice question exercises that accompany the required Latin selections from Vergil's *Aeneid* both prepare students to apply those skills to sight passages and to build a comfort and confidence in doing so. In this workbook we have included three exercises that provide strategies for working with sight passages followed by multiple choice questions. These are followed by an additional nine sight passages and multiple choice questions.

We close with an acknowledgement of all those who helped us, either directly or indirectly, with this project. LeaAnn Osburn, the series editor, initially invited us to prepare this workbook and has offered advice and suggestions at various stages of the writing process. Donald Sprague and Laurel De Vries have worked with us on this second edition and applied their careful reading and critical skills to great advantage in reviewing and standardizing features of the manuscript. AP Latin students at Groton School, furthermore, cheerfully and patiently completed preliminary versions of many of these exercises and scrutinized with keen eyes the final draft. We are greatly indebted to David Ross, who scrupulously read and commented on the entire manuscript; both he and Margaret Brucia proffered guidance, encouragement, and critical support when our spirits flagged. The faith, optimism, and enthusiasm of Matthew McCracken kept spirits up even in the darkest moments; and the Boyds, both

Michael and Rachel, cheered us on as is their wont. And last but not least, we are indebted to all our students past and present, especially those with whom we have had the privilege of reading Vergil, for sharing their insights, enthusiasms, and new questions with us, their teachers. It remains a joy for us, as it ever has been, to discover something new on each rereading of the *Aeneid*.

KATHERINE BRADLEY
Groton School
Groton, Massachusetts

BARBARA WEIDEN BOYD
Bowdoin College
Brunswick, Maine

PREFACE TO THE TEACHER'S MANUAL

A Vergil Workbook Teacher's Manual is intended to complement *A Vergil Workbook* by the same authors. The goal of this handbook is to assist teachers who wish to use the *Workbook* in their classes by offering guidance for the evaluation of their students' work. The *Teacher's Manual* replicates the organization of the *Workbook* in twenty lessons: the selections from Vergil's *Aeneid* and questions relevant to them that are included in the *Workbook* are repeated here, in the identical sequence and numbering. Below we offer some guidelines that, we hope, will clarify the ways in which the supplementary material provided in the *Teacher's Manual* can best be used.

We remind our readers that there are many different types of questions and exercises in *A Vergil Workbook*. Some of these are modeled closely on the format of the Advanced Placement Latin Examination questions (in particular, categories II–IV below); others are not modeled on AP question-types, but offer different ways for students to test their engagement with the poem (see the other question types described below). Teachers wishing to learn more about the format of the AP Latin Examination are urged to consult the publications of the College Entrance Examination Board, available through its website (apcentral.collegeboard.com). These publications also include examples of some of the examinations administered in recent years, and a variety of supplemental materials to support the Advanced Placement experience.

Question Type I: Answers to the Short Answer Questions

These questions lend themselves well to both in-class work and homework assignments. They ask students to look closely at a passage of the *Aeneid* read recently in class and to identify a variety of different features in it. Regular use of a selection of these questions either in or outside of class will help teachers to track their students' comprehension skills. Most of these questions can be answered quickly, sometimes with a single word.

Question Type II: Answers to the Multiple Choice Questions

Some of these questions ask about the same features as do the multiple choice questions on the Advanced Placement Latin Examination: translation or interpretation, grammar, lexical details, allusions and references, meter, and figures of speech. Others focus primarily on comprehension and translation skills, and require a higher degree of precision about grammar and syntax than is normally tested on the AP Latin Examination. In some cases, students are required to choose the correct response from two rather than four options. This is not an AP Latin Examination question type, but offers students an opportunity for quick review.

Question Type III: Answers to Translation Questions

Each lesson contains a translation question. Some of the passages tested are of approximately the same length as those found on the AP Latin Examination; others are longer or shorter. Teachers should train their students to provide a translation that is as literal as possible. Students should be advised not to change active verbs to passive voice or vice versa, or to alter verb tenses. In translating the historical present, students may use either the English present tense for Latin present or consistently convert to past tense in English. Students should be advised to stay as close as possible to the range of standard definitions of words and should not impose from the context a sense that the word does not have. An example of literal translation is provided for each passage, based on the translation in B.W. Boyd, *Vergil's Aeneid: Selected Readings from Books 1, 2, 4, and 6 Teacher's Guide* (Bolchazy-Carducci Publishers, 2012).

We have divided each of the translation passages into grammatical/syntactical units, or "chunks," for scoring; most passages have been broken into eighteen chunks, but some contain fewer or more, depending on the length of the passage in question. Multiple acceptable translations are provided for each "chunk"; no such list can ever be conclusive, however, since many synonyms exist in English for most Latin words and expressions. We therefore encourage teachers to use their discretion. Teachers are reminded that there is no one way to identify such "chunks," and are encouraged to practice this method of grading themselves.

Question Type IV: Answers to Essay Questions

Each section provides an essay question so that students will gain experience with in-depth literary analysis. These essays usually involve the analysis of a single passage from the lesson's Vergil text. For each essay we provide a sample essay answer containing the information that should be included in a comprehensive and thoughtful answer. Of course there will be variation in acceptable answers, and what is offered here is only one approach, not the only acceptable one. These are provided to assist both teacher and student to understand the components of a well developed response.

Essays receiving the highest scores are analytical and interpretive rather than merely descriptive or narrative. These essays require specific reference to the Latin throughout the passage, with appropriate citation, to support and document a student's analysis. For such reference to the Latin, students must write out the Latin and/or cite line numbers. They must also translate, accurately paraphrase, or otherwise make clear in their discussion that they understand the Latin. When referring to a relatively long portion of Latin text, they may either cite the line numbers or use ellipsis ("word . . . word"). When referring only to words or phrases, they should write the Latin out. The responsibility rests with the student to convince the reader that they are drawing conclusions from the Latin text and not from a general recall of the passage. Such careful citation of the Latin is critical as is noted in the essay grading rubrics printed below.

Several other aspects of successful essay writing bear frequent repetition:

- A successful essay has a thesis, which is maintained and supported throughout the essay.
- All parts of a passage on which an essay question is based should be discussed.
- If an essay question asks for the consideration of more than one feature of a passage, all such features should be adequately addressed.
- If an essay question asks students to consider features such as figures of speech or rhetorical devices, these can be used in support of a general thesis but do not usually amount to a substantial response on their own.

The following essay rubrics are adapted from the College Board's *AP Latin Course and Exam Description Effective Fall 2012*. While the rubrics address an essay that discusses two Latin passages, they are readily applied to essays in *A Vergil Workbook* that address a single Latin passage. The AP Latin exam always pairs two passages for discussion and analysis; these pairs consist of one of the following combinations: one passage from Vergil and one from Caesar, two passages from Caesar, or two passages from Vergil. All the essay questions in the student workbook help students prepare for essays that are based in whole or in part on Vergil. With the exception of three essays that require students to discuss two or more passages from Vergil, the essays in the workbook are not identical in format to the current AP Latin exam essay. They do, however, provide excellent preparation for the AP analytical essays.

Essay Scoring Guidelines

5 – Strong

- The essay provides a well-developed, nuanced analysis of the passages.
- The analysis is supported by relevant details and evidence drawn from throughout both passages.
- References to the Latin are accurate, specific, and relevant.
- Inferences made and conclusions drawn fully support the analysis.
- Any examples of language usage and/or stylistic features are well developed and support the analysis.
- Any contextual references are specific and accurate, and support the analysis.

4 – Good

- The essay provides analysis though it may not be nuanced.
- The analysis is supported by the citation of main ideas and some supporting details, with evidence drawn from throughout both passages.
- References to the Latin are accurate, specific, and generally relevant.
- Some inferences may be drawn but the essay relies more on what is directly stated in the passages; occasional errors in inferences may occur.
- Any examples of language usage and/or stylistic features may not be well developed and/or may not support the analysis.
- Any contextual references used to support the argument may not be specific and/or accurate.

3 – Fair

- The essay provides discussion of the question but it may be uneven, inadequately developed, and/or primarily focused on only one of the passages.
- The discussion is supported by main ideas but few supporting details and relies on summary rather than analysis.
- References to the Latin are accurate but may be limited or not connected to the focus of the discussion.
- The essay may show partial understanding of information that is not stated but implied; few inferences are made.

- Any examples of language usage and/or stylistic features may not be connected to the discussion.
- Any contextual references made are not connected effectively to the discussion.

2 – Weak
- The essay provides discussion of the question but the discussion may be confusing and lack organization.
- There may be limited discussion of both passages or an adequate discussion of one passage and failure to recognize the other.
- The discussion consists of summary, not analysis.
- References to the Latin, if any, are limited and there is little or no understanding of the meaning and context.
- Inferences based on the passages are not accurate, and assumptions are incorrect.
- No meaningful examples of language usage and/or stylistic features are provided.
- No meaningful contextual references are made.

1 – Poor
- The essay shows some understanding of the question but contains no meaningful discussion. It provides some correct, relevant information.
- Either no Latin or only individual words are cited; no understanding of the meaning and context of either passage is demonstrated.
- The essay makes no inferences based on the passages.
- No meaningful examples of language usage and/or stylistic features are provided.
- No meaningful contextual references are made.

0 – Unacceptable
- The response is totally irrelevant, totally incorrect, or merely restates the question.
- The response demonstrates no understanding of the Latin in context.

—
- The page is blank or the response is off-task (*e.g.*, drawing, personal letter).

Question Type V: Answers to Scansion Exercises

Scansion questions lend themselves to both in-class practice and homework assignments.

Question Type VI: Answers to Questions on Literary Style

Figures of speech and rhetorical devices are important aspects of Latin poetic language. Recognition of such devices not only can give students enjoyment, but can also help them improve their ability to read Latin. Teachers are reminded to consult a reliable and up-to-date source for the definition of these figures: see, for example, the appendix in Barbara Weiden Boyd, *Vergil's Aeneid: Selected Readings from Books 1, 2, 4, and 6* (Bolchazy-Carducci Publishers, 2012.) Materials available from the College Entrance Examination Board (see weblink above) include a listing of the figures of speech and rhetorical devices currently tested on the AP Latin Examination.

Question Type VI: Answers to Identification Questions Covering Names, Places, and Historical and Mythical Characters and Events

Teachers are encouraged to incorporate as much of this material as time permits into their teaching. Students, even those with otherwise strong Latin skills, often have difficulty with the many proper names and adjectives that appear in the *Aeneid*. While there may be some temptation to de-emphasize them, the ability to distinguish such terms, to translate them, and to use them correctly in English will enhance students' ability to appreciate the poetic achievement of Vergil.

Question Type VIII: Answers to Questions on Grammar and Syntax

Teachers are encouraged to give their students regular opportunities to review grammar and syntax. These exercises are intended to support reading and comprehension, and can be used both in class and as homework assignments.

Sight Passage Exercises and Sight Passages Answers to Multiple Choice Questions

These exercises are provided to help students build both confidence in approaching and skills in working through the sight passages that appear on the AP Latin Exam. We recommend that teachers employ these as in-class assignments over the course of their work with the Vergil section of the AP Latin Exam. Alternatively, teachers could use some of the sight passages with their Vergil lessons and some with their Caesar lessons. The first three excercises should be used in the beginning of the year.

We again thank the colleagues, friends, and family members who supported and encouraged our work on this *Teacher's Manual*, especially Matthew McCracken, David Ross, and Michael and Rachel Boyd. Among the many helpful individuals at Bolchazy-Carducci Publishers, we would like to single out Donald Sprague and Laurel De Vries for their thoughtful and efficient editing. Finally, we want to thank our students, as always, for their answers to these and many other questions like them over the years; and also for their questions, which have inspired us to think anew about the *Aeneid* each and every time we are privileged to teach it.

Katherine Bradley
Groton School
Groton, Massachusetts

Barbara Weiden Boyd
Bowdoin College
Brunswick, Maine

NB: We call your attention to a set of errata on p. 220 for the 2012 printing of the student workbook.

SELECTIONS FROM THE *AENEID* WITH EXERCISES AND ANSWERS

LESSON 1: BOOK 1.1-33

Arma virumque cano, Troiae qui primus ab oris
Italiam fato profugus Laviniaque venit
litora, multum ille et terris iactatus et alto
vi superum, saevae memorem Iunonis ob iram,
5 multa quoque et bello passus, dum conderet urbem
inferretque deos Latio; genus unde Latinum
Albanique patres atque altae moenia Romae.
Musa, mihi causas memora, quo numine laeso
quidve dolens regina deum tot volvere casus
10 insignem pietate virum, tot adire labores
impulerit. Tantaene animis caelestibus irae?
Urbs antiqua fuit (Tyrii tenuere coloni)
Karthago, Italiam contra Tiberinaque longe
ostia, dives opum studiisque asperrima belli,
15 quam Iuno fertur terris magis omnibus unam
posthabita coluisse Samo. Hic illius arma,
hic currus fuit; hoc regnum dea gentibus esse,
si qua fata sinant, iam tum tenditque fovetque.
Progeniem sed enim Troiano a sanguine duci
20 audierat Tyrias olim quae verteret arces;
hinc populum late regem belloque superbum
venturum excidio Libyae; sic volvere Parcas.
Id metuens veterisque memor Saturnia belli,
prima quod ad Troiam pro caris gesserat Argis—
25 necdum etiam causae irarum saevique dolores
exciderant animo; manet alta mente repostum
iudicium Paridis spretaeque iniuria formae
et genus invisum et rapti Ganymedis honores:
his accensa super iactatos aequore toto
30 Troas, reliquias Danaum atque immitis Achilli,
arcebat longe Latio, multosque per annos
errabant acti fatis maria omnia circum.
Tantae molis erat Romanam condere gentem.

Comprehension Questions

NB: Some questions may have several possible correct responses; a sample is given.

1. In the opening line, how does Vergil allude to Homer's *Iliad* and *Odyssey*?

    The word *arma* reflects the *Iliad's* focus on war, and *virum* the *Odyssey's* focus on one man, Odysseus.

2. What does the poet ask the Muse to explain?

    He asks her to explain why Juno (*regina deum*, line 9) was so angry that she forced a good man (*insignem pietate virum*, line 10) to suffer so much (*tot volvere casus*, line 9 and *tot adire labores*, line 10).

3. From lines 1–11, copy out and translate a phrase that characterizes Aeneas.

    ***profugus* (line 2): refugee, exiled, fugitive; *multa . . . passus* (line 5): having suffered/endured so many things/so much; *insignem pietate* (line 10): famous because of his duty, known by his devotion.**

4. In lines 25–29, what are the three reasons Vergil gives for Juno's anger toward the Trojans?

    Juno fears they will destroy the Carthaginian people, her favorites. Juno is insulted because Paris considered Venus more beautiful than she. Jupiter gave the honor of being his cupbearer to the Trojan prince Ganymede rather than to Juno's daughter Hebe.

5. How would you characterize Juno as depicted in this passage? Make sure that you copy out and translate at least three words or phrases that demonstrate features of Juno's character. Provide line references in parentheses for your three Latin choices.

    Students might focus on any one of several qualities of Juno's character as long as the text supports the conclusion the student has drawn.

    Examples:

    Juno picks favorites and looks out for them. *terris magis omnibus unam . . . coluisse* (lines 15–16): which alone Juno is said to have cherished more than all the [other] lands; *hoc . . . regnum . . . gentibus esse . . . tenditque fovetque* (lines 17–18): she intends and cherishes that this be the ruling power for [many] peoples; *arcebat longe Latio* (line 31): she was keeping [the Trojans] far from Latium.

    Juno holds a grudge. *memorem Iunonis ob iram* (line 4): on account of the mindful anger of Juno; *necdum . . . causae irarum . . . exciderant animo* (lines 25–26): not yet had the reasons for her anger fallen from her mind; *manet alta mente repostum* (line 26): it remains buried in her deep mind.

    Juno takes offense deeply and has great anger. *numine laeso* (line 8): her godhead wounded; *quid dolens* (line 9): grieving at what; *tantaene . . . irae* (line 11) [although this explicitly refers to gods in general, by implication it describes Juno]: such great anger.

Multiple Choice Questions *Suggested time: 18 minutes*

1. The word *qui* (line 1) refers to (that is, the antecedent of *qui* is)
   a. *arma* (line 1)
   b. *cano* (line 1)
   c. virum (line 1)
   d. *Troiae* (line 1)

2. The case and number of *superum* (line 4) are
   a. accusative plural
   b. nominative singular
   c. accusative singular
   d. genitive plural

3. In line 5, *dum* is translated
   a. while
   b. until
   c. provided that
   d. then

4. In lines 8–11, Vergil follows the old epic tradition of asking for inspiration from
   a. a muse
   b. the queen
   c. a pious man
   d. a divine will

5. The form of the word *tenuere* (line 12) is
   a. present infinitive
   b. present indicative
   c. perfect infinitive
   d. perfect indicative

6. The word *posthabita* (line 16) modifies
   a. *Iuno* (line 15)
   b. *Samo* (line 16)
   c. *ostia* (line 14)
   d. *arma* (line 16)

7. A figure of speech that occurs in lines 16–17 is
   a. transferred epithet
   b. hendiadys
   c. chiasmus
   d. anaphora

8. In line 19, *duci* is
   a. dative
   b. imperative
   c. infinitive
   d. ablative

9. In lines 19–22, we learn that Juno has heard that the descendants of the Trojans
   a. have destroyed Tyre
   b. would destroy Carthage someday
   c. are coming to the haughty king
   d. have helped a king destroy Libya

10. The antecedent of *quae* (line 20) refers to
    a. *progeniem* (line 19)
    b. *sanguine* (line 19)
    c. *duci* (line 19)
    d. *Tyrias* (line 20)

11. *metuens* in line 23 modifies
    a. *id* (line 23)
    b. *memor* (line 23)
    c. **Saturnia (line 23)**
    d. *prima* (line 24)

12. The metrical pattern for the first four feet of line 28 is
    a. dactyl-dactyl-dactyl-spondee
    b. **dactyl-spondee-spondee-dactyl**
    c. dactyl-spondee-dactyl-spondee
    d. spondee-dactyl-dactyl-spondee

13. *accensa* in line 29 describes
    a. the Fates
    b. Paris
    c. Ganymede
    d. **Juno**

14. In line 30, *reliquias* refers to
    a. **the Trojan refugees**
    b. the Greek conquerers
    c. the hero Achilles
    d. the Latins

15. The clause *multosque per annos / errabant acti fatis maria omnia circum* (lines 31–32) is best translated
    a. and through the years, many wandered, driving the fates around all the seas
    b. and driven by the fates, many wandered through the years and the seas around all
    c. **and driven by the fates they wandered over many years around all the seas**
    d. and many, through the years, were wandering the seas for the fates around all

Translation *Suggested time: 12 minutes*

Translate the passage below as literally as possible.

> Musa, mihi causas memora, quo numine laeso
> quidve dolens regina deum tot volvere casus
> insignem pietate virum, tot adire labores
> impulerit. Tantaene animis caelestibus irae?

Literal Translation
Muse, recall to me the reasons: with what divine power having been wounded [*i.e.*, as the result of harm done to what divine power] or grieving at what did the queen of the gods compel a man outstanding in devotion [*i.e.*, to gods, home, and family] to endure so many misfortunes, confront so many struggles? Do the heavenly spirits possess wrath[s] of such magnitude?

The sections into which a passage is divided are flexible, as are the possible acceptable meanings for any given word. Teachers may prefer a different scheme of "chunking" and range of meanings; what is given below is just one option. Since students must prove to the reader that they understand the grammar of the passage, loose translations are not acceptable, and students should clearly demonstrate the syntactical information provided in parentheses in the column below with the English range of meanings.

12 units
Range of possible meanings followed by notes on grammar and syntax:

Musa	Muse (vocative)
Memora	recount, recall (imperative)
mihi causas	to me the causes/reasons (*mihi* as indirect object; *causas* as direct object of *memora*)
quo numine laeso	with what/which divinity/divine power/godhead [having been] harmed/wounded/struck (ablative absolute)
quidve dolens	or grieving/being vexed at what (*quid* as object of *dolens*; *dolens* modifying *regina*)
regina deum	the queen of the gods (*deum* as genitive)
impulerit	compelled/commanded/forced (*regina* must be subject; perfect tense)
insignem pietate virum	a man/hero famous/known/marked/outstanding in/by duty/loyalty/piety/devotion (object of *impulerit*; *pietate* as ablative of cause or means)
tot volvere casus	to undergo/endure so many mishaps/disasters/misfortunes (*casus* as object of *volvere*)
tot adire labores	to approach/undergo/encounter so many hardships/labors/struggles (*labores* as object of *adire*)
tantaene irae	are the angers/wraths [is the anger/wrath] so great (as nominative subject of understood *sunt*; may be translated as object if *animis caelestibus* is translated as subject)
animis caelestibus	to/for the heavenly/celestial/divine minds/spirits (dative of possession; may be translated as subject, with *tantae irae* as object of English verb "have")

Short Answer Questions

Find, copy out, and provide line references for an example of:

a. metonymy *moenia* **(line 7)**

b. transferred epithet (enallage) *memorem* **(line 4)**

c. anastrophe *Italiam contra* **(line 13);** *maria omnia circum* **(line 32)**

d. anaphora *hic, hic, hoc* **(lines 16–17)**

Match each of these proper names and adjectives with the best description.

1. **M** Achilles — a. ancient city on west coast of Italy near the site of future Rome, named for Latinus's daughter
2. **G** Alba Longa — b. an area of central Italy that includes Rome
3. **N** Danaus — c. a city on the coast of North Africa
4. **C** Karthago — d. a region of North Africa
5. **B** Latium — e. an island where Juno especially was worshipped
6. **A** Lavinium — f. a city in Phoenicia that established a colony in North Africa
7. **D** Libya — g. a city in central Italy, considered the mother of Rome, established by Ascanius
8. **I** Parcae — h. a city in Asia Minor, often associated with Ilium
9. **K** Paris — i. a name for the Fates, Clotho, Lachesis, and Atropos
10. **E** Samos — j. another name for Juno
11. **J** Saturnia — k. son of King Priam of Troy, who brought the Spartan queen to Troy
12. **O** Tiberis — l. anyone from Troy
13. **H** Troia — m. Greek hero who killed many Trojans; a main character of the *Iliad*
14. **L** Tros — n. Greek
15. **F** Tyrus — o. river that runs through Rome to the coast

Essay *Suggested time: 20 minutes*

In this passage Vergil sets forth some of the themes that he will explore in the rest of the poem: the personal cost of founding Rome, Rome's history, the roles that fate and the gods play, and the powerful force of emotion. In a short, well-organized essay, explain how he establishes these themes.

Support your assertions with references drawn from throughout the passage (lines 1–33). All Latin words must be copied or their line numbers provided, AND they must be translated or paraphrased closely enough so that it is clear you understand the Latin. It is your responsibility to convince your reader that you are basing your conclusions on the Latin text and not merely on a general recollection of the passage. Direct your answer to the question; do not merely summarize the passage. Please write your essay on a separate piece of paper.

Students will respond to essay topics in various ways, and different essays, with quite different approaches, may be of equal quality. The following are some possible points students may make.

This essay topic is fairly straightforward, and is designed to give the student practice in choosing words from the text to support an idea. While students may structure their essays however they please, this particular one lends itself to an organization based on the four themes indicated. Phrases, all of which must be translated in student essays, may include the following:

The personal cost, here primarily to Aeneas, of founding Rome: *profugus, multum iactatus, multa passus, tot volvere casus, tot adire labores, reliquias Danaum*

Rome's history: *Troiae ab oris, genus unde Latinum, Albani patres, altae moenia Romae, Tyrias olim verteret arces, venturum excidio Libyae, veteris belli, Tantae molis erat Romanam condere gentem*

The role of fate and the gods: *fato profugus, vi superum, Iunonis ob iram, Iuno fertur coluisse, si fata sinant, Troas arcebat longe Latio, acti fatis*

The powerful force of emotion: *saevae, memorem iram, numine laeso, dolens, Tantaene animis caelestibus irae, terris magis omnibus unam coluisse, tenditque fovetque, metuens, causae irarum saevique dolores, iniuria, invisum, accensa*

See the Scoring Guidelines on pp. xvii–xviii.

Scansion

Scan the following lines.

```
 −  ∪∪ −  ∪ ∪ − −    −    − ∪ ∪ − ×
```
audierat Tyrias olim quae verteret arces   (line 20)

```
 − − −   − − − −    ∪∪  −   ∪∪ − ×
```
errabant acti fatis mari(a) omnia circum   (line 32)

LESSON 2: BOOK 1.34–80

      Vix e conspectu Siculae telluris in altum
35 vela dabant laeti et spumas salis aere ruebant,
      cum Iuno aeternum servans sub pectore vulnus
      haec secum: 'Mene incepto desistere victam
      nec posse Italia Teucrorum avertere regem!
      Quippe vetor fatis. Pallasne exurere classem
40 Argivum atque ipsos potuit submergere ponto
      unius ob noxam et furias Aiacis Oilei?
      Ipsa Iovis rapidum iaculata e nubibus ignem
      disiecitque rates evertitque aequora ventis,
      illum exspirantem transfixo pectore flammas
45 turbine corripuit scopuloque infixit acuto;
      ast ego, quae divum incedo regina Iovisque
      et soror et coniunx, una cum gente tot annos
      bella gero. Et quisquam numen Iunonis adorat
      praeterea aut supplex aris imponet honorem?'
50   Talia flammato secum dea corde volutans
      nimborum in patriam, loca feta furentibus Austris,
      Aeoliam venit. Hic vasto rex Aeolus antro
      luctantes ventos tempestatesque sonoras
      imperio premit ac vinclis et carcere frenat.
55 Illi indignantes magno cum murmure montis
      circum claustra fremunt; celsa sedet Aeolus arce
      sceptra tenens mollitque animos et temperat iras.
      Ni faciat, maria ac terras caelumque profundum
      quippe ferant rapidi secum verrantque per auras;
60 sed pater omnipotens speluncis abdidit atris
      hoc metuens, molemque et montes insuper altos
      imposuit, regemque dedit qui foedere certo
      et premere et laxas sciret dare iussus habenas.
      Ad quem tum Iuno supplex his vocibus usa est:
65 'Aeole (namque tibi divum pater atque hominum rex
      et mulcere dedit fluctus et tollere vento),
      gens inimica mihi Tyrrhenum navigat aequor
      Ilium in Italiam portans victosque penates:
      incute vim ventis submersasque obrue puppes,
70 aut age diversos et dissice corpora ponto.
      Sunt mihi bis septem praestanti corpore Nymphae,
      quarum quae forma pulcherrima Deiopea,
      conubio iungam stabili propriamque dicabo,
      omnes ut tecum meritis pro talibus annos
75 exigat et pulchra faciat te prole parentem.'

Aeolus haec contra: 'Tuus, o regina, quid optes
explorare labor; mihi iussa capessere fas est.
Tu mihi, quodcumque hoc regni, tu sceptra Iovemque
concilias, tu das epulis accumbere divum
80 nimborumque facis tempestatumque potentem.'

Comprehension Questions

NB: Some questions may have several possible correct responses; a sample is given.

1. Juno, in her speech to herself (lines 37–49), expresses her feeling that "it isn't fair." What is it that she wants to do but isn't allowed to? Why is she envious of Minerva?

   She wants to prevent Aeneas and his followers from reaching Italy but is forbidden by the fates; as a result, she has been waging war with the Trojans for many years. Minerva, on the other hand, was allowed to destroy an entire fleet and kill a man, Ajax son of Oileus, just because she was angry at him.

2. Why did Minerva kill Ajax?

   Minerva killed him because in her temple, before the altar of the sanctuary, Ajax had raped her priestess Cassandra.

3. How does Vergil explain the natural phenomenon that the winds sometimes blow and sometimes are calm?

   Their king, Aeolus, keeps them locked in a mountain prison and knows when to restrain them and when to let them loose.

4. Vergil uses a metaphor in lines 62–63 to characterize Aeolus's control of the winds. How does this metaphor illuminate the action it describes?

   Aeolus is a rider controlling his horse, the winds, with reins. In this we can see the power Aeolus wields over the mighty and powerful winds.

5. Identify two things that Juno promises to Aeolus in her speech. What can you infer about epic values concerning marriage and children from this?

   Juno promises Aeolus a most beautiful nymph as a wife and that he will become a father by her. We see that women can be used as objects without their consultation and that fatherhood is highly valued.

6. Given what you know about the background of the Trojan War, why is Juno's bribe ironic?

   Venus used the bribe of a beautiful woman, Helen, to obtain from Paris the outcome she desired, thereby starting the Trojan War.

Multiple Choice Questions *Suggested time: 25 minutes*

1. *vulnus* (line 36) is modified by
   a. *servans* (line 36)
   b. ***aeternum* (line 36)**
   c. *haec* (line 37)
   d. *pectore* (line 36)

2. *Pallas*, in line 39, is another name for
   a. Juno
   b. Teucer
   c. **Minerva**
   d. Ajax

3. The case and number of *Argivum* (line 40) is
   a. nominative singular
   b. accusative singular
   c. **genitive plural**
   d. accusative plural

4. In line 44, *illum* refers to
   a. Jupiter
   b. **Ajax**
   c. Aeneas
   d. Argivus

5. The metrical pattern of the first four feet of line 49 is
   a. dactyl-dactyl-spondee-spondee
   b. dactyl-spondee-dactyl-spondee
   c. spondee-spondee-dactyl-spondee
   d. **dactyl-spondee-spondee-spondee**

6. The word *loca* (line 51) is in apposition to
   a. ***patriam* (line 51)**
   b. *feta* (line 51)
   c. *nimborum* (line 51)
   d. *corde* (line 50)

7. Line 55 contains an example of
   a. chiasmus
   b. **alliteration**
   c. synchysis
   d. litotes

8. In line 59, *-que* connects
   a. *secum* and *verrant* (line 59)
   b. ***ferant* and *verrant* (line 59)**
   c. *verrant* and *per* (line 59)
   d. *secum* and *auras* (line 59)

9. In line 59, *secum* is translated
   a. to himself
   b. with him
   c. to herself
   d. **with them**

10. The antecedent of *qui* (line 62) is
    a. ***regem* (line 62)**
    b. *montes* (line 61)
    c. *foedere* (line 62)
    d. *iussus* (line 63)

11. The phrase *divum . . . rex* (line 65) refers to
    a. Aiax
    b. Priamus
    c. Aeneas
    d. Jupiter

12. The case and number of *fluctus* (line 66) is
    a. nominative singular
    b. accusative plural
    c. nominative plural
    d. genitive singular

13. In line 67, the phrase *gens inimica mihi* describes
    a. Trojans
    b. Greeks
    c. Nymphae
    d. Danai

14. From line 68, we learn that
    a. Penates is bringing Ilium into Italy
    b. the remnants of the Trojan state and its religion are being brought to Italy
    c. Ilium conquered the Penates as they were being carried to Italy
    d. the defeated Trojans are carrying the Penates into Ilium

15. In line 70, *dissice* is
    a. present infinitive
    b. accusative singular
    c. present imperative
    d. ablative singular

16. Why is Deiopea an especially valuable bribe?
    a. she is the most beautiful
    b. she has beautiful offspring
    c. she is fourteen years old
    d. she has performed many duties for Juno

17. The form *iungam* (line 73) is a(n)
    a. perfect participle
    b. present subjunctive
    c. accusative singular
    d. future indicative

18. Line 76 contains a(n)
    a. indirect question
    b. indirect statement
    c. relative clause of purpose
    d. indirect command

19. Lines 78–79 contain the rhetorical device
    a. transferred epithet
    b. chiasmus
    c. metaphor
    d. anaphora

20. In lines 78–80, Aeolus says that he will fulfill Juno's request because
    a. he wants Jupiter's scepter
    b. she has offered him an outstanding bribe
    c. she has given him whatever power he has
    d. he prefers the gods' feasts to having power

Translation *Suggested time: 20 minutes*

Translate the passage below as literally as possible.

>   Ipsa Iovis rapidum iaculata e nubibus ignem
>   disiecitque rates evertitque aequora ventis,
>   illum exspirantem transfixo pectore flammas
>   turbine corripuit scopuloque infixit acuto;
> 5   ast ego, quae divum incedo regina Iovisque
>   et soror et coniunx, una cum gente tot annos
>   bella gero.

Literal Translation
She herself, having hurled the swift fire of Jupiter from the clouds, both scattered the ships and overturned the sea with the winds, and him she snatched up in a whirlwind [as he was] breathing flames from his transfixed breast, and she impaled [him] on a sharp crag. But I, who proceed as queen of the gods and both sister and wife of Jupiter, have been waging war [lit., do wage war] with a single people for so many years [now].

The sections into which a passage is divided are flexible, as are the possible acceptable meanings for any given word. Teachers may prefer a different scheme of "chunking" and range of meanings; what is given below is just one option. Since students must prove to the reader that they understand the grammar of the passage, loose translations are not acceptable, and students should clearly demonstrate the syntactical information provided in parentheses in the column below with the English range of meanings.

18 units
Range of possible meanings followed by notes on grammar and syntax:

Ipsa . . . iaculata e nubibus	she/she herself having hurled/thrown from/out of the clouds (*iaculata* participle modifying *ipsa*)
Iovis rapidum . . . ignem	the swift/rapid/speedy/whirling/consuming fire/lightning (bolt)/flame/light of Jupiter/Jove (*ignem* object of *iaculata*)
disiecitque rates	both scattered/threw apart the ships/boats/rafts
evertitque aequora	and overturned the sea(s)/ocean(s)/waves
ventis	with/by the winds (ablative of means)
illum exspirantem	him/that one breathing (out)/exhaling (object of *corripuit* and *infixit*)
transfixo pectore	from [his] pierced/transfixed heart/chest/breast OR [with] his heart/chest/breast [having been] pierced/transfixed (participle *transfixo* modifies *pectore*; ablative of separation or absolute)
flammas	flames/fire (object of *exspirantem*)
turbine corripuit	snatched (up)/seized with/by/in a whirlwind/storm
infixit	impaled/fastened . . . on (subject is *ipsa*)
scopuloque acuto	and on a sharp/pointed rock/cliff/crag (ablative of means)
ast ego	but/yet/however I

quae . . . incedo	who walk [proudly]/stride
divum regina	[as] queen of the gods/divinities (*divum* genitive; *regina* appositive with *ego* or *quae*)
Iovisque et soror et coniunx	both sister and wife/spouse of Jupiter/Jove
una cum gente	with one people/clan/race/nation (*una* modifies *gente*)
tot annos	for so many years (accusative of duration of time)
bella gero	wage/conduct war(s) (subject *ego*)

Short Answer Questions

NB: More answers may be possible than those given below.

From lines 34–64, find, copy out, and provide line references for:

1. a second declension genitive plural in -*um* **Argivum (line 40);** ***divum* (line 46)**

2. an ablative of separation ***incepto* (line 37),** ***Italia* (line 38)**

3. an appositive ***loca/Aeoliam* (line 51, line 52)**

4. three verbs in the subjunctive ***faciat* (line 58),** ***ferant* (line 59),** ***verrant* (line 59)**

5. three participles NOT in the nominative ***exspirantem* (line 44),** ***incepto* (line 37),** ***flammato* (line 50),** ***luctantes* (line 53)**

6. the objects of these participles:

   servans (line 36) ***vulnus* (line 36)**

   exspirantem (line 44) ***flammas* (line 44)**

   volutans (line 50) ***Talia* (line 50)**

   tenens (line 57) ***sceptra* (57)**

   metuens (line 61) ***hoc* (line 61)**

7. an example of metonymy ***salis* (line 35),** ***aere* (line 35)**

8. a metaphor ***et premere et laxas dare habenas* (line 63)**

9. an example of hendiadys ***vinclis et carcere* (line 54)**

From lines 65–80, find, copy out, and provide line references for:

10. two verbs in the future tense ***iungam* (line 73),** ***dicabo* (line 73)**

11. an example of prolepsis ***submersas obrue puppes* (line 69)**

12. a dative of possession ***mihi* (line 71)**

13. a second declension genitive plural in -*um* ***divum* (line 65, line 79)**

14. an example of anaphora ***tu/tu/tu* (lines 78–79)**

15. two vocatives **Aeole (line 65),** *regina* **(line 76)**

16. four imperatives *incute* **(line 69),** *obrue* **(line 69),** *age* **(line 70),** *dissice* **(line 70)**

17. a superlative adjective *pulcherrima* **(line 72)**

18. an indirect question *quid optes* **(line 76)**

19. an example of alliteration *vim ventis* **(line 69)**

Who or what are the following?

1. Sicilia **a large island off the western coast of Italy and north of North Africa**
2. Pallas **Minerva, goddess of wisdom, war and handicrafts**
3. Aiax Oileus **Greek who desecrated Minerva's temple by raping her priestess Cassandra there**
4. Aeolus **king of the winds**

Essay *Suggested time: 20 minutes*

What can we learn about Juno's character from her speech to Aeolus in lines 65–75? Present your response in a well-organized essay.

Support your assertions with references drawn from throughout this passage (lines 65–75 only). All Latin words must be copied or their line numbers provided, AND they must be translated or paraphrased closely enough so that it is clear you understand the Latin. It is your responsibility to convince your reader that you are basing your conclusions on the Latin text and not merely on a general recollection of the passage. Direct your answer to the question; do not merely summarize the passage. Please write your essay on a separate piece of paper.

Students will respond to essay topics in various ways, and different essays, with quite different approaches, may be of equal quality. The following are some possible points students may make; it is not a sample essay.

   This essay requires the student to draw inferences about Juno on the basis of her speech to Aeolus. While students may refer to other information that they have already gleaned from the poem, it is important for this essay that they focus on this speech. Juno may be seen as flattering since she reminds Aeolus how Jupiter gave Aeolus power, as hostile (*gens inimica mihi*, line 67), as vindictive or violent (*incute vim*, line 69, *obrue puppes*, line 69, *age diversos*, line 70, *dissice corpora*, line 70), and/or scheming, or as a good bargainer since she understands the importance of the exchange of favors (*conubio iungam*, line 73, *propriam dicabo*, line 73, *meritis pro talibus*, line 74). In her role as marriage goddess, she emphasizes *conubio stabili* (line 73) and *omnes annos* (line 74) as well as the production of legitimate offspring (*faciat te prole parentem*, line 75).

See the Scoring Guidelines on pp. xvii–xviii.

Scansion

Scan the following lines.

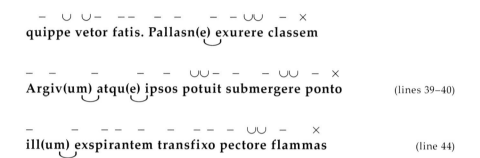

(lines 39–40)

(line 44)

LESSON 3: BOOK 1.81–131

Haec ubi dicta, cavum conversa cuspide montem
impulit in latus: ac venti, velut agmine facto,
qua data porta, ruunt et terras turbine perflant.
Incubuere mari, totumque a sedibus imis
85   una Eurusque Notusque ruunt creberque procellis
Africus, et vastos volvunt ad litora fluctus.
Insequitur clamorque virum stridorque rudentum;
eripiunt subito nubes caelumque diemque
Teucrorum ex oculis; ponto nox incubat atra;
90   intonuere poli, et crebris micat ignibus aether
praesentemque viris intentant omnia mortem.
Extemplo Aeneae solvuntur frigore membra;
ingemit et duplices tendens ad sidera palmas
talia voce refert: 'O terque quaterque beati,
95   quis ante ora patrum Troiae sub moenibus altis
contigit oppetere! O Danaum fortissime gentis
Tydide! Mene Iliacis occumbere campis
non potuisse tuaque animam hanc effundere dextra,
saevus ubi Aeacidae telo iacet Hector, ubi ingens
100 Sarpedon, ubi tot Simois correpta sub undis
scuta virum galeasque et fortia corpora volvit!'
    Talia iactanti stridens Aquilone procella
velum adversa ferit, fluctusque ad sidera tollit.
Franguntur remi; tum prora avertit et undis
105 dat latus, insequitur cumulo praeruptus aquae mons.
Hi summo in fluctu pendent; his unda dehiscens
terram inter fluctus aperit; furit aestus harenis.
Tres Notus abreptas in saxa latentia torquet
(saxa vocant Itali mediis quae in fluctibus Aras,
110 dorsum immane mari summo), tres Eurus ab alto
in brevia et Syrtes urget, miserabile visu,
inliditque vadis atque aggere cingit harenae.
Unam, quae Lycios fidumque vehebat Oronten,
ipsius ante oculos ingens a vertice pontus
115 in puppim ferit: excutitur pronusque magister
volvitur in caput, ast illam ter fluctus ibidem
torquet agens circum et rapidus vorat aequore vertex.
Apparent rari nantes in gurgite vasto,
arma virum tabulaeque et Troia gaza per undas.
120 Iam validam Ilionei navem, iam fortis Achatae,
et qua vectus Abas, et qua grandaevus Aletes,
vicit hiems; laxis laterum compagibus omnes
accipiunt inimicum imbrem rimisque fatiscunt.

```
        Interea magno misceri murmure pontum
125  emissamque hiemem sensit Neptunus et imis
     stagna refusa vadis, graviter commotus, et alto
     prospiciens summa placidum caput extulit unda.
     Disiectam Aeneae toto videt aequore classem,
     fluctibus oppressos Troas caelique ruina;
130  nec latuere doli fratrem Iunonis et irae.
     Eurum ad se Zephyrumque vocat, dehinc talia fatur:
```

Comprehension Questions

NB: Some questions may have several possible correct responses; a sample is given.

1. In the simile in lines 82–83, to what are the rushing winds compared?

   The winds are compared to a battle line.

2. In line 97, Vergil uses a patronymic ("son of . . . ") to refer to an important character, Tydides (lit., "son of Tydeus"). Tydides is the patronymic for whom? Why would Aeneas mention him here?

   Tydides is Diomedes, who would have killed Aeneas on the battlefield at Troy had Venus not saved him.

3. For whom is Aeacides the patronymic? **Aeacides is Achilles.**

4. To what event is Aeneas referring in line 99? **Achilles killed Hector because Hector had killed Patroclus, Achilles's best friend. Achilles then dragged Hector's body around the walls of Troy.**

5. Lines 103 and 105 each contain an example of hyperbole. Give one word from each line that best represents this, and explain the effect of each hyperbole.

   ***sidera, mons.* The waves were so great that they can be imagined as reaching the stars, and the wave that crashed upon the ship can be imagined to be as massive as a mountain. Both heighten the vividness of the scene.**

6. Vergil mentions five ships specifically that were damaged by the storm. With what comrade was each associated?

   1) Orontes; 2) Ilioneus; 3) Achates; 4) Abas; 5) Aletes

7. Line 124 contains a verbal echo of a line of the earlier passage in which Aeolus's control of the wind is described. Identify which line.

   Line 55: *illi indignantes magno cum murmure montis*

8. Why is Neptune upset? **He realizes that there is a storm at sea and he has not approved nor sent it.**

9. Who does he know has caused the storm? **He knows his sister, Juno, has sent it.**

Short Answer Questions

Indicate True or False by marking a "T" or an "F" in the space provided.

1. **F** In line 84, *incubuere* is an infinitive.
2. **T** *ruunt* (line 85) has three subjects.
3. **T** Line 87 describes the sounds of the setting.
4. **F** In line 92, *extemplo* is dative.
5. **T** Aeneas in his speech of lines 94–101 wishes that he were dead.
6. **F** Simois killed Sarpedon.
7. **F** The subject of *dat* (line 105) is *latus* (line 105).
8. **T** In line 110, *dorsum immane* is in apposition to *Aras* (line 109).
9. **F** *visu* (line 111) is a perfect participle.
10. **F** *ipsius* (line 114) refers to *Oronten* (line 113).
11. **T** In lines 115–116, we learn that a ship's pilot is struck because of the storm.
12. **T** Line 118 can be translated "There appear scattered men floating in the huge whirlpool."
13. **F** The object of *vicit* in line 122 is *hiems* (line 122).
14. **F** In line 122, *laterum* is accusative.
15. **T** *sensit* (line 125) governs an indirect statement with three accusative subjects + infinitives.
16. **T** *commotus* (line 126) and *prospiciens* (line 127) both modify *Neptunus* (line 125).
17. **F** Line 128 can be translated "Aeneas sees his fleet scattered on the sea."
18. **T** Line 129 contains hyperbole.
19. **T** In line 130, *latuere* is perfect indicative.
20. **F** We learn that Neptune is angry in line 130.
21. **T** Line 131 contains synizesis.

Copy out an example of each of these figures of speech and provide a line reference in parentheses. (There are several examples of some of these in the passage.)

   a. apostrophe **O terque quaterque beati . . . (line 94); Tydide (line 97)**

   b. hysteron proteron **prospiciens extulit (line 127)**

   c. anaphora (find at least three examples of this) **ubi/ubi/ubi (lines 99–100); tres/tres (lines 108, 110); iam/iam (line 120); qua/qua (line 121)**

   d. alliteration **cavum conversa cuspide (line 81); magno misceri murmure (line 124)**

   e. polysyndeton **clamorque stridorque (line 87); Eurusque Notusque . . . creberque . . . Africus (lines 85–86)**

   f. onomatopoeia **magno misceri murmure pontum (line 124)**

   g. hyperbole **ad sidera (line 103); aquae mons (line 105); caeli ruina (line 129)**

Put the following into one of the categories listed below. (Some names appear in earlier lines.)

Achates	Achilles	Aeolia	Africus	Aias
Aquilo	Arae	Auster	Diomedes	Eurus
Hector	Ilioneus	Lavinium	Libya	Notus
Orontes	Paris	Priam	Sarpedon	Simois
Tiberis	Tyrrhenia	Zephyrus		

Greek heroes/allies **Achilles, Aias, Diomedes**

Trojan heroes/allies **Achates, Hector, Ilioneus, Paris, Priam, Orontes, Sarpedon**

Winds **Africus, Aquila, Auster, Eurus, Notus, Zephyrus**

Places **Aeolia, Arae, Libya, Lavinium, Simois, Tiberis, Tyrrhenia**

Translation *Suggested time: 15 minutes*

Translate the following lines as literally as possible.

> Interea magno misceri murmure pontum
> emissamque hiemem sensit Neptunus et imis
> stagna refusa vadis, graviter commotus, et alto
> prospiciens summa placidum caput extulit unda.
> 5 Disiectam Aeneae toto videt aequore classem,
> fluctibus oppressos Troas caelique ruina;
> nec latuere doli fratrem Iunonis et irae.

Literal Translation
Meanwhile, Neptune, gravely disturbed, sensed that the sea was being confused with a great rumbling and that a storm [had been] sent forth and that the still waters [had been] poured back from [or to] the depths of the sea, and looking out over the deep sea he raised [his] peaceful head from the top of the water. He sees the fleet of Aeneas scattered on the entire sea, [and] the Trojans overwhelmed by waves and the downfall of heaven; nor did the tricks and wrath of Juno escape the notice of [her] brother.

The sections into which a passage is divided are flexible, as are the possible acceptable meanings for any given word. Teachers may prefer a different scheme of "chunking" and range of meanings; what is given below is just one option. Since students must prove to the reader that they understand the grammar of the passage, loose translations are not acceptable, and students should clearly demonstrate the syntactical information provided in parentheses in the column below with the English range of meanings.

18 units
Range of possible meanings followed by notes on grammar and syntax:

interea . . . sensit Neptunus	meanwhile Neptune sensed/perceived/felt (perfect tense)
magno . . . murmure	with a large/great roar/rumble/murmur
misceri . . . pontum	[that] the sea/ocean/water was being mixed/confused/stirred (indirect statement; *pontum* subject of *misceri*)
emissamque hiemem	and [that] a storm had been sent forth/sent out (indirect statement; *hiemem* subject of *emissam* [*esse*]
imis . . . vadis	from the lowest/very bottom shallows/shoals/depths
et . . . stagna refusa	and [that] the still waters/depths had been poured back (indirect statement; *stagna* object of *refusa* [*esse*]
graviter commotus	[having been] seriously/gravely/heavily/violently/greatly moved/upset/disturbed (*commotus* modifies *Neptunus*)
et alto prospiciens	and looking out (on)/seeing the deep/deep sea/sea/ocean OR from the deep/deep sea/sea/ocean (*prospiciens* modifies *Neptunus*)
placidum caput extulit	he raised/lifted (up) [his] calm/quiet/peaceful head (*Neptunus* is subject of *extulit*)

summa . . . unda	from the top of/highest/uppermost wave/billow/water/sea
videt	he sees/watches (*Neptunus* is subject)
disiectam Aeneae . . . classem	[that] Aeneas's scattered/dispersed fleet OR [that] Aeneas's fleet has been scattered/dispersed
toto . . . aequore	on/over the whole sea/ocean/waves
oppressos Troas	[and] the Trojans overwhelmed/crushed OR [and that] the Trojans have been overwhelmed/crushed
fluctibus . . . caelique ruina	by/with the waves/water/sea/flood and by/with the downfall/ruin/fall of the sky/heaven (ablative of means)
nec latuere	did not lie hidden [from]/escape the notice [of] (perfect tense)
doli . . . Iunonis et irae	the deceit(s)/wiles/tricks/fraud(s) and anger(s)/wrath(s) of Juno (*doli* and *irae* nominative; *Iunonis* genitive)
fratrem	[her] brother (object of *latuere*)

Essays *Suggested time: 40 minutes (20 minutes per essay)*

1. In lines 81–91, Vergil establishes a vivid and violent setting for the events that follow. In a short, well-organized essay, explain how he creates this setting.

2. The first appearance of Aeneas in the poem occurs in lines 92–101. In a short, well-organized essay, describe how Vergil characterizes Aeneas in this passage.

For each essay above, support your assertions with references drawn from throughout the passage indicated by each essay, that is, lines 81–91 only for essay #1 and lines 92–101 only for essay #2. All Latin words must be copied or their line numbers provided, AND they must be translated or paraphrased closely enough so that it is clear you understand the Latin. It is your responsibility to convince your reader that you are basing your conclusions on the Latin text and not merely on a general recollection of the passage. Direct your answer to the question; do not merely summarize the passage. Please write your essays on a separate piece of paper.

Students will respond to essay topics in various ways, and different essays, with quite different approaches, may be of equal quality. The following are some possible points students may make; they are not sample essays.

Essay #1: While the essay asks students to explain how Vergil creates the setting, it also gives some direction with the use of the words "vivid and violent." Students should be sure to write a thesis statement and then support it. Ideas and phrases, <u>all of which must be translated</u> in student essays, may include the following: the use of a simile, in which the winds are compared to an army line (*agmine facto*, line 82); the repetition of the word *ruunt* (lines 83 and 85); the use of the superlative *imis* (line 84); the description of the *fluctus* as *vastos* (both, line 86). In addition to visual imagery, Vergil uses aural imagery with *clamor* and *stridor* (both, line 87), and later with *intonuere* (line 90). The clouds violently snatch away (*eripiunt*, line 88) the daytime sky, and the day is described as becoming *nox atra* (line 89). Frequent lightning (*crebris ignibus*, line 90) flashes (*micat*, line 90). The final line is framed by the threatening phrase *praesentem mortem* (line 91).

Essay #2: Students are asked how Aeneas is characterized in these ten lines, so the essay should begin with a thesis that states what qualities the student believes are being presented. Ideas and phrases, <u>all of which must be translated</u> in student essays, may include the following. Aeneas appears to be fearful and in a state of despair. The first description of him, *Aeneae solvuntur frigore membra* (line 92), emphasizes his fear. He is stretching his hands to the sky (*duplices tendens ad sidera palmas*, line 93) in prayer as a suppliant. He sees so little hope for his situation that he thinks that those who have died are lucky (*terque quaterque beati*, line 94), even if it meant that they died in front of their fathers (*ante ora patrum*, line 95). He wishes that he had been killed (*occumbere*, line 97; *animam effundere*, line 98) in Troy by Diomedes (*Tydide*, line 97). He seems to feel that it would have been better to die in a familiar place (*Iliacis campis*, line 97) with familiar people (*Hector*, line 99; *Sarpedon*, line 100) than at sea.

See the Scoring Guidelines on pp. xvii–xviii.

Scansion

Scan the following lines.

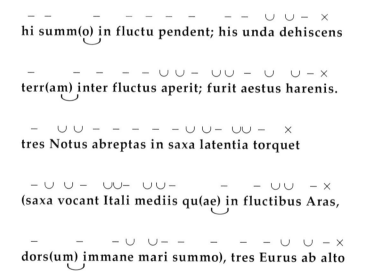

(lines 106–110)

A bit trickier:

$$-\ \ \cup\cup\ \ \ -\cup\cup\ -\ \ -\ -\ \ \ -\ \ \ -\cup\ \cup\ \ -\ \times$$
iam valid(am) Ilionei navem, iam fortis Achatae   (line 120)

LESSON 4: BOOK 1.132–179

'Tantane vos generis tenuit fiducia vestri?
Iam caelum terramque meo sine numine, venti,
miscere et tantas audetis tollere moles?
135 Quos ego—sed motos praestat componere fluctus.
Post mihi non simili poena commissa luetis.
Maturate fugam regique haec dicite vestro:
non illi imperium pelagi saevumque tridentem,
sed mihi sorte datum. Tenet ille immania saxa,
140 vestras, Eure, domos; illa se iactet in aula
Aeolus et clauso ventorum carcere regnet.'
  Sic ait, et dicto citius tumida aequora placat
collectasque fugat nubes solemque reducit.
Cymothoe simul et Triton adnixus acuto
145 detrudunt naves scopulo; levat ipse tridenti
et vastas aperit Syrtes et temperat aequor
atque rotis summas levibus perlabitur undas.
Ac veluti magno in populo cum saepe coorta est
seditio saevitque animis ignobile vulgus
150 iamque faces et saxa volant, furor arma ministrat;
tum, pietate gravem ac meritis si forte virum quem
conspexere, silent arrectisque auribus astant;
ille regit dictis animos et pectora mulcet:
sic cunctus pelagi cecidit fragor, aequora postquam
155 prospiciens genitor caeloque invectus aperto
flectit equos curruque volans dat lora secundo.
  Defessi Aeneadae quae proxima litora cursu
contendunt petere, et Libyae vertuntur ad oras.
Est in secessu longo locus: insula portum
160 efficit obiectu laterum, quibus omnis ab alto
frangitur inque sinus scindit sese unda reductos.
Hinc atque hinc vastae rupes geminique minantur
in caelum scopuli, quorum sub vertice late
aequora tuta silent; tum silvis scaena coruscis
165 desuper, horrentique atrum nemus imminet umbra.
Fronte sub adversa scopulis pendentibus antrum;
intus aquae dulces vivoque sedilia saxo,
Nympharum domus. Hic fessas non vincula naves
ulla tenent, unco non alligat ancora morsu.
170 Huc septem Aeneas collectis navibus omni
ex numero subit, ac magno telluris amore
egressi optata potiuntur Troes harena
et sale tabentis artus in litore ponunt.

Ac primum silici scintillam excudit Achates
175 suscepitque ignem foliis atque arida circum
nutrimenta dedit rapuitque in fomite flammam.
Tum Cererem corruptam undis Cerealiaque arma
expediunt fessi rerum, frugesque receptas
et torrere parant flammis et frangere saxo.

Comprehension Questions

NB: Some questions may have several possible correct responses; a sample is given.

1. How is Neptune's mood illustrated in lines 132–141? Provide line references in parentheses for any Latin you cite.

   He is angry and feels that the winds have infringed upon his domain.

   In his anger, he asks them if they dare (*audetis*, line 134) to create a storm without his permission (*meo sine numine*, line 133). He breaks off his speech (*aposiopesis*) in anger, realizing that he must take action before further railing agains the winds. He states that power over the sea is his (*imperium mihi datum*, lines 138–139), not Aeolus's (*non illi*, line 138).

2. How does Neptune defend his sphere of influence? **He sends off the winds (*maturate fugam*, line 137) with a threat (*non simili poena commissa luetis*, 136) and the message for Aeolus that he should remain in his own realm (*illa in aula*, line 140). Neptune then calms the seas (*aequora placat*, line 142).**

3. Who are Cymothoe and Triton? **Cymothoe is a sea nymph, and Triton is a minor sea god.**

4. What action in the narrative is enhanced by the simile (lines 148–153)?

   In a reversal of the usual Homeric simile, forces of nature are compared to human action. The winds settle down and obey Neptune (*pelagi cecidit fragor*, line 154) just as a raging, angry mob (*saevit ignobile vulgus*, line 149) pays attention to a man who is serious with a sense of duty (*pietate gravem*, line 151) and who is able to calm the mob (*animos et pectora mulcet*, line 153).

5. Why do Aeneas and his followers beach their ships where they do?

   They beach where they do because it is the nearest shore (*proxima litora*, line 157) and because the waters are calm there (*aequora tuta silent*, line 164).

6. In the ecphrasis (lines 159–169), Vergil uses language that suggests both a peaceful and a threatening atmosphere. Which words (with their line numbers) connote peacefulness and which a threat?

   Peacefulness is connoted by *aequora tuta silent* (line 164), *intus aquae dulces* (line 167), *non vincula . . . tenent* (lines 168–169), *non alligat ancora* (line 169). Threat is connoted by *vastae* and *minantur* (line 162), *horrenti, atrum, imminet* (line 165).

7. What does the phrase *magno telluris amore* (line 171) tell us about the shipwrecked Trojans?

   The phrase shows how weary of the sea the men are, and how eager they are to spend time on land.

8. Why do Achates's actions in lines 174–176 receive so much emphasis from Vergil?

   Achates is shown taking care of the men by performing the basic step necessary for the preparation of food, *i.e.*, the making of a fire.

9. Why does Vergil remind the reader of the importance of fire and the preparation of food at this point in the plot?

   After the devasting storm that the men heroically survive, we see that they are still very much human, with all the basic needs of humans. They need to be warm and dry, and they need sustenance to survive.

Multiple Choice Questions *Suggested time: 18 minutes*

1. *domos* (line 140) is in apposition to
   - a. *immania* (line 139)
   - b. *vestras* (line 140)
   - c. *Eure* (line 140)
   - **d. *saxa* (line 139)**

2. The tense and mood of *iactet* (line 140) is
   - **a. present indicative**
   - b. present subjunctive
   - c. future indicative
   - d. perfect subjunctive

3. The form of *citius* (line 142) is
   - a. comparative adjective
   - **b. comparative adverb**
   - c. positive adverb
   - d. positive adjective

4. The best translation of lines 142–143 (*Sic . . . reducit*) is
   - **a. Thus he speaks, and more quickly than a word he calms the swollen seas and puts to flight the gathered clouds and brings back the sun.**
   - b. Thus he speaks, and with his rather quick word he calms the swollen seas and sends off the collected clouds and leads back the sun.
   - c. He speaks thus, and with his speech he calms the swift, swelling seas and sends away the collected clouds and leads back the sun.
   - d. He speaks thus, and he placates the swollen seas with his swift word and puts to flight the gathered clouds and brings back the sun.

5. The case and number of *vulgus* (line 149) is
   - a. accusative plural
   - **b. nominative singular**
   - c. accusative singular
   - d. nominative plural

6. Vergil makes the point in line 150 that
   a. only crazy people will throw weapons in a crowd
   b. people will throw torches if they are ignoble
   c. weapons increase the anger of a crowd
   d. when a mob is angry, it will use anything as a weapon

7. In line 153, *ille* refers to
   a. *virum* (line 151)
   b. *pietate* (line 151)
   c. Triton (understood)
   d. *fragor* (line 154)

8. The *-que* in line 155 connects
   a. *genitor* and *invectus* (line 155)
   b. *prospiciens* (line 155) and *flectit* (line 156)
   c. *caelo* and *aperto* (line 155)
   d. *prospiciens* and *invectus* (line 155)

9. The case of *curru* (line 156) is
   a. ablative
   b. nominative
   c. dative
   d. accusative

10. The best translation of lines 157–158 (*Defessi . . . oras*) is
    a. Aeneas's tired followers strive toward the shores in their course, which is very near, and they are turned toward Libya's coast.
    b. Aeneas's tired followers, who are nearest to the shore in their course, aim toward it, and they are turned toward Libya's coast.
    c. The weary followers of Aeneas strive to seek with their course the shores which are nearest, and they are turned toward the coast of Libya.
    d. The weary followers of Aeneas seek in their haste the nearest shores, which they strive toward, and they are turned toward the coast of Libya.

11. The antecedent of *quibus* (line 160) is
    a. *laterum* (line 160)
    b. *obiectu* (line 160)
    c. *omnis* (line 160)
    d. *sinus* (line 161)

12. The case and number of *sinus* (line 161) is
    a. nominative singular
    b. genitive singular
    c. nominative plural
    d. accusative plural

13. The metrical pattern of the first four feet of line 162 is
    a. dactyl-dactyl-dactyl-spondee
    b. dactyl-spondee-spondee-spondee
    c. spondee-spondee-spondee-dactyl
    d. spondee-dactyl-spondee-dactyl

14. In line 170, *omni* modifies
    a. *huc* (line 170)
    b. *septem* (line 170)
    c. *numero* (line 171)
    d. *amore* (line 171)

15. A figure of speech that occurs in line 177 is
    a. personification
    b. anaphora
    c. aposiopesis
    d. **metonymy**

Translation *Suggested time: 20 minutes*

Translate the following lines as literally as possible.

       Huc septem Aeneas collectis navibus omni
       ex numero subit, ac magno telluris amore
       egressi optata potiuntur Troes harena
       et sale tabentis artus in litore ponunt.
5   Ac primum silici scintillam excudit Achates
       suscepitque ignem foliis atque arida circum
       nutrimenta dedit rapuitque in fomite flammam.

Literal Translation
Aeneas enters this place with seven ships gathered from the entire number [i.e., of ships], and, disembarking, the Trojans take possession of the longed-for sand with a great love for (of) land, and set [their] bodies [lit., limbs] dripping with salt [i.e., salt-water] on the shore. And first of all, Achates struck a spark from a flint, and took up the fire with leaves, and gave around [i.e., scattered] dry nourishment[s] [i.e., kindling], and caught the flame in the timber.

The sections into which a passage is divided are flexible, as are the possible acceptable meanings for any given word. Teachers may prefer a different scheme of "chunking" and range of meanings; what is given below is just one option. Since students must prove to the reader that they understand the grammar of the passage, loose translations are not acceptable, and students should clearly demonstrate the syntactical information provided in parentheses in the column below with the English range of meanings.

18 units
Range of possible meanings followed by notes on grammar and syntax:

huc Aeneas subit	hither/to this place Aeneas enters/goes
septem collectis navibus	with seven ships/boats/barks [having been] collected/gathered [together] (*septem* and *collectis* modify *navibus*; ablative absolute)
omni ex numero	from/out of the whole/all [the] number (*omni* modifies *numero*)
magno telluris amore	with great/large/big love/fondness for/of the land/earth (ablative of description; *telluris* genitive)
egressi	having gone out/disembarked/stepped out (participle, modifies *Troes*)
potiuntur Troes	the Trojans gain possession of/get hold of/win (*Troes* subject)

optata harena	the hoped for/chosen/desired sand/beach/coast/land (participle modifies *harena*; object of *potiuntur*)
tabentis artus	limbs dripping/soaking/melting (direct object of *ponunt*)
sale	with/by salt/salt-sea-water/salt-water
in litore ponunt	they place/put/set on the shore/beach (subject *Troes*)
ac primum	and first/at first/initially (adverbial)
scintillam excudit Achates	Achates struck a spark/flash
silici	from the flint (dative of separation)
suscepitque ignem	and took up/caught (up)/received fire/flame (-*que* connects *excudit* and *suscepit*; *Achates* subject)
foliis	with/by the leaves (ablative of means)
atque	and (connects *suscepit* and *dedit*)
arida circum nutrimenta dedit	gave dry nourishment/food around/all around (*arida* modifies *nutrimenta*; *circum* adverbial; *Achates* subject)
rapuitque in fomite flammam	and caught/seized/took a flame/fire in the tinder/fuel/shaving (-*que* connects *dedit* and *rapuit*; *Achates* subject)

Short Answer Questions

Each of these lines contains at least one figure of speech. Identify one figure of speech in each line.

1. *Post mihi non simili poena commissa luetis* **litotes (line 136)**

2. *conspexere, silent arrectisque auribus astant* **chiasmus, alliteration, assonance (line 152)**

3. *frangitur inque sinus scindit sese unda reductos* **alliteration (line 161)**

4. *Nympharum domus. Hic fessas non vincula naves* **personification (line 168)**

5. *Tum Cererem corruptam undis Cerealiaque arma* **metonymy (line 177)**

Essay *Suggested time: 20 minutes*

In his simile in lines 148–153, whom is Vergil describing? To whom else may he be referring (consider line 10 of the poem)? From your knowledge of Roman history, why might this simile particularly resonate with a Roman reader? Present your response in a well-organized essay.

Support your assertions with references drawn from throughout this passage (lines 148–153 only). All Latin words must be copied or their line numbers provided, AND they must be translated or paraphrased closely enough so that it is clear you understand the Latin. It is your responsibility to convince your reader that you are basing your conclusions on the Latin text and not merely on a general recollection of the passage. Direct your answer to the question; do not merely summarize the passage. Please write your essay on a separate piece of paper.

(See Lesson 9 for an additional essay on this passage.)

Students will respond to essay topics in various ways, and different essays, with quite different approaches, may be of equal quality. The following are some possible points students may make; it is not a sample essay.

In this essay, students are asked to consider the famous simile in which Neptune is compared to a *gravem virum* (line 151). The topic is less defined than earlier ones, and students will have a slightly greater challenge formulating a thesis. Ideas and phrases, <u>all of which must be translated</u> in student essays, may include the following. The phrase *pietate gravem* (line 151) may recall the description of Aeneas as *insignem pietate* at 1.10. The Romans valued oratory highly, and so the ability of a man to calm (*animos et pectora mulcet*, line 153) an angry mob (*seditio, saevit . . . vulgus*, line 149) through speech would have been recognized and respected. Riots had been a regular part of Roman political life, for example, after the murder of Caesar, and so this part of the simile, too, would have been familiar to the Roman reader. Students who begin to see that similes can operate on several levels, and are not always just in a one-to-one correspondence, will have a richer experience reading the poem. A Roman reader might think of Augustus, who "calmed" the riots of Rome by ending its civil wars.

See the Scoring Guidelines on pp. xvii–xviii.

Scansion

Scan the following lines.

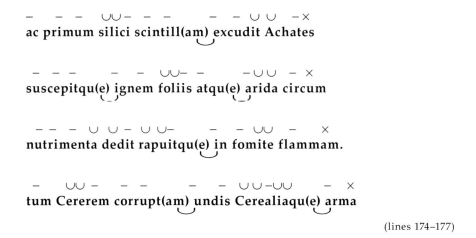

(lines 174–177)

LESSON 5: BOOK 1.180–209

```
180    Aeneas scopulum interea conscendit, et omnem
       prospectum late pelago petit, Anthea si quem
       iactatum vento videat Phrygiasque biremes
       aut Capyn aut celsis in puppibus arma Caici.
       Navem in conspectu nullam, tres litore cervos
185    prospicit errantes; hos tota armenta sequuntur
       a tergo et longum per valles pascitur agmen.
       Constitit hic arcumque manu celeresque sagittas
       corripuit fidus quae tela gerebat Achates,
       ductoresque ipsos primum capita alta ferentes
190    cornibus arboreis sternit, tum vulgus et omnem
       miscet agens telis nemora inter frondea turbam;
       nec prius absistit quam septem ingentia victor
       corpora fundat humi et numerum cum navibus aequet;
       hinc portum petit et socios partitur in omnes.
195    Vina bonus quae deinde cadis onerarat Acestes
       litore Trinacrio dederatque abeuntibus heros
       dividit, et dictis maerentia pectora mulcet:
            'O socii (neque enim ignari sumus ante malorum),
       o passi graviora, dabit deus his quoque finem.
200    Vos et Scyllaeam rabiem penitusque sonantes
       accestis scopulos, vos et Cyclopia saxa
       experti: revocate animos maestumque timorem
       mittite; forsan et haec olim meminisse iuvabit.
       Per varios casus, per tot discrimina rerum
205    tendimus in Latium, sedes ubi fata quietas
       ostendunt; illic fas regna resurgere Troiae.
       Durate, et vosmet rebus servate secundis.'
            Talia voce refert curisque ingentibus aeger
       spem vultu simulat, premit altum corde dolorem.
```

Comprehension Questions

NB: Some questions may have several possible correct responses; a sample is given.

1. How many ships survive the storm? **seven**

2. How does Aeneas demonstrate concern for his men? **He gets food for them and brings it to their ships, and he gives them an encouraging speech.**

3. Where is Phrygia? **Troy, the near East**

4. Where is the *litus Trinacrium*? **Sicily**

5. Where is Latium? **Central Italy**

6. In lines 184–194, what words suggest that a military metaphor is being employed?

    ***agmen* (line 186), *arcum, sagittas* (line 187), *ductores* (line 189), *telis* (line 191), *victor* (line 192), *fundat* (line 193)**

7. In line 197, Vergil uses the phrase *pectora mulcet*. He used the same phrase, in the same position in the line, in line 153. What implicit comparison does he expect the reader to make?

    Aeneas has the same ability to soothe his men as the speaker in the simile has with the crowd, and Neptune has with the winds.

8. What other epic hero and his followers encountered Scylla and the Cyclops? **Odysseus**

9. In his speech, Aeneas encourages his men by referring to the past and to the future. How does he recollect the past? What events in the future does he choose to speak about in hopes of buoying up his comrades' spirits? How does he himself feel about what he's saying?

    Aeneas recollects the past with the phrases *neque ignari sumus ante malorum* (line 198), *passi graviora* (line 199), *Scyllaeam rabiem* (line 200), *sonantes scopulos* (lines 200–201), *Cyclopia saxa* (line 201).

    He refers to the future with the phrases *forsan haec olim meminisse iuvabit* (line 203), *tendimus in Latium* (line 205), *sedes fata quietas ostendunt* (lines 205–206), *fas regna resurgere Troiae* (line 206).

    He himself is feigning such hopefulness (*spem vultu simulat*, line 209); in reality he is worried (*premit altum corde dolorem*, line 209).

10. What specific phrases in Aeneas's speech suggest the theme of Rome's establishment?

    ***sedes ubi fata quietas ostendunt* (lines 205–206); *fas regna resurgere Troiae* (line 206)**

Short Answer Questions

Choose the best translation by circling the appropriate letter.

1. *Navem in conspectu nullam, tres litore cervos / prospicit errantes* (lines 184–185)
    a. **he sees no ship in sight, but three stags wandering on the shore**
    b. no ship is in sight, but he catches sight of stags wandering on the shore in three places

2. *ductoresque ipsos primum capita alta ferentes / cornibus arboreis sternit* (lines 189–190)
    a. **he first lays low the leaders themselves bearing their heads tall with branching antlers**
    b. he lays low the leaders and the first of those bearing high heads with tree-like antlers

3. *nec prius absistit quam septem ingentia victor / corpora fundat humi et numerum cum navibus aequet* (lines 192–193)
   a. nor does he stop earlier, and the huge victor lays low the seven bodies that were on the ground, and he equals the number with the ships
   b. nor does he stop before, as victor, he lays low seven huge bodies onto the ground and makes equal their number with the ships

4. *Vina bonus quae deinde cadis onerarat Acestes / litore Trinacrio dederatque abeuntibus heros / dividit* (lines 195–197)
   a. the wines that good Acestes then had loaded in jars the hero divides on the Sicilian shore and gives to them as they depart
   b. he divides the wine that the good hero Acestes had then loaded into jars on the Sicilian shore and had given to them as they departed

5. *Vos et Scyllaeam rabiem penitusque sonantes / accestis scopulos, vos et Cyclopia saxa / experti* (lines 200–202)
   a. You yourselves have experienced Scylla's rage deeply and the crags resounding with your approach, and you tested yourselves with the Cyclyops' rocks
   b. You have both approached the rage of Scylla and the deeply resounding crags and you have experienced the rocks of the Cyclops

6. *forsan et haec olim meminisse iuvabit* (line 203)
   a. by chance and someday this will be pleasing to have remembered
   b. perhaps someday it will be pleasing to remember even these things

What figure of speech occurs in each of the following lines?

1. *Navem in conspectu nullam, tres litore cervos* (line 184)
   a. zeugma
   c. asyndeton
   b. metonymy
   d. enallage

2. *Vina bonus quae deinde cadis onerarat Acestes / litore Trinacrio dederatque abeuntibus heros / dividit* (lines 195–197)
   a. personification
   b. synchysis
   c. chiasmus
   d. hyperbaton

3. *Per varios casus, per tot discrimina rerum / tendimus in Latium* (lines 204–205)
   a. tmesis
   b. polysyndeton
   c. litotes
   d. anaphora

4. *spem vultu simulat, premit altum corde dolorem* (line 209)
   a. anaphora
   b. chiasmus
   c. prolepsis
   d. synecdoche

What noun does each of these adjectives/participles modify?

a. *iactatum* (line 182) **Anthea (line 181)**

b. *tres* (line 184) **cervos**

c. *errantes* (line 185) **cervos (line 184)**

d. *celeres* (line 187) **sagittas**

e. *ferentes* (line 189) **ductores**

f. *ingentia* (line 192) **corpora (line 193)**

g. *omnes* (line 194) **socios**

h. *bonus* (line 195) **Acestes**

i. *passi* (line 199) **socii (line 198)**

j. *sonantes* (line 200) **scopulos (line 201)**

k. *quietas* (line 205) **sedes**

What two items does each *-que* connect?

a. line 187 (first *-que*) **constitit (line 187)** and **corripuit (line 188)**

b. line 187 (second *-que*) **arcum** and **sagittas**

c. line 189 **corripuit (line 188)** and **sternit (line 190)**

d. line 208 **refert (line 208)** and **simulat (line 209)**

What is the object(s) of these verbs/participles?

a. *sequuntur* (line 185) **hos**

b. *ferentes* (line 189) **capita**

c. *dederat* (line 196) **quae (line 195)**

d. *passi* (line 199) **graviora**

e. *refert* (line 208) **talia**

Translation *Suggested time: 15 minutes*

Translate the following lines as literally as possible.

> 'O socii (neque enim ignari sumus ante malorum),
> o passi graviora, dabit deus his quoque finem.
> Vos et Scyllaeam rabiem penitusque sonantes
> accestis scopulos, vos et Cyclopia saxa
> 5   experti: revocate animos maestumque timorem
> mittite; forsan et haec olim meminisse iuvabit.'

Literal translation
"O companions (for neither are we ignorant of troubles before), o men having suffered more severe things, the god will give a limit to these [things], too. You have approached the Scyllaean rage and the deeply resounding cliffs, and you [have] experienced the Cyclopian rocks. Call back your spirits and let go of sorrowful fear; perhaps at some time [in the future] it will be pleasing to remember even these things."

The sections into which a passage is divided are flexible, as are the possible acceptable meanings for any given word. Teachers may prefer a different scheme of "chunking" and range of meanings; what is given below is just one option. Since students must prove to the reader that they understand the grammar of the passage, loose translations are not acceptable, and students should clearly demonstrate the information given under "notes."

15 units
Range of possible meanings followed by notes on grammar and syntax:

o socii	Oh allies/comrades/companions, friends (vocative)
neque enim ignari sumus	for neither are we unknowing/ignorant/unaware/inexperienced
ante malorum	of troubles/evils/difficulties, bad [things] earlier, before, in the past (*ante* as adverb)
o passi graviora	O [you] having endured/suffered/experienced worse, more serious, weightier, heavier [things] (*passi* vocative participle; *graviora* object of *passi*)
dabit deus his quoque finem	god will also/too give/grant an end/limit/boundary to/for these [things]
vos accestis	you have approached (*vos* subject; *accestis* perfect)
et Scyllaeam rabiem	both Scylla's rage/madness/fury
penitusque sonantes scopulos	and the rocks/crags/cliffs resounding/sounding/roaring deeply/wholly/within (object of *accestis*; *penitus* modifies *sonantes*)
vos et experti	and you have experienced/tried (*vos* nominative)
Cyclopia saxa	the Cyclops'/Cyclopes'/Cyclopean rocks (object of *experti* [*estis*])
revocate animos	recall/restore [your] spirits/courage/minds (imperative)

maestumque timorem mittite	and send away/dismiss/let go [your] sad/grievous/gloomy fear (*maestum* modifies *timorem*)
forsan	perhaps/perchance/possibly (adverb)
olim meminisse iuvabit	someday/in the future it will be pleasing/helpful to remember/recall (*et* is not conjunction; *haec* is object of *meminisse*)
et haec	even these [things] (*iuvabit* future; defective verb *meminisse* translated as present infinitive)

Essay *Suggested time: 20 minutes*

This passage recalls several episodes in the *Odyssey*: Odysseus killing a deer for his men, his encounters with Scylla and the Cyclops, and the detailed description of the preparation of food. Given these epic allusions, Aeneas's brief "private moment" in lines 208–209 stands out. Why does Vergil show Aeneas as having these two facets, the heroic and the human? Present your response in a well-organized essay.

Support your assertions with references drawn from throughout this passage (lines 180–222). All Latin words must be copied or their line numbers provided, AND they must be translated or paraphrased closely enough so that it is clear you understand the Latin. It is your responsibility to convince your reader that you are basing your conclusions on the Latin text and not merely on a general recollection of the passage. Direct your answer to the question; do not merely summarize the passage. Please write your essay on a separate piece of paper.

This essay is quite sophisticated, as it asks why the author has depicted Aeneas as he has. There is no "correct" answer to the question, so students will need to feel confident that they are able to support their theses. Ideas and phrases drawn from the Latin text <u>must all be translated</u> in student essays in order to receive credit.

Students will respond to essay topics in various ways, and different essays, with quite different approaches, may be of equal quality. The following are three essay responses that high school Latin students wrote. These essays have not been edited but left as they were written. A brief critique follows each.

Student response #1:
These two lines really allow the audience to connect with Aeneas in that they too would feel the immense pain from such a situation, while at the same time the audience admires Aeneas's heroism in that he is able to feign hope for the benefit of his comrades. Vergil also uses chiasmus in line 209 to accentuate the conflicting emotions felt by Aeneas: pain on the inside, hope on the outside.

Also, it was common for heroes, back then, to display their emotions openly. By these lines the audience can see that he still feels the emotions but decides it is better for his comrades to display a hopeful expression.

Not an adequate reply, since the student does not follow the instructions and writes only about lines 208–209. The entire passage provides important information for answering the question. This essay would likely earn a score of 1.

Student response #2:
To his men, Aeneas is a leader. They have all just endured many hardships including the loss of comrades. They are down trodden, and need inspiration to be able to continue on their journey. Aeneas provides this inspiration for them. He goes out alone in search of food, and kills enough deer for them to feast on. He gives them a speech, telling them to dismiss their fears and "prepare for following matters." Since Aeneas has no one to confide in, the readers are the only people who get to see Aeneas's true feelings. Aeneas has endured just as much as his men have, so he is just as afraid. No one is there to give him a pep talk, so he is forced to suppress his pain and grieve in silence. While looking out on the sea, Aeneas sees nothing of his lost comrades. However, he continues to lead his men, mourning the lost souls to himself.

Better than response #1, but still not adequate; the student has referred specifically to only one phrase in the passage. His/her observations about the reader's unusual perspective could, if more fully developed, make this essay much stronger. This essay would likely earn a score of 2.

Student response #3:
Vergil shows Aeneas as having two sides because throughout the story, Aeneas has always been an accidental/unwilling hero. When he first speaks, he wishes he could have died along with his countrymen defending Troy. But since he is an accidental hero, it would be unlikely that suddenly he becomes heroic in every scene and show no signs of weakness. In addition, the duality of his character makes him more human and real. It is hard to imagine anyone who has just had his country conquered and been forced to leave his home and on his way to a new land, lose even more of his men, and come out emotionally unscathed. He takes care of his men by giving them food/meat (*socios partitur in omnes*) and drink (*vina dividit*), and by encouraging them (*revocate animos*). The fact that he, too, mourns for his friends with a heavy heart (*Praecipue pius Aeneas nunc acris Oronti, nunc Amyci casum gemit . . . Cloanthum*) shows he is compassionate and a good leader; a good leader cares about the lives and well-being of his followers. This also shows that Aeneas has self-control, another leadership trait; he can put on a front (*spem vultu simulat*) to encourage his men and keep his own doubts and woes deep in his heart (*premit altum corde dolorem*).

A very good answer, since the student realizes what the question is getting at and uses citation from the Latin text, along with paraphrase, effectively and accurately. This essay would likely earn a score of 5.

Scansion

Scan the following lines.

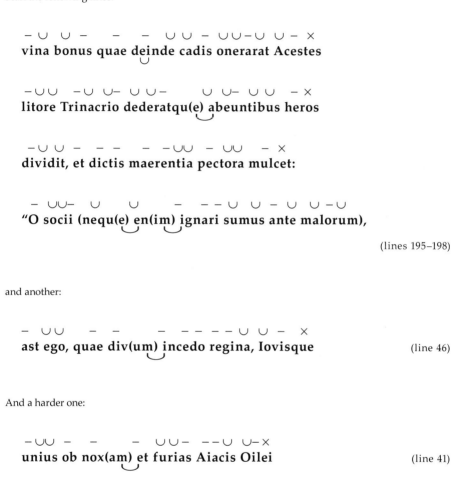

(lines 195–198)

and another:

(line 46)

And a harder one:

(line 41)

LESSON 6: BOOK 1.418–440

```
       Corripuere viam interea, qua semita monstrat.
       Iamque ascendebant collem, qui plurimus urbi
420    imminet adversasque adspectat desuper arces.
       Miratur molem Aeneas, magalia quondam,
       miratur portas strepitumque et strata viarum.
       Instant ardentes Tyrii: pars ducere muros
       molirique arcem et manibus subvolvere saxa,
425    pars optare locum tecto et concludere sulco;
       iura magistratusque legunt sanctumque senatum.
       Hic portus alii effodiunt; hic alta theatris
       fundamenta locant alii, immanesque columnas
       rupibus excidunt, scaenis decora alta futuris.
430    Qualis apes aestate nova per florea rura
       exercet sub sole labor, cum gentis adultos
       educunt fetus, aut cum liquentia mella
       stipant et dulci distendunt nectare cellas,
       aut onera accipiunt venientum, aut agmine facto
435    ignavum fucos pecus a praesepibus arcent;
       fervet opus redolentque thymo fraglantia mella.
       'O fortunati, quorum iam moenia surgunt!'
       Aeneas ait et fastigia suspicit urbis.
       Infert se saeptus nebula (mirabile dictu)
440    per medios, miscetque viris neque cernitur ulli.
```

Comprehension Questions

NB: Some questions may have several possible correct responses; a sample is given.

1. What is the effect of the anaphora in lines 421–422? **It emphasizes Aeneas's amazement at Dido's achievements.**

2. In lines 418–429, what phrases show that the various aspects of city life are all being established in Carthage? (Make sure you translate and provide the line references for the phrases that you use to answer the question.)

   - **protection:** *portas* (line 422), gates; *arcem* (line 424), citadel; *muros* (line 423), walls
   - **roads:** *strata viarum* (line 422), pavements for roads
   - **legal system:** *iura, magistratus, senatum* (line 426), laws, magistrates, senate
   - **maritime trade:** *portus* (line 427), harbors
   - **entertainment:** *theatris* (line 427), theaters
   - **dwellings:** *molem, magalia quondam* (line 421), mass [of the city], formerly huts; *tecto* (line 425), building(s)

3. What events in the narrative are enhanced by the extended simile (lines 430–436)?

   The simile makes more vivid the division of labor among the Carthaginians and the number of people involved in the building of the city.

4. What is Aeneas's reaction when he first sees Carthage? **He is amazed (*miratur*) and envious (*fortunati!*).**

Multiple Choice Questions *Suggested time: 15 minutes*

1. In line 418, *corripuere* is
   a. future perfect indicative
   b. perfect infinitive
   c. present infinitive
   d. perfect indicative

2. *urbi* (line 419) is dative
   a. indirect object
   b. with *imminet* (line 420)
   c. with *plurimus* (line 419)
   d. of agent

3. *Miratur* (line 422) has how many direct objects?
   a. 0
   b. 1
   c. 2
   d. 3

4. *legunt* (line 426) has how many direct objects?
   a. 1
   b. 2
   c. 3
   d. 4

5. One thing Vergil does NOT mention the Carthaginians building (lines 421–429) is
   a. temples
   b. theaters
   c. roads
   d. harbors

6. In line 429, *decora* is in apposition to
   a. *scaenis* (line 429)
   b. *alta* (line 429)
   c. *rupibus* (line 429)
   d. *columnas* (line 428)

7. The subject of *exercet* (line 431) is
   a. *apes* (line 430)
   b. *labor* (line 431)
   c. *rura* (line 430)
   d. *qualis* (line 430)

8. In line 432, *fetus* is
   a. genitive singular
   b. nominative plural
   c. accusative plural
   d. nominative singular

9. Lines 431–432 (*cum . . . fetus*) are best translated
   a. **when they lead out the adult offspring of the tribe**
   b. when the adults of the tribe lead out the offspring
   c. when the offspring lead out the adult tribes
   d. the offspring lead out the adults with the tribes

10. The first four feet of line 434 are scanned
    a. spondee-spondee-dactyl-dactyl
    b. dactyl-spondee-dactyl-spondee
    c. dactyl-dactyl-dactyl-dactyl
    d. **dactyl-dactyl-dactyl-spondee**

11. *dictu* (line 439) is translated
    a. by saying
    b. **to say**
    c. with a word
    d. than a word

12. In line 440, *ulli* is
    a. genitive singular
    b. nominative plural
    c. ablative singular
    d. **dative singular**

Translation *Suggested time: 15 minutes*

Translate the passage below as literally as possible.

> Corripuere viam interea, qua semita monstrat.
> Iamque ascendebant collem, qui plurimus urbi
> imminet adversasque adspectat desuper arces.
> Miratur molem Aeneas, magalia quondam,
> 5   miratur portas strepitumque et strata viarum.

Literal Translation
Meanwhile they hastened on the road in any way the path shows, and now they were climbing a hill, which, very large, menaces the city and looks at the facing citadels from above. Aeneas wonders at the mass, once huts, he wonders at the gates and the uproar and the pavements of the roads.

The sections into which a passage is divided are flexible, as are the possible acceptable meanings for any given word. Teachers may prefer a different scheme of "chunking" and range of meanings; what is given below is just one option. Since students must prove to the reader that they understand the grammar of the passage, loose translations are not acceptable, and students should clearly demonstrate the information given under "notes."

18 units
Range of possible meanings followed by notes on grammar and syntax:

interea	meanwhile, meantime (adverb)
Corripuere viam	they hastened upon/took hold of/snatched up the road/way (3rd person perfect; *viam* is object)

qua	where(by), in any way
semita monstrat	the path shows/points out (*semita* is subject of *monstrat*)
Iamque	and now, and then, at this point (adverb)
ascendebant collem	they were climbing/ascending/going up a hill/mountain (imperfect tense)
qui	which (antecedent is *collem*)
plurimus	very large, with imposing size, in its great size (modifies *qui*)
urbi imminet	threatens/menaces/hangs over the city (*urbi* is object of *imminet*)
desuper	from above (adverb)
adspectat adversasque arces	and looks at/faces/views/sees the facing/opposite citadels (subject is *qui*; -*que* connects *adspectat* and *imminet*; *adversas* modifies *arces*)
Aeneas	Aeneas (subject of *miratur*)
Miratur molem	wonders at/is amazed at/admires the mass/structure (*molem* is object of *miratur*)
quondam	once, once upon a time (adverb)
magalia	huts (in apposition to *molem*)
miratur portas	wonders at/is amazed at/admires the gates (*portas* is object of *miratur*)
strepitumque	and the noise/uproar (*et* connects *strepitum* and *strata*; *strata* is object of *miratur*)
et strata viarum	and the beds/pavements of the streets/roads/ways

Short Answer Questions

Matching

1. **F** ablative of time when a. *plurimus* (line 419)
2. **D** accusative plural noun b. *subvolvere* (line 424)
3. **J** dative of agent c. *tecto* (line 425)
4. **C** dative of purpose d. *portus* (line 427)
5. **B** historical infinitive e. *alta* (line 429)
6. **H** neuter accusative noun f. *aestate* (line 430)
7. **E** neuter adjective g. *venientum* (line 434)
8. **G** present participle h. *pecus* (line 435)
9. **A** superlative adjective i. *dictu* (line 439)
10. **I** supine j. *ulli* (line 440)

Essay *Suggested time: 20 minutes*

What activities described in lines 421–429 does Vergil highlight with the extended simile of lines 430–436? How does the extended simile make the previous lines more vivid? Present your response in a well-organized essay.

All Latin words must be copied or their line numbers provided, AND they must be translated or paraphrased closely enough so that it is clear you understand the Latin. It is your responsibility to convince your reader that you are basing your conclusions on the Latin text and not merely on a general recollection of the passage. Direct your answer to the question; do not merely summarize the passage. Please write your essay on a separate piece of paper.

Students will respond to essay topics in various ways, and different essays, with quite different approaches, may be of equal quality. The following are some possible points students may make; it is not a sample essay.

This essay asks students to demonstrate an understanding of the role of an extended simile in epic. Students should formulate a thesis and then support it with Latin. Some ideas and phrases, <u>all of which must be translated</u> in student essays, may include the following: Vergil emphasizes the extent of the work and the division of labor of the Tyrians by comparing them to the work of bees and the distinct roles they play. The Tyrians have constructed a city (*molem*, line 421), complete with gates and roads (*portas, strata viarum*, line 422). Their work is divided: some (*pars*, line 423) are building the city's defenses (*ducere muros*, line 423; *moliri arcem*, line 424) while others (*pars*, line 425) are building homes (*optare locum tecto*, line 425). Some (*alii*, line 427) are building the port (*portus effodiunt*, line 427) while others (*alii*, line 428) are constructing a theater (*fundamenta locant*, line 428). In the simile, the challenge of the work (*labor*, line 431) is emphasized (*exercet*, line 431). Some lead out (*educunt*, line 432) the grown offspring (*adultos fetus*, lines 431–432), while others fill the hive with honey (*liquentia mella stipant, distendunt nectare cellas*, lines 432–433). Some receive the pollen that the others bring in (*onera accipiunt venientum*, line 434), while others keep the drones from the hive (*ignavum pecus a praesepibus arcent*, line 435). Just as the bees' work is fervent (*fervet opus*, line 436), the Tyrians work fervently to build Carthage. Vergil is asking the reader to acknowledge the challenge of building the various aspects of a city, perhaps with a nod to the extensive rebuilding program in which Augustus was involved.

See the Scoring Guidelines on pp. xvii–xviii.

Scansion

Scan the following lines.

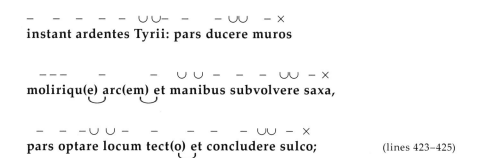

(lines 423–425)

LESSON 7: BOOK 1.494–538

      Haec dum Dardanio Aeneae miranda videntur,
495 dum stupet obtutuque haeret defixus in uno,
      regina ad templum, forma pulcherrima Dido,
      incessit magna iuvenum stipante caterva.
      Qualis in Eurotae ripis aut per iuga Cynthi
      exercet Diana choros, quam mille secutae
500 hinc atque hinc glomerantur Oreades; illa pharetram
      fert umero gradiensque deas supereminet omnes
      (Latonae tacitum pertemptant gaudia pectus):
      talis erat Dido, talem se laeta ferebat
      per medios instans operi regnisque futuris.
505 Tum foribus divae, media testudine templi,
      saepta armis solioque alte subnixa resedit.
      Iura dabat legesque viris, operumque laborem
      partibus aequabat iustis aut sorte trahebat:
      cum subito Aeneas concursu accedere magno
510 Anthea Sergestumque videt fortemque Cloanthum
      Teucrorumque alios, ater quos aequore turbo
      dispulerat penitusque alias avexerat oras.
      Obstipuit simul ipse, simul percussus Achates
      laetitiaque metuque; avidi coniungere dextras
515 ardebant, sed res animos incognita turbat.
      Dissimulant et nube cava speculantur amicti
      quae fortuna viris, classem quo litore linquant,
      quid veniant; cunctis nam lecti navibus ibant
      orantes veniam et templum clamore petebant.
520 Postquam introgressi et coram data copia fandi,
      maximus Ilioneus placido sic pectore coepit:
      'O regina, novam cui condere Iuppiter urbem
      iustitiaque dedit gentes frenare superbas,
      Troes te miseri, ventis maria omnia vecti,
525 oramus: prohibe infandos a navibus ignes,
      parce pio generi, et propius res aspice nostras.
      Non nos aut ferro Libycos populare penates
      venimus, aut raptas ad litora vertere praedas;
      non ea vis animo nec tanta superbia victis.
530 Est locus, Hesperiam Grai cognomine dicunt,
      terra antiqua, potens armis atque ubere glaebae;
      Oenotri coluere viri; nunc fama minores
      Italiam dixisse ducis de nomine gentem.
      Hic cursus fuit,

535 cum subito adsurgens fluctu nimbosus Orion
     in vada caeca tulit penitusque procacibus Austris
     perque undas superante salo perque invia saxa
     dispulit; huc pauci vestris adnavimus oris.

Comprehension Questions

NB: Some questions may have several possible correct responses; a sample is given.

1. What is Aeneas doing when Dido enters the temple? **He is transfixed, gazing at the amazing pictures on the temple walls.**

2. In the simile (lines 498–502), to whom or what is the *magna iuvenum stipante caterva* compared?

    The throng of youths surrounding Dido is compared to the chorus of Oreads who accompany Diana.

3. Why is Leto happy? **She is proud of her daughter Diana.**

4. Why does Vergil depict Dido performing the acts she does in lines 507–508? **He shows that she is a good and fair leader.**

5. What is the *res incognita* of line 515? **How Dido will react to Aeneas's comrades.**

6. What are Aeneas's comrades doing in lines 518–519? **Coming to the temple to ask Dido for mercy.**

7. How does Ilioneus compliment Dido in the opening of his speech? **He says that she has been able to establish a new city and to restrain haughty peoples.**

8. What three requests does Ilioneus make? **He asks her not to burn their ships, to spare his people, and to look carefully at their situation.**

9. In lines 527–529, how does Ilioneus reassure Dido of the Trojans' good intentions?

    He explains that the Trojans do not intend to destroy her people or plunder her property, and that, as conquered people, do not have power or pride.

10. How does the etymological explanation in line 533 contribute to the theme of Ilioneus's speech?

    In his use of "*Italiam gentem*" Vergil reminds his reader that Ilioneus is speaking of the Romans' own land and at the same time he emphasizes the long-lasting importance of leadership, since the land has been named for its leader.

11. How, according to Ilioneus, did the Trojans reach the Libyan shore? **After being blown toward Libya by the storm winds, a few men swam to shore.**

Short Answer Questions

1. How is *dum* (lines 494 and 495) translated? **while**
2. What case is *Aeneae* (line 494)? **dative**
3. What case is *forma* (line 496)? **ablative**
4. How is the phrase *magna iuvenum stipante caterva* (line 497) translated? **with a great crowd of youths crowding about**
5. What poetic device does *qualis* (line 498) introduce? **simile**
6. What is the antecedent of *quam* (line 499)? **Diana (line 499)**
7. What does *secutae* (line 499) modify? **Oreades (line 500)**
8. Who/what is *illa* (line 500)? **Diana**
9. What is the subject of *pertemptant* (line 502)? **gaudia**
10. Who/what does *saepta* (line 506) describe? **Dido**
11. Who/what is the subject of *aequabat* (line 508)? **Dido**
12. Why is *accedere* (line 509) in the infinitive? **indirect statement**
13. Who/what is the antecedent of *quos* (line 511)? **alios (line 511) or Teucrorum (line 511)**
14. Who is *ipse* (line 513)? **Aeneas**
15. Who/what does *avidi* (line 514) describe? **Aeneas and Achates**
16. Why are *linquant* (line 517) and *veniant* (line 518) in the subjunctive? **indirect question**
17. Who/what does *lecti* (line 518) describe? **men/comrades of Aeneas (from the twleve saved ships)**
18. What part of speech is *fandi* (line 520)? **gerund**
19. What are the case and use of *cui* (line 522)? **dative, indirect object**
20. How can you tell by scansion what case *iustitia* (line 523) is? **the final -a must be long because it's the first syllable of the dactyl; therefore the word is ablative.**
21. What word does *miseri* (line 524) modify? **Troes**
22. What use of the dative is *generi* (line 526)? **with *parce*, a special verb**
23. What part of speech is *propius* (line 526)? **comparative adverb**
24. What part of speech is *victis* (line 529)? **perfect passive participle**
25. *Terra* (line 531) is in apposition with what Latin word? **locus (line 530)**
26. How can you tell by scansion what case *fama* (line 532) is? **the final -a must be short because it's the second syllable of the dactyl; therefore the word is nominative.**

27. What use of the infinitive is *dixisse* (line 533)? **indirect statement**

28. What word does *adsurgens* (line 535) modify? **Orion**

29. What part of speech is *penitus* (line 536)? **adverb**

30. What use of the ablative is *salo* (line 537)? **ablative absolute**

Translation *Suggested time: 20 minutes*

Translate the following passage as literally as possible.

> Iura dabat legesque viris, operumque laborem
> partibus aequabat iustis aut sorte trahebat:
> cum subito Aeneas concursu accedere magno
> Anthea Sergestumque videt fortemque Cloanthum
> 5 Teucrorumque alios, ater quos aequore turbo
> dispulerat penitusque alias avexerat oras.

Literal Translation
She gave rights and laws to men, and she equalized the labor of the works in equal parts or drew [the work assignments] by lot—when suddenly Aeneas sees approaching in a great crowd Antheas and Sergestus and brave Cloanthus and others of the Trojans whom the black whirlwind at sea had driven apart and had deep within carried to other shores.

The sections into which a passage is divided are flexible, as are the possible acceptable meanings for any given word. Teachers may prefer a different scheme of "chunking" and range of meanings; what is given below is just one option. Since students must prove to the reader that they understand the grammar of the passage, loose translations are not acceptable, and students should clearly demonstrate the information given under "notes."

18 units
Range of possible meanings followed by notes on grammar and syntax:

dabat viris	she was giving/granting the men/to the men (indirect object)
Iura legesque	justice/rights and laws (*-que* connecting the two direct objects)
-que aequabat	and she was making equal/equalizing/dividing equally (*-que* connecting *dabat* and *aequabat*)
operum laborem	the hardship/labor/effort of the works/jobs/undertakings (*operum* genitive, *laborem* direct object)
partibus iustis	in equal/fair/just parts/divisions
aut sorte trahebat	or [she] was drawing/taking/dragging [them] by lot
cum subito	when suddenly
Aeneas videt	Aeneas sees
concursu magno	in/with a great/large/big crowd/throng/gathering
accedere Anthea	[that] Antheas approaches/is approaching/approaching (*Anthea* subject of *accedere*)

Sergestumque	and Sergestus (*-que* connects *Anthea* and *Sergestum*; *Sergestum* subject of *accedere*)
fortemque Cloanthum	and brave/strong/hearty Cloanthus (*-que* connects *Sergestum* and *Cloanthum*; *fortem* modifies *Cloanthum*; *Cloanthum* subject of *accedere*)
Teucrorumque alios	and others of the Trojans/Teucrians (*-que* connects *Cloanthum* and *alios*; *Teucrorum* genitive)
ater turbo	black/dark/gloomy whirlwind/storm/tornado (*ater* modifies *turbo*)
quos dispulerat	whom [*ater turbo*] had scattered/dispelled (antecedent of *quos* is *Teucrorum* or *alios*; pluperfect tense)
aequore	on the sea (ablative)
penitusque avexerat	and had carried off/transported off completely/deeply/altogether (*penitus* adverb; pluperfect tense)
alias oras	to other shores (accusative of place to which)

Essays *Suggested time: 60 minutes (20 minutes per essay)*

1. By comparing Dido to Diana (lines 498–504), what does Vergil suggest about Dido? Present your response in a well-organized essay.

2. What is Aeneas feeling in lines 513–519? Present your response in a well-organized essay.

3. What background information about the Trojans does Ilioneus provide in lines 522–538, and how does he expect this to influence Dido?

For each essay above, support your assertions with references drawn from throughout the passage indicated by each essay, that is, lines 498–504 for essay #1, lines 513–519 for essay #2, and lines 522–538 for essay #3. All Latin words must be copied or their line numbers provided, AND they must be translated or paraphrased closely enough so that it is clear you understand the Latin. It is your responsibility to convince your reader that you are basing your conclusions on the Latin text and not merely on a general recollection of the passage. Direct your answer to the question; do not merely summarize the passage. Please write your essays on a separate piece of paper.

Students will respond to essay topics in various ways, and different essays, with quite different approaches, may be of equal quality. The following are some possible points students may make; they are not sample essays.

Essay #1: This topic may present a challenge because a strong answer must incorporate general knowledge about both Dido and Diana, not simply the information provided in this passage. Students should be sure to write a thesis statement and then support it. Ideas and phrases, all of which must be translated in student essays, may include the following. Diana's role as leader of her chorus of Oreads is emphasized in the simile (*deas supereminet omnes*, line 501), thereby underscoring Dido's abilities as a leader. Students may also discuss Diana's hearty, self-confident nature in comparison to Dido's. Some students familiar with the rest of the poem and with mythology may find ironic the comparison of chaste Diana to Dido, who blames herself for having had two "husbands."

Essay #2 asks students to describe Aeneas's feelings. Students may present weak responses if they limit themselves to only one emotion. Students should be sure to write a thesis statement and then support it. Ideas and phrases, all of which must be translated in student essays, may include the following. Aeneas is amazed at what he is seeing (*obstipuit*, line 513); he and Achates feel both joyous (*laetitia*, line 514) and fearful (*metu*, line 514). They are eager (*avidi*, line 514) to join their friends, but are held back from doing so by lack of certainty about the situation (*res animos incognita turbat*, line 515). They remain enclosed in safety in their cloud and learn what has happened to their comrades. We see here that Aeneas has a natural, human range of responses to a heroic/epic situation.

Essay #3 asks students to analyze the motivations for Ilioneus's appeal to Dido. A strong answer should address the rhetorical effectiveness of the entire passage and should answer both parts of the question. Students may include that Ilioneus is trying to evoke sympathy from Dido by including background about their journey (*Troes te miseri, ventis maria omnia vecti*, line 524), the destination they hope to reach (*Est locus, Hesperiam Grai cognomine dicunt*, line 530), and the storm at sea (lines 535–538).

See the Scoring Guidelines on pp. xvii–xviii.

Scansion

Scan the following lines.

```
  —    ∪ ∪ —  — —      — —  — — ∪ ∪  — ×
dum stupet obtutuqu(e) haeret defixus in uno,

 — —     —  —      —   — —    —  — ∪ ∪  — ×
regin(a) ad templum, forma pulcherrima Dido,
```

(lines 495–96)

and another:

```
 —     —   —  ∪ ∪—     — — —  — ∪ ∪ — ×
saept(a) armis solioqu(e) alte subnixa resedit.
```

(line 506)

LESSON 8: BOOK 1.539–578

Quod genus hoc hominum? Quaeve hunc tam barbara morem
540　permittit patria? Hospitio prohibemur harenae;
bella cient primaque vetant consistere terra.
Si genus humanum et mortalia temnitis arma,
at sperate deos memores fandi atque nefandi.
Rex erat Aeneas nobis, quo iustior alter
545　nec pietate fuit, nec bello maior et armis.
Quem si fata virum servant, si vescitur aura
aetheria neque adhuc crudelibus occubat umbris,
non metus, officio nec te certasse priorem
paeniteat. Sunt et Siculis regionibus urbes
550　armaque Troianoque a sanguine clarus Acestes.
Quassatam ventis liceat subducere classem
et silvis aptare trabes et stringere remos,
si datur Italiam sociis et rege recepto
tendere, ut Italiam laeti Latiumque petamus;
555　sin absumpta salus, et te, pater optime Teucrum,
pontus habet Libyae, nec spes iam restat Iuli,
at freta Sicaniae saltem sedesque paratas,
unde huc advecti, regemque petamus Acesten.'
Talibus Ilioneus; cuncti simul ore fremebant
560　Dardanidae.
Tum breviter Dido vultum demissa profatur:
'Solvite corde metum, Teucri, secludite curas.
Res dura et regni novitas me talia cogunt
moliri, et late fines custode tueri.
565　Quis genus Aeneadum, quis Troiae nesciat urbem,
virtutesque virosque aut tanti incendia belli?
Non obtunsa adeo gestamus pectora Poeni,
nec tam aversus equos Tyria Sol iungit ab urbe.
Seu vos Hesperiam magnam Saturniaque arva
570　sive Erycis fines regemque optatis Acesten,
auxilio tutos dimittam opibusque iuvabo.
Vultis et his mecum pariter considere regnis?
Urbem quam statuo, vestra est; subducite navis;
Tros Tyriusque mihi nullo discrimine agetur.
575　Atque utinam rex ipse Noto compulsus eodem
adforet Aeneas! Equidem per litora certos
dimittam et Libyae lustrare extrema iubebo,
si quibus eiectus silvis aut urbibus errat.'

Comprehension Questions

1. How does Ilioneus feel he and his comrades have been treated? Copy out words and phrases from lines 539–543 to support your answer.

   He feels they have been treated poorly. He wonders what country allows such treatment (*morem permittit*, lines 539–540). He says they have been prevented from landing (*hospitio prohibemur*, line 540), and that the Carthaginians stirred up wars (*bella cient*, line 541) and prevented the Trojans from landing (*vetant consistere terra*, line 541). He argues that even if the Carthaginians scorn humans (*genus humanum ... temnitis*, line 542), they should consider that the gods take notice of right and wrong (*deos memores fandi atque nefandi*, line 543).

2. Ilioneus says Dido will not regret helping the Trojans (line 549) under what condition?

   If Aeneas is alive (*si fata virum servant, si vescitur aura*, line 546), (*neque adhuc crudelibus occubat umbris*, line 547).

3. In lines 551–558 Ilioneus presents two options that the Trojans may have. What are they?

   They may either go to Italy (*si datur Italiam ... tendere*, lines 553–554) if Aeneas is alive, or to Sicily (*freta Sicaniae sedesque paratas ... regemque petamus Acesten*, lines 557–558) if Aeneas is dead.

4. What reason does Dido give for the treatment given the Trojans? **Her situation is difficult (*res dura*, line 563) and because her kingdom is new (*regni novitas*, line 563), she must guard her borders carefully (*late fines custode tueri*, line 564).**

5. Why is Dido willing to help the Trojans? **Because she knows of them (*genus Aeneadum*), their city (*Troiae urbem*), their courage (*virtutes*), their men (*viros*) and the destruction of war (*incendia belli*). (All from lines 565–566).**

6. What does Dido wish for in lines 575–576? What does she say she will do? **She wishes Aeneas were present (*utinam adforet Aeneas*). She says she will send out men (*certos dimittam*) and order them to look for Aeneas (*lustrare iubebo*).**

Multiple Choice Questions *Suggested time: 25 minutes*

1. In line 540, *hospitio* is
   a. ablative of means
   b. ablative of separation
   c. dative, indirect object
   d. dative with special verb

2. The case, number, and gender of *prima* (line 541) are
   a. nominative plural neuter
   b. accusative plural neuter
   c. nominative singular feminine
   d. ablative singular feminine

3. The case of *memores* (line 543) is
   a. nominative
   b. genitive
   c. accusative
   d. ablative

4. In line 543, *fandi* is
   a. participle
   b. gerund
   c. gerundive
   d. adjective

5. The best translation of lines 544–545 (*rex . . . armis*) is
   a. Aeneas had been the king for us, because of whom another was not more just in duty nor greater in war and weapons.
   b. We had Aeneas as our king, because of whose devotion each was neither more just nor greater in war and weapons.
   c. For us Aeneas was the king, for whom there was neither any fairer sense of duty nor greater war and weapons.
   d. Aeneas was our king, than whom another was neither more righteous in duty nor greater in war and arms.

6. In line 546, *aura* is
   a. ablative object of *vescitur* (line 546)
   b. ablative of separation
   c. accusative object of *vescitur* (line 546)
   d. nominative subject of *vescitur* (line 546)

7. The best translation of line 551 (*quassatam . . . classem*) is
   a. Let us be permitted to beach our fleet shattered by the winds.
   b. It is permitted to lead our fleet broken by the winds.
   c. May it be permitted to lead our broken fleet down from the winds.
   d. Let the shattered fleet be beached by the winds.

8. In line 555, *te* refers to
   a. Aeneas
   b. Dido
   c. Teucer
   d. Jupiter

9. Line 555 contains an example of
   a. synecdoche
   b. apostrophe
   c. hendiadys
   d. anastrophe

10. In line 557, *saltem* is a(n)
    a. accusative, singular adjective
    b. accusative, singular noun
    c. adverb
    d. present subjunctive

11. *Acesten* (line 558) was originally
    a. Italian
    b. Greek
    c. Trojan
    d. Libyan

12. The metrical pattern of the first four feet of line 564 is
    a. dactyl-dactyl-spondee-spondee
    b. spondee-dactyl-spondee-dactyl
    c. dactyl-spondee-dactyl-spondee
    d. spondee-spondee-spondee-spondee

13. In line 565, *nesciat* is a
    a. deliberative subjunctive
    b. future indicative
    c. subjunctive in an indirect question
    d. subjunctive in a relative clause of purpose

14. *Saturnia arva* (line 569) refers to
    a. Tyre
    b. Troy
    c. Italy
    d. Sicily

15. *Erycis* (line 570) is
    a. a city near Carthage
    b. a city near Troy
    c. a city in Latium
    d. a city in Sicily

16. In line 571, *dimittam* is
    a. future indicative
    b. accusative singular
    c. present subjunctive
    d. an adverb

17. From line 574 we understand that
    a. neither Trojan nor Tyrian has committed any crime against Dido
    b. the Trojans and Tyrians will not enter into any contests with one another
    c. Dido will treat the Trojans and Carthaginians in the same way
    d. Tros and Tyrius will not be allowed to enter into a lawsuit

18. *Adforet* (line 576) is subjunctive in a(n)
    a. indirect question
    b. wish (optative)
    c. purpose clause
    d. possibility (potential)

19. *Equidem* (line 576) means
    a. a certain
    b. several
    c. an equal
    d. indeed

20. In line 578, *eiectus* modifies
    a. *Tros* (understood)
    b. *Aeneas* (understood)
    c. the subject of *iubebo* (line 577)
    d. *Ilioneus* (understood)

Translation *Suggested time: 20 minutes*

Translate the following passage as literally as possible.

> Rex erat Aeneas nobis, quo iustior alter
> nec pietate fuit, nec bello maior et armis.
> Quem si fata virum servant, si vescitur aura
> aetheria neque adhuc crudelibus occubat umbris,
> 5   non metus, officio nec te certasse priorem
> paeniteat. Sunt et Siculis regionibus urbes
> armaque Troianoque a sanguine clarus Acestes.

Literal Translation
Aeneas was our king/Aeneas was the king for us, than whom another was not fairer in duty nor greater in war and weapons. If the fates protect this man, if he feeds upon the ethereal air and does not yet lie among the cruel shades, there [should be] no fear, nor should you regret/it be a source of regret for you to have vied [to be] first in kindness. There are also in the Sicilian regions cities and weapons and famous Acestes from Trojan blood.

The sections into which a passage is divided are flexible, as are the possible acceptable meanings for any given word. Teachers may prefer a different scheme of "chunking" and range of meanings; what is given below is just one option. Since students must prove to the reader that they understand the grammar of the passage, loose translations are not acceptable, and students should clearly demonstrate the information given under "notes."

20 units
Possible range of meanings:

Rex erat Aeneas	Aeneas was a king, [our] king was Aeneas, we had Aeneas as our king, Aeneas was the king (correct tense)
nobis	for us, to us; our; we (when translated as subject of sentence, showing understanding of dative of possession; *nobis* as dative of possessor)
quo	than whom (ablative of comparison)
iustior alter fuit	another [person/man] was more fair/juster/more righteous
nec pietate	neither in [respect to] duty/loyalty/devotion (ablative of specification)
nec maior	nor greater/bigger
bello et armis	in [respect to] war/fighting and arms/weapons (ablative of specification)
si fata servant	if the fates protect/preserve/save (*fata* subject of *servant*)
Quem virum	this man/hero (*quem* modifies *virum*; direct object of *servant*)
si vescitur aura aetheria	if he feeds on/lives on/breathes the ethereal/upper air/breeze (*aura aetheria* object of *vescitur*)
neque adhuc occubat	nor/and does not yet lie/lie dead
crudelibus umbris	among/in the cruel/heartless shades/shadows (ablative of place where)
non metus	[there is/there should be] no fear

nec te paeniteat	nor should you regret/feel shame; nor should it repent you/ nor should it shame you (subjunctive)
certasse priorem	to have strived/vied/fought [to be] first
officio	in duty/kindness/office (ablative of specification)
Sunt et urbes armaque	there are [for us] also/even cities and weapons
Siculis regionibus	in the Sicilian regions (ablative place where)
clarus Acestes	and famous/well-known/illustrious Acestes
Troianoque a sanguine	from Trojan blood/bloodline/stock

Essay *Suggested time: 20 minutes*

In her speech (lines 562–578) Dido both defends the actions of her people and offers help to the Trojans. Explain how she does this and whether or not she is acting as a responsible leader.

All Latin words must be copied or their line numbers provided, AND they must be translated or paraphrased closely enough so that it is clear you understand the Latin. It is your responsibility to convince your reader that you are basing your conclusions on the Latin text and not merely on a general recollection of the passage. Direct your answer to the question; do not merely summarize the passage. Please write your essay on a separate piece of paper.

Students will respond to essay topics in various ways, and different essays, with quite different approaches, may be of equal quality. The following are some possible points students may make; it is not a sample essay.

   This essay asks students to analyze how Dido defends the hostile actions of her people and what offers of assistance she gives the Trojans and to use that analysis to argue about her effectiveness as a leader. She defends the actions of her people by explaining that their difficult situation (*res dura*, line 563) and that the newness of her kingdom (*regni novitas*, line 563) compel her to plan such things (*talia cogunt moliri*, lines 563–564) as keeping visitors from landing and treating them with hostility; they also force her to protect her territory far and wide with guards (*late fines custode tueri*, line 564). She offers to send the Trojans off with help (*auxilio tutos dimittam opibusque iuvabo*, line 571). She also offers to allow them to remain with her (*vultis mecum pariter considere*, line 572), where she will treat them as her own people (*Tros Tyriusque mihi nullo discrimine agetur*, line 574). Finally, she says she will send scouts to look for Aeneas (*certos lustrare iubebo*, lines 576–577) in case he is wandering about (*eiectus errat*, line 578). Her explanation of her people's behavior shows she is being a responsible leader. Students might argue that her offers of help and quick acceptance of the Trojans into her kingdom, based solely on their reputation, is not responsible; on the other hand, it may demonstrate that she is helping her city by accepting tried and true men who can assist with its building and protection.

See the Scoring Guidelines on pp. xvii–xviii.

Scansion

Scan the following lines.

```
 −      ∪∪ −   − −∪ ∪− −   −  ∪ ∪− ×
Atqu(e) utinam rex ipse Noto compulsus eodem
```

```
 − ∪ ∪  − − − ∪  ∪ −    − −∪∪ − ×
adforet Aeneas! Equidem per litora certos
```

```
 − −       − ∪ ∪− − −   −  − ∪ ∪ − ×
dimitt(am) et Libyae lustrar(e) extrema iubebo,
```

```
 −  ∪ ∪ − − − −  −  − ∪ ∪ − ×
si quibus eiectus silvis aut urbibus errat.
```

(lines 575–579)

LESSON 9: BOOK 2.40–56

40   Primus ibi ante omnes magna comitante caterva
Laocoon ardens summa decurrit ab arce,
et procul "O miseri, quae tanta insania, cives?
Creditis avectos hostis? Aut ulla putatis
dona carere dolis Danaum? Sic notus Ulixes?
45   Aut hoc inclusi ligno occultantur Achivi,
aut haec in nostros fabricata est machina muros,
inspectura domos venturaque desuper urbi,
aut aliquis latet error; equo ne credite, Teucri.
Quidquid id est, timeo Danaos et dona ferentes."
50   Sic fatus validis ingentem viribus hastam
in latus inque feri curvam compagibus alvum
contorsit. Stetit illa tremens, uteroque recusso
insonuere cavae gemitumque dedere cavernae.
Et, si fata deum, si mens non laeva fuisset,
55   impulerat ferro Argolicas foedare latebras,
Troiaque nunc staret, Priamique arx alta maneres.

Comprehension Questions

1. What case does Laocoon make (lines 42–49) for not accepting the horse into the city?

    He says the Greeks are known for their deceptiveness and this situation is no different. He suspects the horse is a war machine and that Greeks are hiding within it.

2. What does Laocoon do in lines 51–52? **He hurls his spear at the side of the wooden horse.**

3. The contrary to fact condition in lines 54–56 evokes what emotions? **Regret; if the Trojans had listened to Laocoon, Troy would not have been destroyed.**

Multiple Choice Questions *Suggested time: 6 minutes*

1. Line 45 contains an example of
   a. alliteration
   b. **metonymy**
   c. anastrophe
   d. hyperbaton

2. *Teucri* in line 48 is
   a. genitive
   b. nominative
   c. **vocative**
   d. ablative

3. In line 52, *illa* refers to
   a. **hastam (line 50)**
   b. *curvam* (line 51)
   c. *cavae* (line 53)
   d. *alvum* (line 51)

4. In line 56, *staret* is translated
   a. was standing
   b. **would stand**
   c. will stand
   d. might have stood

5. Line 56 contains an example of
   a. anaphora
   b. hyperbole
   c. **apostrophe**
   d. hendiadys

Translation *Suggested time: 15 minutes*

Translate the following passage as literally as possible.

>   Aut hoc inclusi ligno occultantur Achivi,
>   aut haec in nostros fabricata est machina muros,
>   inspectura domos venturaque desuper urbi,
>   aut aliquis latet error; equo ne credite, Teucri.
> 5   Quidquid id est, timeo Danaos et dona ferentes."

Literal Translation
Either Greeks are hidden enclosed in this wood or this machine was fashioned against our walls, to look into [our] homes and to come into our city from above, or some deceit lies hidden; do not trust the horse, Trojans. Whatever it is, I fear Greeks even bearing gifts.

The sections into which a passage is divided are flexible, as are the possible acceptable meanings for any given word. Teachers may prefer a different scheme of "chunking" and range of meanings; what is given below is just one option. Since students must prove to the reader that they understand the grammar of the passage, loose translations are not acceptable, and students should clearly demonstrate the information given under "notes."

14 units
Range of possible meanings followed by notes on grammar and syntax:

Aut occultantur Achivi	either the Greeks/Achaeans lie hidden/are hidden/are concealed/are secreted
hoc inclusi ligno	[having been] enclosed/confined in this wood/horse (*hoc* modifies *ligno*; *inclusi* modifies *Achivi*)
aut haec machina	or this [war] machine/device/engine (nominative)
fabricata est	has been/was fashioned/made/created/fabricated
in nostros muros	against/toward our walls/city
inspectura domos	about to/intending to/to look into [our] homes/houses (future participle, *domos* direct object of *inspectura*)
venturaque desuper	and about to/intending to/to come from above (future participle)
urbi	to [our] city (dative of direction)
aut aliquis latet error	or some deceit/trick/error lies [hidden] (*aliquis* modifies *error*)
equo ne credite	do not trust/believe the horse (imperative; *equo* object of *credite*)
Teucri	Trojans/Teucrians (vocative)
Quidquid id est	whatever it is
timeo Danaos	I fear Greeks/Danaans
et dona ferentes	even/also bearing/carrying/bringing gifts (*et* for *etiam*; *dona* object of *ferentes*)

Short Answer Questions

Provide the answers as required.

1. *caterva* (line 40): what use of the ablative? **ablative absolute**

2. *summa* (line 41): what does it modify? ***arce* (line 41)**

3. *cives* (line 42): what case? **vocative**

4. *hostis* (line 43): what case and use? **accusative subject of indirect statement**

5. *dolis* (line 44): what use of the ablative? **separation or with *carere*, a verb that takes the ablative**

6. *inspectura* (line 47): what is its object? ***domos* (line 47)**

7. *equo* (line 48): what case and use? **dative with *credite* (line 48)**

8. *ferentes* (line 49): what is its direct object? ***dona* (line 49)**

9. *curvam* (line 51): what does it modify? ***alvum* (line 51)**

10. *contorsit* (line 52): what is its direct object? ***hastam* (line 50)**

11. *insonuere* (line 53): what is its subject? ***cavernae* (line 53)**

12. *dedere* (line 53): what is its direct object? ***gemitum* (line 53)**

Essay *Suggested time: 20 minutes*

> Ac veluti magno in populo cum saepe coorta est
> seditio saevitque animis ignobile vulgus
> iamque faces et saxa volant, furor arma ministrat;
> tum, pietate gravem ac meritis si forte virum quem
> 5   conspexere, silent arrectisque auribus astant;
> ille regit dictis animos et pectora mulcet:
> sic cunctus pelagi cecidit fragor, aequora postquam
> prospiciens genitor caeloque invectus aperto
> flectit equos curruque volans dat lora secundo.
>   (Book 1.148–156)

The passage above and the one included in this lesson (Book 2.40–56) depict characters trying to bring order to a chaotic situation. How does Vergil intertwine mortal and divine concerns in these two depictions?

Support your assertions with references drawn from throughout both passages (1.148–156 and 2.40–56). All Latin words must be copied or their line numbers provided, AND they must be translated or paraphrased closely enough so that it is clear you understand the Latin. It is your responsibility to convince your reader that you are basing your conclusions on the Latin text and not merely on a general recollection of the passages. Direct your answer to the question; do not merely summarize the passages. Please write your essay on a separate piece of paper.

Students will respond to essay topics in various ways, and different essays, with quite different approaches, may be of equal quality. The following are some possible points students may make; it is not a sample essay.

This essay contains an implicit expectation that students will compare two passages, and discuss the ways both human and divine affairs are depicted in each. Students should be sure to write a thesis statement and then support it. Ideas and phrases, <u>all of which must be translated</u> in student essays, may include the following. Some students may see the *virum* (line 151 or line 4) of the first passage and Laocoon as similarly protective and pious leaders, while others may feel that that in the first passage the *virum* gains control of the chaos because of his reputation (*pietate gravem ac meritis*, line 151 or line 4), but Laocoon is ineffective because after his speech he hurls his weapon, and does not calm nor persuade the crowd. Some students may contrast the two passages, pointing out that in the first the leader stops the mob from hurling weapons, while in the second the leader is the one who takes up arms. In the first passage, the leader is known for his *pietas*, and because of his loyalty or duty to his fellow man and to the gods, he is effective. In the simile, Neptune is compared to this human, and the stormy seas to the human mob, thus connecting the divine and the mortal. In the second passage, Laocoon, a priest of Neptune (though this detail is not included in the passage), gives a speech that is true, yet his efforts are completely ineffective, showing that even a dutiful priest cannot change the course of events, and that the *fata deum* (line 54) are more powerful than a priest.

See the Scoring Guidelines on pp. xvii–xviii.

Scansion

Scan the following lines.

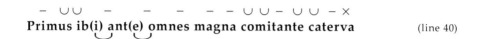
Primus ib(i) ant(e) omnes magna comitante caterva   (line 40)

1. How does scansion show what case *magna* is? **The final -a of *magna* scans long, so it must be ablative.**

Laocoon ardens summa decurrit ab arce,   (line 41)

2. How does scansion show what case *summa* is? **The final -a of *summa* scans long, so it must be ablative.**

– ∪ ∪   – ∪ ∪–   – –   – ∪∪ – ×
et procul 'O miseri, quae tant(a) insania, cives?   (line 42)

3. How does scansion show what case *insania* is? **The final -a of *insania* scans short, so it must be nominative.**

LESSON 10: BOOK 2.201-249

Laocoon, ductus Neptuno sorte sacerdos,
sollemnes taurum ingentem mactabat ad aras.
Ecce autem gemini a Tenedo tranquilla per alta
(horresco referens) immensis orbibus angues
205 incumbunt pelago pariterque ad litora tendunt;
pectora quorum inter fluctus arrecta iubaeque
sanguineae superant undas, pars cetera pontum
pone legit sinuatque immensa volumine terga.
Fit sonitus spumante salo; iamque arva tenebant
210 ardentesque oculos suffecti sanguine et igni
sibila lambebant linguis vibrantibus ora.
Diffugimus visu exsangues. Illi agmine certo
Laocoonta petunt; et primum parva duorum
corpora natorum serpens amplexus uterque
215 implicat et miseros morsu depascitur artus;
post ipsum auxilio subeuntem ac tela ferentem
corripiunt spirisque ligant ingentibus; et iam
bis medium amplexi, bis collo squamea circum
terga dati superant capite et cervicibus altis.
220 Ille simul manibus tendit divellere nodos
perfusus sanie vittas atroque veneno,
clamores simul horrendos ad sidera tollit:
qualis mugitus, fugit cum saucius aram
taurus et incertam excussit cervice securim.
225 At gemini lapsu delubra ad summa dracones
effugiunt saevaeque petunt Tritonidis arcem,
sub pedibusque deae clipeique sub orbe teguntur.
Tum vero tremefacta novus per pectora cunctis
insinuat pavor, et scelus expendisse merentem
230 Laocoonta ferunt, sacrum qui cuspide robur
laeserit et tergo sceleratam intorserit hastam.
Ducendum ad sedes simulacrum orandaque divae
numina conclamant.
Dividimus muros et moenia pandimus urbis.
235 Accingunt omnes operi pedibusque rotarum
subiciunt lapsus, et stuppea vincula collo
intendunt: scandit fatalis machina muros
feta armis. Pueri circum innuptaeque puellae
sacra canunt funemque manu contingere gaudent;
240 illa subit mediaeque minans inlabitur urbi.
O patria, o divum domus Ilium et incluta bello
moenia Dardanidum! Quater ipso in limine portae

```
           substitit atque utero sonitum quater arma dedere;
           instamus tamen immemores caecique furore
    245    et monstrum infelix sacrata sistimus arce.
           Tunc etiam fatis aperit Cassandra futuris
           ora dei iussu non umquam credita Teucris.
           Nos delubra deum miseri, quibus ultimus esset
           ille dies, festa velamus fronde per urbem.
```

Comprehension Questions

NB: Some questions may have several possible correct responses; a sample is given.

1. What was Laocoon doing when the snakes were coming ashore? **He was sacrificing a bull.**

2. What two Greek leaders do the two snakes (lines 203–204) symbolize? **They represent Agamemnon and Menelaus.**

3. What event in the narrative is enhanced by the simile (lines 223–224)? **Laocoon's screams as he is being killed.**

4. What is the result of Laocoon's death? **The Trojans are convinced to bring the horse into the city.**

5. What omen/sign do the Trojans ignore as they drag the horse into the city? **The horse halted four times on the threshold of the city gate, and four times the arms within the horse made a sound.**

6. From throughout the passage, find all the words related to snakes or snake imagery. Provide line references in parentheses.

   Much of lines 203–211 contains descriptions of the snakes, but especially vivid are the phrases *immensis orbibus angues; iubae sanguineae; sinuat immensa volumine terga; sibila lambebant linguis vibrantibus ora*. Elsewhere in the passage are *amplexus*, line 214; *implicat*, line 215; *spiris ingentibus*, line 217; *amplexi*, line 218; *lapsu*, line 225; *dracones*, line 225; *insinuat*, line 229; *lapsus*, line 236; *inlabitur*, line 240.

Multiple Choice Questions *Suggested time: 25 minutes*

1. Lines 201–202 (*Laocoon . . . aras*) tell us that Laocoon
   a. had been led to Neptune's priest
   b. was solemn before the temple of Neptune
   c. had led a bull to Neptune
   d. **was sacrificing a bull**

2. The case and number of *fluctus* (line 206) is
   a. **accusative plural**
   b. nominative plural
   c. nominative singular
   d. genitive singular

3. What part of speech is *pone* (line 208)?
   a. noun
   b. verb
   c. adverb
   d. adjective

4. From line 212 (*diffugimus . . . exsangues*), we can infer that
   a. the snakes were bloodless
   b. the Trojans were afraid
   c. most Trojans escaped from the snakes
   d. the snakes were bloody in their sight

5. From lines 213–215 (*et . . . artus*), we can infer that
   a. Laocoon's sons were young
   b. the bodies of the snakes were small
   c. Laocoon loved his sons
   d. Lacoon's sons embraced each other in their fear

6. The words *miseros . . . artus* (line 215) are translated
   a. the limb with respect to the wretched ones is fed upon with a bite
   b. [each] feeds upon the limbs with a wretched bite
   c. the limbs of the wretched ones are fed upon with a bite
   d. [each] feeds upon the wretched limbs with its bite

7. In line 221, *perfusus* describes
   a. *sanie* (line 221)
   b. *nodos* (line 220)
   c. *ille* (line 220)
   d. *vittas* (line 221)

8. Lines 223–224 (*qualis . . . securim*) tell us that
   a. the bull Laocoon was sacrificing fled
   b. Laocoon was screaming like a wounded bull
   c. Laocoon, wounded, fled to the altar
   d. the bull fled with uncertainty because it was wounded

9. Another name for *Tritonidis* (line 226) is
   a. Minerva
   b. Juno
   c. Triton
   d. Neptune

10. Lines 229–230 (*et . . . ferunt*) tell us that
    a. the Trojans carried off Laocoon's body after he died
    b. Laocoon had carefully considered his wrongdoing
    c. the Trojans felt Laocoon deserved his death
    d. the Trojans mourned for Laocoon because of his penalty

11. The tense and mood of *laeserit* (line 231) is
    a. perfect indicative
    b. pluperfect subjunctive
    c. future perfect indicative
    d. perfect subjunctive

12. The metrical pattern of the first four feet of line 232 is
    a. spondee-spondee-dactyl-dactyl
    b. spondee-spondee-dactyl-spondee
    c. dactyl-dactyl-dactyl-spondee
    d. dactyl-dactyl-spondee-dactyl

13. In line 232, *simulacrum* refers to
    a. the spear
    b. the statue of the goddess
    c. the horse
    d. Laocoon

14. The words *scandit . . . armis* (lines 237–238) are translated
    a. the machine climbs the deadly walls, pregnant with arms
    b. the deadly machine, pregnant with weapons, climbs the walls
    c. the machine, pregnant with deadly weapons, climbs the walls
    d. the walls are mounted by the machine pregnant with deadly weapons

15. In line 240, *illa* refers to
    a. *machina* (line 237)
    b. *puellae* (line 238)
    c. *sacra* (line 239)
    d. *urbi* (line 240)

16. What figure of speech occurs in lines 241–242 (*o . . . Dardanidum*)?
    a. hendiadys
    b. tmesis
    c. zeugma
    d. apostrophe

17. Line 244 (*instamus . . . furore*) tells us that the Trojans
    a. thought Laocoon was heedless and furious
    b. were not thinking clearly
    c. were furious
    d. pressed on although they remembered Laocoon's madness

18. The word *Teucris* (line 247) is translated
    a. for the Trojans
    b. of the Trojans
    c. by the Trojans
    d. with the Trojans

19. In line 248, *quibus* refers to
    a. *nos* (line 248)
    b. *delubra* (line 248)
    c. *dies* (line 249)
    d. *dei* (line 247)

Translation *Suggested time: 15 minutes*

Translate the following lines as literally as possible.

        Ille simul manibus tendit divellere nodos
        perfusus sanie vittas atroque veneno,
        clamores simul horrendos ad sidera tollit:
        qualis mugitus, fugit cum saucius aram
5   taurus et incertam excussit cervice securim.

Literal Translation
At that very moment that one [*i.e.*, Laocoon] tries to pull apart the knots with [his] hands, his headbands soaked [lit., having been soaked with respect to his headbands] with gore and black poison, at that very moment he raises horrifying cries to the stars. Of such a sort is the mooing, when a wounded bull has fled the altar and has shaken off from [his] neck the ill-aimed axe.

The sections into which a passage is divided are flexible, as are the possible acceptable meanings for any given word. Teachers may prefer a different scheme of "chunking" and range of meanings; what is given below is just one option. Since students must prove to the reader that they understand the grammar of the passage, loose translations are not acceptable, and students should clearly demonstrate the information given under "notes."

15 units
Range of possible meanings followed by notes on grammar and syntax:

ille simul tendit	That one/he at the same time/at that moment aims/tries
divellere nodos	to rip/tear apart/pluck/remove the knots (complementary infinitive with *tendit*)
manibus	with [his] hands (ablative of means)
perfusus	[having been] suffused/soaked/drenched (participle modifying *ille*)
vittas	as to/in respect to [his] fillets/ribbons/garlands/bands (accusative of respect or specification)
sanie	with/by blood/gore
atroque veneno	and with/by black/dark/gloomy poison
simul tollit	at the same time/then he lifts/raises
clamores horrendos	horrible/horrifying shouts/clamors/screams
ad sidera	to/toward the stars/planets
qualis mugitus	such/just like/of such a sort [is] the mooing/lowing/bellowing/roaring
cum saucius taurus	when a wounded/harmed/hurt bull/ox
fugit aram	has fled/run from the altar (perfect tense)
et incertam excussit securim	and has shaken off the unsure/uncertain/ill-aimed axe (perfect tense)
cervice	from his neck (ablative of separation)

Essays *Suggested time: 40 minutes (20 minutes per essay)*

1. The description of the snakes and their actions (lines 203–227) is extraordinarily vivid. How does Vergil achieve this effect? What senses does his description include? Present your response in a well-organized essay.

2. In lines 234–249, Aeneas emphasizes with regret the rashness of the Trojans in bringing the horse into their city. How does he convey this? Present your response in a well-organized essay.

For each essay above, support your assertions with references drawn from throughout the passage indicated by each essay, that is, lines 203–227 only for essay #1 and lines 234–249 for essay #2. All Latin words must be copied or their line numbers provided, AND they must be translated or paraphrased closely enough so that it is clear you understand the Latin. It is your responsibility to convince your reader that you are basing your conclusions on the Latin text and not merely on a general recollection of the passage. Direct your answer to the question; do not merely summarize the passage. Please write your essays on a separate piece of paper.

In Essay #1 students are asked to think about how Vergil has crafted his description of the snakes. Most students will begin with the notion that the description is vivid and will use this as their thesis. After they have written a thesis, students must support it with evidence from the Latin. Ideas and phrases, <u>all of which must be translated</u> in student essays, may include the following. By introducing the passage with the word *Ecce*, addressed to the reader, Vergil makes the following description more immediate. Aeneas says that he shudders just recalling the event, *horresco referens* (line 204), and he underlines the bloodthirsty nature of the serpents by the use of words like *sanguineae* (line 207), *sanguine* (line 210), and *exsangues* (line 212). We hear the serpents, *fit sonitus* (line 209), *sibila . . . ora* (line 211), and Laocoon's desperate roar, *clamores horrendas* (line 222), which is likened to the roar of a wounded sacrificial ox (line 223). The sinuous curves of the snakes are emphasized by *orbibus* (line 204), *sinuat* (line 208), *volumine* (line 208), *implicat* (line 215), *spiris* (line 217), and *nodos* (line 220). Students might also write about how the reader is made to feel sympathy for the boys by the use of *parva corpora* (lines 213–214) and *miseros* (line 215). The essay lends itself to a wide variety of answers, many of which would suitably address the topic.

    Essay #2 asks students to show how we see the regret Aeneas and the other Trojans feel. Possible responses might include the apostrophe in lines 241–242; his description of himself and townspeople as *immemores* (line 244), *caeci furore* (line 244), and *miseri* (line 248); the epithet *infelix* (line 245) for the horse, and the use of *monstrum* (line 245) for the horse. The juxtaposition of the joy people feel in lines 238–239 with the destructive nature of the horse (*fatalis*, line 237; *minans*, line 240) heightens the reader's sympathy for the Trojans and underscores Aeneas's sense of regret.

See the Scoring Guidelines on pp. xvii–xviii.

Scansion

Scan the following lines.

```
  −   −    −    ∪∪ −  ∪ ∪−       −    −∪∪ −   ×
incumbunt pelago pariterqu(e) ad litora tendunt;

 −  ∪∪    −       −   −   −   −  − ∪∪   −   ×
pectora quor(um) inter fluctus arrecta iubaeque

 −    ∪ ∪−  ∪ ∪−     −    −     −    −∪∪  −   ×
sanguineae superant undas, pars cetera pontum

 − ∪ ∪ −  ∪∪−       −    − ∪  ∪−  ∪∪  −  ×
pone legit sinuatqu(e) immensa volumine terga.
```

(lines 205–208)

Notes

LESSON 11: BOOK 2.268–297

      Tempus erat quo prima quies mortalibus aegris
incipit et dono divum gratissima serpit.
270 In somnis, ecce, ante oculos maestissimus Hector
visusque adesse mihi largosque effundere fletus,
raptatus bigis ut quondam, aterque cruento
pulvere perque pedes traiectus lora tumentes.
Ei mihi, qualis erat, quantum mutatus ab illo
275 Hectore qui redit exuvias indutus Achilli
vel Danaum Phrygios iaculatus puppibus ignes;
squalentem barbam et concretos sanguine crines
vulneraque illa gerens, quae circum plurima muros
accepit patrios. Ultro flens ipse videbar
280 compellare virum et maestas expromere voces:
"O lux Dardaniae, spes o fidissima Teucrum,
quae tantae tenuere morae? Quibus Hector ab oris
exspectate venis? Ut te post multa tuorum
funera, post varios hominumque urbisque labores
285 defessi aspicimus! Quae causa indigna serenos
foedavit vultus? Aut cur haec vulnera cerno?"
Ille nihil, nec me quaerentem vana moratur,
sed graviter gemitus imo de pectore ducens,
"Heu fuge, nate dea, teque his" ait "eripe flammis.
290 Hostis habet muros; ruit alto a culmine Troia.
Sat patriae Priamoque datum: si Pergama dextra
defendi possent, etiam hac defensa fuissent.
Sacra suosque tibi commendat Troia penates;
hos cape fatorum comites, his moenia quaere
295 magna, pererrato statues quae denique ponto."
Sic ait et manibus vittas Vestamque potentem
aeternumque adytis effert penetralibus ignem.

Comprehension Questions

1. How does Hector look when he appears to Aeneas? Why does he look this way?

    He appears defiled, bloody, and wounded because he has been killed by Achilles and then dragged around the walls of Troy by him.

2. What is Aeneas's reaction when he sees Hector? **Aeneas is happy and relieved (*exspectate*, line 283) to see his friend (*lux, spes*, line 281), but is also confused, because in his dream he does not appear to remember Achilles's defilement of Hector.**

3. What instructions does Hector give Aeneas? **Hector tells Aeneas to flee from the city.**

4. Hector boasts a bit in lines 291–292. What does he say? **He says that Troy is falling, and that if it had been possible for Troy to be saved, he himself would have done it.**

5. What does Hector do in the final two lines of this passage? What do you think the significance of this is?

   He removes the ever-burning hearth fire, symbolizing home and security, from its shrine and entrusts it to Aeneas. Hector thereby indicates that it is time to abandon Troy and to establish a new home elsewhere.

Short Answer Questions

Indicate True or False. Place a "T" or "F" as appropriate in the line provided.

1. **F**   In line 268 *quo* is translated "by which."
2. **T**   *gratissima* (line 269) modifies *quies* (line 268).
3. **F**   *fletus* in line 271 is nominative singular.
4. **F**   *Phrygios* (line 276) refers to the Greeks.
5. **T**   In line 279, *ipse* is translated "I myself."
6. **T**   *spes* (line 281) refers to Hector.
7. **F**   *quae* in line 285 is accusative, plural, neuter.
8. **T**   In line 287, *vana* is the object of *quaerentem*.
9. **F**   *dea* (line 289) is vocative.
10. **F**   *commendat* in line 293 is present subjunctive.
11. **F**   *potentem* (line 296) and *aeternum* (line 297) both modify *ignem* (line 297).

Translation *Suggested time: 15 minutes*

Translate the following passage as literally as possible.

> "Sat patriae Priamoque datum: si Pergama dextra
> defendi possent, etiam hac defensa fuissent.
> Sacra suosque tibi commendat Troia penates;
> hos cape fatorum comites, his moenia quaere
> 5   magna, pererrato statues quae denique ponto."

Literal translation
Enough [has been] given to the homeland and to Priam; if Troy were able to be defended by [any] hand, it would indeed have been defended by this [one]. Troy entrusts [her] holy things [i.e., rituals] and her household gods to you; take these [as] companions of [your] fates; seek for these great walls, which you will establish at last, the sea having been thoroughly wandered.

The sections into which a passage is divided are flexible, as are the possible acceptable meanings for any given word. Teachers may prefer a different scheme of "chunking" and range of meanings; what is given below is just one option. Since students must prove to the reader that they understand the grammar of the passage, loose translations are not acceptable, and students should clearly demonstrate the information given under "notes."

12 units
Range of possible meanings followed by notes on grammar and syntax:

sat datum	enough has been given/granted (*datum* [*est*])
patriae Priamoque	to the country/fatherland/homeland and to Priam (dative)
si Pergama defendi possent	if Pergamum/Troy/the citadels of Troy were able to be defended/protected (present contrary to fact protasis)
dextra	by a right [hand]/by a hand/by any hand (ablative of means)
etiam defensa fuissent	indeed/even they/it would have been defended (past contrary to fact apodosis)
hac	by this [one/hand] (ablative of means)
commendat Troia	Troy entrusts/commits
sacra suosque tibi penates	the sacred rites/things/objects and its Penates/household gods to you (*sacra* and *penates* are objects of *commendat*)
hos cape fatorum comites	take these [as] companions/comrades of [your] fates
his moenia quaere magna	seek/look for great/large/big walls for these (*his* is dative of reference)
statues quae denique	which you will establish/found/build/set up finally/at last (*statues* is future; antecedent of *quae* is *moenia*)
pererrato ponto	[with] the sea/ocean/water [having been] wandered [through]/traversed (ablative absolute)

Short Answer Questions

Find, copy out, and provide line references in parentheses for:

1. an ablative absolute **pererrato ponto (line 295)**
2. two neuter relative pronouns **quae (line 295), quae (line 278)**
3. a verb in the future tense **statues (line 295)**
4. a passive infinitive **defendi (line 292)**
5. a perfect passive participle in the vocative **exspectate (line 283)**
6. four superlative adjectives **fidissima (line 281), gratissima (line 269), maestissimus (line 270), imo (line 288)**
7. three nouns in the vocative **lux, spes (line 281), nate (line 289)**
8. three objects of *gerens* (line 278) **barbam (line 277), crines (line 277), vulnera (line 278)**
9. a reflexive pronoun in the accusative **te (line 289)**
10. a reflexive adjective in the accusative **suos (line 293)**
11. the object of *ducens* (line 288) **gemitus (line 288)**

Translation and Analysis Questions

1. Why do you think Vergil used the verb *serpit* (line 269)? **The sleep, which will lead to the destruction of Troy, slithers in as the snakes did.**

2. From lines 270–279, copy out and translate the phrases that describe Hector's appearance. How does his appearance affect the reader?

    The description of Hector's wounds evokes the reader's sympathy: *squalentem barbam*, **line 277 (filthy beard);** *concretos sanguine crines*, **line 277 (hair matted with blood);** *vulnera gerens*, **line 278 (bearing wounds).**

3. What effect do the lines 274–276 have? **These lines recall how heroic Hector once had been, just as Troy once was.**

4. What feelings about Hector does Aeneas express in his speech (lines 281–286)? Copy out and translate three phrases to support your answer.

    Aeneas admires Hector (*lux Dardaniae***, line 281), considers him a hero (***spes fidissima Teucrum***, line 281), and misses him (***exspectate***, line 283).**

5. How does Hector's statement at line 293 support an aspect of Aeneas's character that Vergil has emphasized earlier in the poem?

    Troy entrusts its religion, the centerpiece of its identity, to Aeneas, emphasizing Aeneas's sense of *pietas*.

Essay *Suggested time: 20 minutes*

How does the appearance of Hector's ghost to Aeneas mark a transition between the past and the future?

Support your assertions with references drawn from throughout the passage (lines 268–297). All Latin words must be copied or their line numbers provided, AND they must be translated or paraphrased closely enough so that it is clear you understand the Latin. It is your responsibility to convince your reader that you are basing your conclusions on the Latin text and not merely on a general recollection of the passage. Direct your answer to the question; do not merely summarize the passage. Please write your essay on a separate piece of paper.

This essay asks students to read closely to recognize not just how Hector's ghost is described, but how the appearance of the ghost symbolizes a transition from the past to the future. Students may refer to the past heroism of Hector (*quantum mutatus . . . ignes*, lines 274–276) as contrasted with his current state (*squalentem barbam . . . gerens*, lines 277–278). Students may also see the past glory of Hector as symbolizing the past glory of Troy, and his destroyed state as symbolizing Troy's destruction. The arrival of Hector's ghost marks a transition to the future as he enjoins Aeneas to escape from Troy (*Heu fuge*, line 289) because it has been taken by the enemy (*Hostis . . . Troia*, line 290), and to seek a new life elsewhere (*his . . . ponto*, lines 294–295). It is at this point that Aeneas begins to turn his thoughts to the future.

See the Scoring Guidelines on pp. xvii-xviii.

Scansion

Scan the following lines. NB: They are not consecutive lines but three discrete selections.

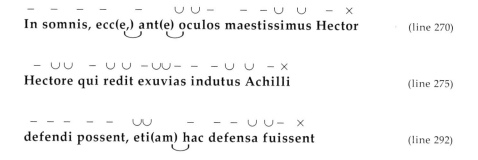

LESSON 12: BOOK 2.559–620

      At me tum primum saevus circumstetit horror.
560 Obstipui; subiit cari genitoris imago,
      ut regem aequaevum crudeli vulnere vidi
      vitam exhalantem, subiit deserta Creusa
      et direpta domus et parvi casus Iuli.
      Respicio et quae sit me circum copia lustro.
565 Deseruere omnes defessi, et corpora saltu
      ad terram misere aut ignibus aegra dedere.
      [Iamque adeo super unus eram, cum limina Vestae
      servantem et tacitam secreta in sede latentem
      Tyndarida aspicio; dant claram incendia lucem
570 erranti passimque oculos per cuncta ferenti.
      Illa sibi infestos eversa ob Pergama Teucros
      et Danaum poenam et deserti coniugis iras
      praemetuens, Troiae et patriae communis Erinys,
      abdiderat sese atque aris invisa sedebat.
575 Exarsere ignes animo; subit ira cadentem
      ulcisci patriam et sceleratas sumere poenas.
      "Scilicet haec Spartam incolumis patriasque Mycenas
      aspiciet, partoque ibit regina triumpho?
      Coniugiumque domumque patris natosque videbit
580 Iliadum turba et Phrygiis comitata ministris?
      Occiderit ferro Priamus? Troia arserit igni?
      Dardanium totiens sudarit sanguine litus?
      Non ita. Namque etsi nullum memorabile nomen
      feminea in poena est, habet haec victoria laudem;
585 exstinxisse nefas tamen et sumpsisse merentes
      laudabor poenas, animumque explesse iuvabit
      ultricis †famam et cineres satiasse meorum."
      Talia iactabam et furiata mente ferebar,]
      cum mihi se, non ante oculis tam clara, videndam
590 obtulit et pura per noctem in luce refulsit
      alma parens, confessa deam qualisque videri
      caelicolis et quanta solet, dextraque prehensum
      continuit roseoque haec insuper addidit ore:
      "Nate, quis indomitas tantus dolor excitat iras?
595 Quid furis? Aut quonam nostri tibi cura recessit?
      Non prius aspicies ubi fessum aetate parentem
      liqueris Anchisen, superet coniunxne Creusa
      Ascaniusque puer? Quos omnes undique Graiae
      circum errant acies et, ni mea cura resistat,
600 iam flammae tulerint inimicus et hauserit ensis.

Non tibi Tyndaridis facies invisa Lacaenae
culpatusve Paris, divum inclementia, divum
has evertit opes sternitque a culmine Troiam.
Aspice (namque omnem, quae nunc obducta tuenti
605 mortales hebetat visus tibi et umida circum
caligat, nubem eripiam; tu ne qua parentis
iussa time neu praeceptis parere recusa):
hic, ubi disiectas moles avulsaque saxis
saxa vides, mixtoque undantem pulvere fumum,
610 Neptunus muros magnoque emota tridenti
fundamenta quatit totamque a sedibus urbem
eruit. Hic Iuno Scaeas saevissima portas
prima tenet sociumque furens a navibus agmen
ferro accincta vocat.
615 Iam summas arces Tritonia, respice, Pallas
insedit nimbo effulgens et Gorgone saeva.
Ipse pater Danais animos viresque secundas
sufficit, ipse deos in Dardana suscitat arma.
Eripe, nate, fugam finemque impone labori;
620 nusquam abero et tutum patrio te limine sistam."

Comprehension Questions

NB: Some questions may have several possible correct responses; a sample is given.

1. What prompts Aeneas to think of his own father in line 560? **As Aeneas watches Priam die, he thinks of his own father, who is the same age as Priam.**

2. What three reasons does Vergil give (lines 571–574) for Helen to have hidden herself?

   She fears the Trojans because she is hateful to the Trojans because of the destruction of their city, and she fears both the punishment from the Greeks and anger of her husband.

3. In lines 575–587, what does Aeneas want to do to Helen? How does he convince himself that it is an acceptable course of action?

   Aeneas wants to kill her, and although he knows killing a woman does not bring long-lasting glory, he feels in this case he will be praised for taking vengeance.

4. What people does Venus recall first to Aeneas's attention in lines 594–598?

   Anchises, Creusa, and Iulus.

84 • VERGIL

5. In lines 598–603, who does Venus say are NOT to blame for the downfall of Troy?

   Helen and Paris.

6. What four divinities does Venus name as responsible for Troy's destruction (lines 604–618)?

   Neptune, Juno, Athena, and Jupiter.

7. What is ironic about Venus's command in line 619? **Although she tells him to put an end to his labor/hardship, he has much more ahead of him.**

8. How does Venus reassure Aeneas in line 620? **She says she will always be present and she will make sure he arrives home safely.**

Multiple Choice Questions *Suggested time: 41 minutes*

1. The subject of *obstipui* (line 560) is
   a. *Creusa* (understood)
   b. *imago* (line 560)
   c. *horror* (line 559)
   d. *Aeneas* (understood)

2. In line 562, *exhalantem* modifies
   a. *vitam* (line 562)
   b. *regem* (line 561)
   c. *aequaevum* (line 561)
   d. *Creusa* (line 562)

3. Line 564 contains an example of
   a. anastrophe
   b. hendiadys
   c. apostrophe
   d. anaphora

4. In line 565, *saltu* is a(n)
   a. noun
   b. participle
   c. adverb
   d. adjective

5. Lines 567–569 (*Iamque . . . aspicio*) are best translated
   a. And now I go forth and in addition was alone, and I spy the daughter of Tyndarus protecting herself with Vesta's thresholds and, silent, lurking in the remote seat.
   b. And already I was the only one, when I catch sight of silent Helen saving herself at the thresholds of Vesta and secretly hiding in that seat.
   c. And already I am going forth and was left alone, when look at the thresholds of Vesta and the silent daughter of Tyndarus saving herself and hiding in the secret location.
   d. And at that point indeed I alone was left, when I see Helen keeping Vesta's thresholds and, silent, hiding in the remote location.

6. In line 571, *sibi* refers to
   a. **Helen**
   b. Vesta
   c. the Trojans
   d. Aeneas

7. In line 572, *poenam* is the accusative
   a. subject of indirect statement
   b. object of *ob* (line 571)
   c. **object of *praemetuens* (line 573)**
   d. object of *eversa* (line 571)

8. *Erinys* (line 573) is one of the
   a. Fates
   b. Muses
   c. Graces
   d. **Furies**

9. The metrical pattern of the first four feet of line 574 is
   a. dactyl-spondee-dactyl-spondee
   b. **dactyl-spondee-spondee-spondee**
   c. spondee-dactyl-spondee-dactyl
   d. dactyl-spondee-spondee-dactyl

10. In line 577, *scilicet* is
    a. a present subjunctive verb
    b. a present indicative verb
    c. **an adverb**
    d. an adjective

11. In lines 577–578 (*scilicet . . . aspiciet*), Aeneas is
    a. stating that Mycenae is permitting Helen to return to Sparta
    b. acknowledging that Sparta and Mycenae were unharmed in the war
    c. **expressing his anger that Helen will see Greece again**
    d. sharing his grief about the loss of Sparta and Mycenae

12. Lines 579–580 (*coniugium . . . ministris*) are best translated
    a. **Will she, accompanied by a throng of Trojan women and Phrygian attendants, see her husband and her father's home and her sons?**
    b. Will she see her husband and the home of her father and her sons with a throng of Trojan women and Phrygian attendants having been accompanied?
    c. Will the accompanying throng of Trojan women and their Phrygian attendants see her husband and her house and the sons of her father?
    d. Will her husband see her in the house of her father and her sons when she will have been accompanied by a throng of Trojan women and Phrygian attendants?

13. In line 582, the mood and tense of *sudarit* are
    a. present indicative
    b. present subjunctive
    c. **future perfect indicative**
    d. imperfect subjunctive

14. The implication of the phrase *nullum memorabile nomen* in line 583 is
    a. a woman cannot earn an everlasting name
    b. no name is memorable if not accompanied by glory
    c. the name of Troy will not be long remembered
    d. there is no lasting glory in killing a woman

15. In line 584, *feminea* is a(n)
    a. ablative adjective modifying *poena* (line 584)
    b. nominative adjective modifying *victoria* (line 584)
    c. ablative noun, object of *in* (line 584)
    d. nominative noun, subject of *habet* (line 584)

16. The form of *satiasse* in line 587 is
    a. neuter nominative adjective
    b. perfect active infinitive
    c. ablative singular participle
    d. singular imperative

17. In line 589, *se* refers to
    a. Aeneas's anger
    b. Helen
    c. Aeneas
    d. Venus

18. In line 590, *pura* modifies
    a. *se* (line 589)
    b. *luce* (line 590)
    c. *parens* (line 591)
    d. *alma* (line 591)

19. In line 592, *dextra* refers to
    a. the right way of doing things
    b. standing to the right
    c. the right hand
    d. the right way of speaking

20. In line 592, *prehensum* modifies
    a. *noctem* (line 590)
    b. *deam* (line 591)
    c. *haec* (line 593)
    d. *me* (understood)

21. In line 593, *-que* connects
    a. *continuit* and *roseo* (line 593)
    b. *roseo* and *haec* (line 593)
    c. *continuit* and *addidit* (line 593)
    d. *roseo* and *ore* (line 593)

22. Lines 596–598 (*Non . . . puer*) are best translated
    a. **Will you not first see where you left your father, Anchises, weary with age, and whether your wife, Creusa, and the boy, Ascanius, survive?**
    b. Should you not see sooner when your parent, Anchises, tired with age, was left, and whether your wife, Creusa, and the boy, Ascanius, remain?
    c. When you will not first see that your father, Anchises, is weary with age, and is not to be left, and that Creusa, your wife, and Ascanius, your son, survive?
    d. Will you leave your father, Anchises, weary with age, where you did not see him before, and where your wife, Creusa, and your son, Ascanius remain?

23. In line 599, *resistat* is
    a. present subjunctive in a negative purpose clause
    b. **present subjunctive in a condition**
    c. present indicative in a subordinate clause
    d. perfect indicative in a condition

24. *Tyndaridis* (line 601) is an example of
    a. metonymy
    b. synecdoche
    c. **patronymic**
    d. metaphor

25. In line 602, *divum* is
    a. **genitive plural**
    b. accusative singular
    c. nominative singular
    d. genitive singular

26. In line 602, *inclementia* is
    a. ablative of means with *culpatus* (line 602)
    b. ablative modifying *culmine* (line 603)
    c. accusative object of *evertit* and *sternit* (line 603)
    d. **nominative subject of *evertit* and *sternit* (line 603)**

27. In line 607, *recusa* is
    a. singular ablative
    b. singular nominative
    c. **singular imperative**
    d. plural accusative

28. Line 609 contains an example of
    a. synecdoche
    b. chiasmus
    c. **synchysis**
    d. anastrophe

29. The *-que* in line 611 connects
    a. *fundamenta* and *urbem* (line 611)
    b. *totam* and *a* (line 611)
    c. *quatit* and *totam* (line 611)
    d. ***quatit* (line 611) and *eruit* (line 612)**

30. In line 616, *effulgens* modifies
    a. *nimbo* (line 616)
    b. **Pallas (line 615)**
    c. *saeva* (line 616)
    d. the subject of *respice* (line 615)

31. The use of *Gorgone* in line 616 recalls
    a. Medea
    b. **Medusa**
    c. Ariadne
    d. Penthesilea

32. In line 618, *Dardana* refers to
    a. the Greeks
    b. Pallas
    c. Jupiter
    d. **the Trojans**

33. The metrical pattern of the first four feet of line 620 is
    a. **dactyl-spondee-dactyl-spondee**
    b. dactyl-dactyl-spondee-spondee
    c. spondee-dactyl-dactyl-dactyl
    d. dactyl-spondee-spondee-dactyl

34. In line 620, *sistam* is a(n)
    a. accusative singular noun
    b. **future indicative verb**
    c. present subjunctive verb
    d. accusative singular adjective

Translation *Suggested time: 25 minutes*

Translate the following passage as literally as possible.

> At me tum primum saevus circumstetit horror.
> Obstipui; subiit cari genitoris imago,
> ut regem aequaevum crudeli vulnere vidi
> vitam exhalantem, subiit deserta Creusa
> 5   et direpta domus et parvi casus Iuli.
> Respicio et quae sit me circum copia lustro.
> Deseruere omnes defessi, et corpora saltu
> ad terram misere aut ignibus aegra dedere.

Literal Translation
And then first fierce horror surrounded me. I stood agape; the image of my dear father came [to mind] as I saw the king of the same age exhaling his life from the cruel wound, deserted Creusa and my plundered home and the misfortune of little Iulus came [to mind]. I look back and survey what forces are around me. All, exhausted, have deserted and thrown their bodies to the earth or given them, sick, to the fires.

The sections into which a passage is divided are flexible, as are the possible acceptable meanings for any given word. Teachers may prefer a different scheme of "chunking" and range of meanings; what is given below is just one option. Since students must prove to the reader that they understand the grammar of the passage, loose translations are not acceptable, and students should clearly demonstrate the information given under "notes."

18 units
Range of possible meanings followed by notes on grammar and syntax:

At tum primum	and/but then/at that time first (*primum* is adverb)
saevus circumstetit horror me	cruel/fierce/savage horror/alarm/shuddering surrounded/stood around me (*saevus* modifies *horror*)
obstipui	I stood agape/was dazed
subiit imago	the image/picture/likeness entered (*imago* is subject of *subiit*)
cari genitoris	of [my] dear/beloved/fond father/parent (genitive, dependent on *imago*)
ut regem aequaevum vidi	as I saw the king of equal age (*ut* = "as/when"; *regem* is object of *vidi*)
vitam exhalantem	exhaling/breathing out [his] life (*vitam* object of *exhalantem*, which modifies *regem*)
crudeli vulnere	with/by/from the cruel/bloody/bitter wound (ablative of means, instrument, or separation)
subiit deserta Creusa	Creusa [having been] deserted/forsaken entered (*deserta* modifies *Creusa*)
et direpta domus	and [the/my] [having been] ravaged/plundered home/house (*direpta* modifies *domus*; *domus* is nominative)

et casus parvi Iuli	and the misfortune/chance/fall of small/little Iulus (*casus* is nominative; *parvi* modifies *Iuli*)
Respicio et lustro	I look back and I survey
quae sit me circum copia	what troop(s) is (are) around me (*quae* modifies *copia*)
Deseruere omnes defessi	all/every weary/exhausted/worn have deserted/forsaken (*deseruere* is perfect; *omnes defessi* subject)
et corpora misere ad terram	and have sent/thrown [their] bodies to/toward the earth/land (*corpora* accusative; *misere* perfect)
saltu	with/by a leap/jump (ablative of means)
aut aegra dedere	or have given [their] weary/sick/wretched [bodies] (*aegra* modifies *corpora*; *dedere* perfect)
ignibus	to the fires/conflagrations (dative indirect object)

Translation and Analysis Questions

Translate any Latin used in the question and then answer the question.

1. A standard feature of epic poetry is a description of a hero's *aristeia*, his "display of glory on the battlefield," and Vergil does in fact include several passages of this sort later in the poem. How do the lines *subiit cari genitoris imago, / ut regem aequaevum crudeli vulnere vidi / vitam exhalantem, subiit deserta Creusa / et direpta domus et parvi casus Iuli* (lines 560–563) focus the reader's attention on a contrasting vision of war?

    Aeneas recalls, "The image of my dear father came [to mind] as I saw the king of the same age breathing out his life, deserted Creusa came [to mind] and so did the ravaged house and the misfortune of little Iulus." This personal account of the devastation of war contrasts deeply with the celebration of heroism depicted in an account of an *aristeia*.

2. How do the lines *deseruere omnes defessi, et corpora saltu / ad terram misere aut ignibus aegra dedere* (lines 565–566) show yet another contrast with the concept of *aristeia*?

    "All the weary [men] departed and sent their bodies to the ground with a leap or gave them, weary, to the fires." Soldiers who are so exhausted and weary that they kill themselves contrast greatly with those whose exploits are celebrated in epic.

3. What can we tell about Aeneas's feelings for Helen from these words and phrases: *tacitam secreta in sede latentem* (line 568); *sibi infestos eversa ob Pergama Teucros* (line 571); *Troiae et patriae communis Erinys / abdiderat sese atque aris invisa sedebat* (lines 573–574)?

    By calling Helen "silent(ly) lying hidden in remote seat," stating that "the Trojans are hostile to her on account of Troy having been destroyed," and declaring that "the curse common to Troy and [her own] country had hidden herself and, hateful, was sitting at the altars," Aeneas shows his contempt and anger for Helen. He says that she is fearful from all sides, emphasizing how she is untrustworthy and deserving of punishment.

4. Aeneas emphasizes a contrast between Helen's future and that of the Trojans with *'Scilicet haec Spartam incolumis patriasque Mycenas / aspiciet, partoque ibit regina triumpho? / Coniugiumque domumque patris natosque videbit / Iliadum turba et Phrygiis comitata ministris? / Occiderit ferro Priamus? Troia arserit igni? / Dardanium totiens sudarit sanguine litus?'* (lines 577–582). What is this contrast? What does it reveal about Aeneas's emotions?

    Aeneas's series of questions, "Indeed will this one safe(ly) see Sparta and her ancestral Mycenae, and will she go as a queen with a triumph produced? Will she, accompanied by a throng of Trojan women and Phrygian attendants see her husband and father's home and [her] children?" shows how fortunate Helen will be, and how she will not only pay no penalty for her wrongdoing, but she will even return home in triumph and with Trojan slaves. On the other hand, the questions, "Will Priam have died by the sword? Will Troy have burned with fire? Will the Dardanian shore have sweated so often with blood?" show the destruction the war resulting from Helen's actions has had on Troy. As Aeneas asks himself these questions, his rage increases, and he begins to feel justified in killing Helen as if she were an enemy soldier.

5. What does *Namque etsi nullum memorabile nomen / feminea in poena est, habet haec victoria laudem* (lines 583–584) tell us about Roman values about war?

    "For even if there is no long-lasting glory in punishing a woman, this victory holds praise" shows that glory can be gained in punishing or killing an enemy, but not a woman.

6. Venus herself makes a contrast by asking first, *'Nate, quis indomitas tantus dolor excitat iras? / Quid furis?'* (lines 594–595) and then, *'Aut quonam nostri tibi cura recessit? / Non prius aspicies ubi fessum aetate parentem / liqueris Anchisen, superet coniunxne Creusa / Ascaniusque puer?'* (lines 595–598). What distinction is Venus making, and what action is she hoping Aeneas will take as a result of these contrasting questions?

    Venus first asks Aeneas about his anger: "Son, what so great grief stirs up unrestrained rage? Why do you rage?" and then reminds him about his family, "Or where has your care for us gone? Will you not first look where you left [your] father Anchises, weary with age, or whether [your] wife Creusa and [your] boy Ascanius survive?" By first addressing his rage, then making him think about his family, she is hoping he will calm down and go look after them.

7. What aspects of the gods' character is Venus emphasizing with her use of *Neptunus muros magnoque emota tridenti / fundamenta quatit* (lines 610–611), *Iuno . . . saevissima . . . furens . . . / . . . ferro accincta* (lines 612–614), *Pallas . . . Gorgone saeva* (lines 615–616), and *ipse deos in Dardana suscitat arma* (line 618)?

    In each of these, the warlike qualities of the god is emphasized: "Neptune shakes the wall and the foundations, wrenched away with his great trident"; "Juno . . . most savage . . . raging . . . girt with her sword"; "Pallas . . . with the savage Gorgon"; "[Jupiter] himself stirs up the gods against the Trojan arms."

Essay *Suggested time: 20 minutes*

Throughout lines 559–607, Vergil uses language associated with darkness and light, seeing and not seeing. How does he do this, and what is the effect of this cinematic vividness on Aeneas's narrative? Present your response in a well-organized essay.

Support your assertions with references drawn from throughout the passage. All Latin words must be copied or their line numbers provided, AND they must be translated or paraphrased closely enough so that it is clear you understand the Latin. It is your responsibility to convince your reader that you are basing your conclusions on the Latin text and not merely on a general recollection of the passage. Direct your answer to the question; do not merely summarize the passage. Please write your essay on a separate piece of paper.

(See Lesson 19 for an additional essay on this passage.)

Students will respond to essay topics in various ways, and different essays, with quite different approaches, may be of equal quality. The following are some possible points students may make; it is not a sample essay.

This essay provides students with ample opportunity to use evidence from the text to support a general conclusion about the imagery associated with war. Students should be sure to write a thesis statement and then support it. Ideas and phrases, <u>all of which must be translated</u> in student essays, may include the following. Many references to seeing, not seeing, the light of fire, and darkness pervade these lines. Among the references to seeing, students might cite Aeneas's recollection of his father, wife, home, and son as an example of a type of seeing: *imago subiit* (line 560) and/or *subiit deserta Creusa / et direpta domus et parvi casus Iuli* (lines 562–563). Specific references to sight, such as *vidi* (line 561), *aspicio* (line 569), *aspiciet* (line 578), *videbit* (line 579), *non ante oculis tam clara, videndam* (line 589), *videri* (line 591), *aspicies* (line 596), *aspice* (line 604), and *visus* (line 605), emphasize that the reader is to be thinking of the visual aspects of this episode. Images of light and fire as a force of destruction include *ignibus* (line 566), *Troia arserit igni* (line 581), and *flammae tulerint* (600). More positive connotations of light include *dant claram incendia lucem* (line 569) and *pura per noctem in luce refulsit* (line 590). There may be a play on words about seeing with *invisa* (line 574 and again at 601). Strong students may look to lines 604–606 (*Aspice . . . eripiam*) to draw the conclusion that Aeneas is unable to see or understand and that his mother is enlightening him.

See the Scoring Guidelines on pp. xvii–xviii.

Scansion

Scan the following lines.

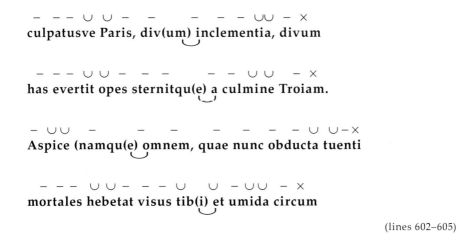

(lines 602–605)

LESSON 13: BOOK 4.160–218

160 Interea magno misceri murmure caelum
incipit, insequitur commixta grandine nimbus,
et Tyrii comites passim et Troiana iuventus
Dardaniusque nepos Veneris diversa per agros
tecta metu petiere; ruunt de montibus amnes.
165 Speluncam Dido dux et Troianus eandem
deveniunt. Prima et Tellus et pronuba Iuno
dant signum; fulsere ignes et conscius aether
conubiis summoque ululanunt vertice Nymphae.
Ille dies primus leti primusque malorum
170 causa fuit; neque enim specie famave movetur
nec iam furtivum Dido meditatur amorem:
coniugium vocat, hoc praetexit nomine culpam.
Extemplo Libyae magnas it Fama per urbes,
Fama, malum qua non aliud velocius ullum:
175 mobilitate viget viresque adquirit eundo,
parva metu primo, mox sese attollit in auras
ingrediturque solo et caput inter nubila condit.
Illam Terra parens ira inritata deorum
extremam, ut perhibent, Coeo Enceladoque sororem
180 progenuit pedibus celerem et pernicibus alis,
monstrum horrendum, ingens, cui quot sunt corpore plumae,
tot vigiles oculi subter (mirabile dictu),
tot linguae, totidem ora sonant, tot subrigit aures.
Nocte volat caeli medio terraeque per umbram
185 stridens, nec dulci declinat lumina somno;
luce sedet custos aut summi culmine tecti
turribus aut altis, et magnas territat urbes,
tam ficti pravique tenax quam nuntia veri.
Haec tum multiplici populos sermone replebat
190 gaudens, et pariter facta atque infecta canebat:
venisse Aenean Troiano sanguine cretum,
cui se pulchra viro dignetur iungere Dido;
nunc hiemem inter se luxu, quam longa, fovere
regnorum immemores turpique cupidine captos.
195 Haec passim dea foeda virum diffundit in ora.
Protinus ad regem cursus detorquet Iarban
incenditque animum dictis atque aggerat iras.
Hic Hammone satus rapta Garamantide nympha
templa Iovi centum latis immania regnis,
200 centum aras posuit vigilemque sacraverat ignem,
excubias divum aeternas, pecudumque cruore

pingue solum et variis florentia limina sertis.
Isque amens animi et rumore accensus amaro
dicitur ante aras media inter numina divum
205 multa Iovem manibus supplex orasse supinis:
'Iuppiter omnipotens, cui nunc Maurusia pictis
gens epulata toris Lenaeum libat honorem,
aspicis haec? An te, genitor, cum fulmina torques
nequiquam horremus, caecique in nubibus ignes
210 terrificant animos et inania murmura miscent?
Femina, quae nostris errans in finibus urbem
exiguam pretio posuit, cui litus arandum
cuique loci leges dedimus, conubia nostra
reppulit ac dominum Aenean in regna recepit.
215 Et nunc ille Paris cum semiviro comitatu,
Maeonia mentum mitra crinemque madentem
subnexus, rapto potitur: nos munera templis
quippe tuis ferimus famamque fovemus inanem.'

Comprehension Questions

NB: Some questions may have several possible correct responses; a sample is given.

1. The description of the storm in lines 160–164 recalls what earlier passage in the poem?

    It recalls Juno's speech (lines 120–125), in which she says she will create the storm.

2. How does Vergil employ natural phenomena to recreate a typical wedding ceremony?

    Mother Earth presides over the marriage, Juno is the matron of honor, the lightning acts as the wedding torch, the *aether* is the witness, and the nymphs sing the wedding song.

3. What do lines 169–172 foreshadow? **They foreshadow Dido's betrayal and destruction.**

4. In the personification of Fama (lines 173–190), Vergil gives one of the most vivid descriptions of a monster in ancient literature. Though Fama has a frightening appearance, its greatest destructiveness appears in lines 188–190. What is it that makes Fama so harmful?

    Because Fama mixes real information with invented information, it is believable and therefore more destructive.

5. Who are Iarbas's parents? **The god Hammon/Ammon and a nymph of the Garamantes.**

6. Why does Iarbas refer to Aeneas as *ille Paris* (line 215)? **Iarbas calls Aeneas "that Paris" because Aeneas has, in Iarbas's view, come as a stranger and won Dido's heart, just as Paris came as a stranger to Greece and won Helen's heart.**

7. In your opinion, is Iarbas angrier because he has lost Dido or because he has lost her kingdom? Copy out and translate at least one phrase to support your answer.

   Because he has lost Dido: *conubia nostra reppulit*, **lines 213–214 (she has rejected my/our marriage);** *dominum Aenean in regna recepit*, **line 214 (she has received into her kingdom Aeneas as master). Because he has lost her kingdom:** *rapto potitur*, **line 217 (he/Aeneas possesses [it/her kingdom] having been taken).**

8. What is the tone of Iarbas's prayer in lines 206–218? What is he feeling? **The tone of Iarbas's prayer is bitter as he feels angry and betrayed.**

Multiple Choice Questions

1. The case of *commixta* (line 161) is
   a. nominative
   b. ablative

2. The phrase *Troiana iuventus Dardaniusque nepos Veneris* (lines 162–163) is translated
   a. the Dardanian youth from Troy and the grandson of Venus
   b. the Trojan youth and the Dardanian grandson of Venus

3. In line 164, the case of *tecta* is
   a. nominative
   b. accusative

4. In line 167, *fulsere* is
   a. indicative
   b. infinitive

5. In line 168, *ululurunt* is
   a. perfect
   b. present

6. In line 170, *-ve* connects
   a. *fama* and *movetur* (line 170)
   b. *specie* and *fama* (line 170)

7. The case of *hoc* (line 172) is
   a. accusative
   b. ablative

8. In line 173, *extemplo* is a(n)
   a. verb
   b. adverb

9. In line 174, *qua* is
   a. ablative of means
   b. ablative of comparison

10. In line 174, the gender of *velocius* is
    a. masculine
    b. neuter

11. Line 175 (*mobilitate . . . eundo*) is best translated
    a. with movement the strength increases and it gains speed for going
    b. it flourishes with motion and gains strength by going

12. In line 176, the case of *parva* is
    a. ablative
    b. nominative

13. In line 178, *illam* is the object of
    a. *perhibent* (line 179)
    b. *progenuit* (line 180)

14. In line 179, the case of *Encelado* is
    a. dative
    b. ablative

15. In line 180, *celerem* modifies
    a. *monstrum* (line 181)
    b. *sororem* (line 179)

16. In line 181, the gender of *ingens* is
    a. neuter
    b. feminine

17. In line 183, the case of *ora* is
    a. nominative
    b. accusative

18. In line 183, the case of *aures* is
    a. nominative
    b. accusative

19. In line 184, *-que* connects
    a. *medio* and *terrae* (line 184)
    b. *caeli* and *terrae* (line 184)

20. In line 185, *dulci* modifies
    a. *somno* (line 185)
    b. *lumina* (line 185)

21. In line 186, *luce* is ablative of
    a. time when
    b. means

22. The case and number of *nuntia* (line 188) are
    a. nominative singular
    b. accusative plural

23. In line 191, *venisse* is a(n)
    a. complementary infinitive
    b. infinitive in indirect statement

24. In line 192, *se* refers to
    a. **Dido**
    b. Aeneas

25. In line 193, *fovere* is a(n)
    a. **infinitive in indirect statement**
    b. complementary infinitive

26. In line 194, *-que* connects
    a. *turpi* and *cupidine* (line 194)
    b. ***immemores* and *captos* (line 194)**

27. The case of *virum* (line 195) is
    a. **genitive**
    b. accusative

28. In line 196, the case of *cursus* is
    a. nominative
    b. **accusative**

29. In line 198, *rapta* modifies
    a. *nympha* (line 198)
    b. ***Hammone* (line 198)**

30. The phrase *pecudumque cruore / pingue solum* (lines 201–202) is best translated
    a. **and the ground with the rich gore of animals**
    b. and the ground rich with the gore of animals

31. *dicitur* (line 204) is best translated
    a. **he is said**
    b. it is said

32. *cui* (line 206) is best translated
    a. whose
    b. **to whom**

33. In line 208, *torques* is
    a. **accusative plural**
    b. present indicative

34. In line 209, *caeci* modifies
    a. *ignes* (line 209)
    b. **the subject of *horremus* (line 209)**

35. In line 211, the form of *quae* is
    a. nominative singular feminine
    b. **accusative plural neuter**

36. In line 214, the tense of *reppulit* is
    a. present
    b. **perfect**

37. *comitatu* (line 215) is best translated
    a. having been accompanied
    b. company

38. *mentum* (line 216) is best translated
    a. as to his chin
    b. of minds

39. In line 217, the case of *rapto* is
    a. dative
    b. ablative

Translation *Suggested time: 15 minutes*

Translate the following passage as literally as possible.

> Extemplo Libyae magnas it Fama per urbes,
> Fama, malum qua non aliud velocius ullum:
> mobilitate viget viresque adquirit eundo,
> parva metu primo, mox sese attollit in auras
> 5   ingrediturque solo et caput inter nubila condit.

Literal Translation
Immediately Rumor goes through the great cities of Libya, Rumor, than which no other evil [lit., bad thing] is swifter: she thrives on movement and acquires strength by going, small at first on account of fear, [but] soon she raises herself into the air[s] and steps on the earth and hides [her] head among the clouds.

The sections into which a passage is divided are flexible, as are the possible acceptable meanings for any given word. Teachers may prefer a different scheme of "chunking" and range of meanings; what is given below is just one option. Since students must prove to the reader that they understand the grammar of the passage, loose translations are not acceptable, and students should clearly demonstrate the information given under "notes."

15 units
Range of possible meanings followed by notes on grammar and syntax:

extemplo it Fama	immediately/at once/suddenly Rumor/report goes (*extemplo* adverb)
Libyae magnas per urbes	through the great/large cities/towns of Libya
Fama	Rumor/report
qua	than which (ablative of comparison)
malum non aliud ullum	not [any] other evil/bad [thing]
velocius	more swiftly/swifter (comparative)
mobilitate viget	it grows/thrives/flourishes by/with [its] movement/mobility
viresque adquirit	and it acquires/gains strength/power (*vires* accusative)

eundo	by going (gerund)
parva metu	small because of fear/anxiety/fright (*metu* ablative of cause)
primo	first/at first (adverb or adjective modifying *metu*)
mox sese attollit in auras	soon it raises/lifts/rears itself into the breezes/airs
ingrediturque solo	and it goes/progresses/walks/proceeds upon/on the earth
et caput inter nubila condit	and establishes/buries/hides [its] head amidst/among/between the clouds

Short Answer Questions

From lines 160–177, find, copy out, and provide line references in parentheses for:

1. an example of epanalepsis **Fama, Fama (lines 173 and 174)**
2. three deponent verbs in the indicative **insequitur (line 161), meditatur (line 171), ingreditur (line 177)**
3. a gerund **eundo (line 175)**
4. a reflexive pronoun **sese (line 176)**
5. a passive infinitive **misceri (line 160)**
6. an ablative of comparison **qua (line 174)**
7. an ablative absolute **commixta grandine (line 161)**
8. a passive indicative verb **movetur (line 170)**
9. five verbs in the perfect indicative **petiere (line 164), fulsere (line 167), ululaurunt (line 168), fuit (line 170), praetexit (line 172)**

From lines 178–194, find, copy out, and provide line references in parentheses for:

1. two present participles **stridens (line 185), gaudens (line 190)**
2. three lines that contain two elisions **line 179, line 181, line 190**
3. two infinitives in indirect statement **venisse (line 191), fovere (line 193)**
4. an example of anaphora **tot/tot/tot (lines 182–183)**
5. a perfect passive participle in the nominative singular **inritata (line 178)**
6. a fourth declension noun **luxu (line 193)**
7. a supine **dictu (line 182)**
8. an example of chiasmus **extremam, ut perhibent, Coeo Enceladoque sororem (line 179); Aenean Troiano sanguine cretum (line 191)**

9. an ablative of time when *nocte* **(line 184)**
10. a dative of possession *cui* **(line 181)**

From lines 195–218, find, copy out, and provide line references in parentheses for:
1. an ablative object of a deponent verb *rapto (potitur)* **(line 217)**
2. an example of chiasmus *variis florentia limina sertis* **(line 202);** *terrificant animos et inania murmura miscent* **(line 210)**
3. a vocative noun *Iuppiter* **(line 206),** *genitor* **(line 208)**
4. three feminine relative pronouns *quae* **(line 211),** *cui* **(line 212),** *cui* **(line 213)**
5. an example of anaphora *quae/cui/cui* **(lines 211–213),** *centum* **(lines 199–200)**
6. a line with three elisions **line 203**
7. two nouns in apposition to one another *regem Iarbam* **(line 196);** *ignem/excubias* **(lines 200–201);** *dominum Aenean* **(line 214)**
8. a second declension genitive plural ending in *-um* *virum* **(line 195),** *divum* **(line 201)**
9. a perfect infinitive *orasse* **(line 205)**
10. an example of metonymy *Lenaeum honorem* **(line 207)**

Essay *Suggested time: 20 minutes*

How does Vergil create a sense of foreboding in lines 160–172? And what is its effect on the reader? Present your response in a well-organized essay.

Support your assertions with references drawn from throughout this passage (lines 160–72 only). All Latin words must be copied or their line numbers provided, AND they must be translated or paraphrased closely enough so that it is clear you understand the Latin. It is your responsibility to convince your reader that you are basing your conclusions on the Latin text and not merely on a general recollection of the passage. Direct your answer to the question; do not merely summarize the passage. Please write your essay on a separate piece of paper.

Students will respond to essay topics in various ways, and different essays, with quite different approaches, may be of equal quality. The following are some possible points students may make; it is not a sample essay.

    This essay asks students to explore the setting of a passage, and they are given some direction with the use of the word "foreboding." Students should be sure to write a thesis statement and then support it. Ideas and phrases, <u>all of which must be translated</u> in student essays, may include the following. The storm and attendant darkness are ominous. The sound of the storm is described (*magno misceri murmure caelum*, line 160) with language that recalls earlier moments of disaster. The hunters are all described as fearful (*metu*, line 164). The language of the storm/"wedding" is also foreboding, with lightning flashing (*fulsere ignes*, line 167) and the nymphs shrieking (*ululurunt*, line 168). Finally, the use of the words *leti* and *malorum* (line 169), and the use of *culpam* (line 172) as the concluding word of the passage, leave the reader with a sense of bad things to come.

See the Scoring Guidelines on pp. xvii–xviii.

Scansion

Indicate whether or not each line is scanned properly. In the line provided, mark a "Y" for yes or an "N" for no as appropriate. NB: These are not consecutive lines but five discrete selections.

1. **N**   Īllĕ dĭ|ēs prĭmŭs| lētī| prīmūs|quē mā|lōrŭm

2. **N**   pārvă mĕ|tū prī|mō, (mo)x sē|s(e) āttōl|līt īn |āūrās

3. **Y**   īncēn|dītqu(e) ănĭ|mūm dīc|tīs āt|qu(e) āggĕrăt| īrās.

4. **N**   nēquī|quām hōr|rēmŭs|, cāecĭqu(e) ĭn |nūbĭbŭs |īgnēs

5. **Y**   Māeŏnĭ|ā mēn|tūm mīt|rā crī|nēmquĕ mă|dēntēm

LESSON 14: BOOK 4.259–299

Ut primum alatis tetigit magalia plantis,
260 Aenean fundantem arces ac tecta novantem
conspicit. Atque illi stellatus iaspide fulva
ensis erat Tyrioque ardebat murice laena
demissa ex umeris, dives quae munera Dido
fecerat, et tenui telas discreverat auro.
265 Continuo invadit: 'Tu nunc Karthaginis altae
fundamenta locas pulchramque uxorius urbem
exstruis? Heu, regni rerumque oblite tuarum!
Ipse deum tibi me claro demittit Olympo
regnator, caelum et terras qui numine torquet,
270 ipse haec ferre iubet celeres mandata per auras:
quid struis? Aut qua spe Libycis teris otia terris?
Si te nulla movet tantarum gloria rerum
[nec super ipse tua moliris laude laborem,]
Ascanium surgentem et spes heredis Iuli
275 respice, cui regnum Italiae Romanaque tellus
debetur.' Tali Cyllenius ore locutus
mortales visus medio sermone reliquit
et procul in tenuem ex oculis evanuit auram.
At vero Aeneas aspectu obmutuit amens,
280 arrectaeque horrore comae et vox faucibus haesit.
Ardet abire fuga dulcesque relinquere terras,
attonitus tanto monitu imperioque deorum.
Heu quid agat? Quo nunc reginam ambire furentem
audeat adfatu? Quae prima exordia sumat?
285 Atque animum nunc huc celerem nunc dividit illuc
in partisque rapit varias perque omnia versat.
Haec alternanti potior sententia visa est:
Mnesthea Sergestumque vocat fortemque Serestum,
classem aptent taciti sociosque ad litora cogant,
290 arma parent et quae rebus sit causa novandis
dissimulent; sese interea, quando optima Dido
nesciat et tantos rumpi non speret amores,
temptaturum aditus et quae mollissima fandi
tempora, quis rebus dexter modus. Ocius omnes
295 imperio laeti parent et iussa facessunt.
At regina dolos (quis fallere possit amantem?)
praesensit, motusque excepit prima futuros
omnia tuta timens. Eadem impia Fama furenti
detulit armari classem cursumque parari.

Comprehension Questions

NB: Some questions may have several possible correct responses; a sample is given.

1. What is Aeneas wearing when Mercury sees him in lines 260–264? **Aeneas is wearing a decorative sword and a purple and gold cloak that Dido had made. She gave him both as gifts.**

2. In lines 265–276, Mercury chastises Aeneas for delaying in Carthage, and prompts him to leave. Identify at least three words in the speech that indicate Mercury's tone. What is the most important reason Aeneas should depart, according to Mercury? Support your answer with specific references to the text.

   Mercury scolds Aeneas by questioning his building Carthage (*Tu . . . exstruis?*, lines 265–267). He then calls Aeneas forgetful of his realm (*regni . . . tuarum*, line 267). Mercury also repeats Jupiter's calling into question Aeneas's motives for not moving on to Italy (*quid . . . terris*, line 271). Mercury reminds Aeneas that even if he does not worry about his own glory (line 272), he should consider Ascanius and any possible future descendants of his (lines 274–275), adding that the realm of Italy is owed to Ascanius (lines 275–276).

3. How does Vergil emphasize Aeneas's divided feelings in lines 279–286? Provide line references and translate any words or phrases you use to support your answer.

   The phrases "*nunc huc . . . nunc illuc*" (now this way . . . now that, line 285) show Aeneas's divided mind. He wants to leave (*ardet abire*, line 281), he wonders what he should do (*quid agat*, line 283), he doesn't know with what words he dare approach the queen (*quo nunc reginam ambire furentem audeat adfatu*, lines 283–284), and he sends his thoughts into different directions (*partis varias*, line 286). Vergil uses symptoms of fear (for example, *vox faucibus haesit*, line 280, his voice sticks in his throat), the deliberative subjunctives in lines 283–284, and the anaphora (mentioned above) of line 285 to show how mixed Aeneas's feelings are.

4. Why does Aeneas tell his men to carry out his orders "silently" (line 289) and that they should "pretend otherwise" (line 291)?

   Aeneas is worried that Dido will discover his plan before he has a chance to speak with her.

5. How does Vergil explain Dido's awareness of Aeneas's plans? Identify at least two ways Vergil does this by writing out the relevant words or phrases and providing line references for them in parentheses.

   ***quis fallere possit amantem?* (line 296); *eadem impia Fama furenti detulit* (lines 298–299).**

Multiple Choice Questions *Suggested time: 25 minutes*

1. Line 260 contains an example of
   a. hendiadys
   b. alliteration
   c. synchysis
   d. chiasmus

2. In line 261, *illi* is
   a. genitive of possession
   b. dative of possession
   c. nominative subject
   d. dative with *ardebat* (line 262)

3. *dives quae munera Dido / fecerat* (lines 263–264) is best translated
   a. which gifts rich Dido had made
   b. which rich gifts Dido had made
   c. which gifts rich Dido would have made
   d. which rich gifts Dido would have made

4. In line 267, *oblite* is best translated
   a. forget
   b. by forgetting
   c. having forgotten
   d. don't forget

5. In line 269, the antecedent of *qui* is
   a. *deum* (line 268)
   b. *me* (line 268)
   c. *regnator* (line 269)
   d. *caelum* (line 269)

6. *Aut qua spe Libycis teris otia terris* (line 271) is best translated
   a. or in (your) hope what leisure are you wearing away in the Libyan lands
   b. or where are you aiming with leisurely hope in the Libyan lands
   c. or with what (sort of) leisure are you wasting your hope in the Libyan lands
   d. or with what hope are you wearing away (your) leisure in the Libyan lands

7. In line 275, *cui* is best translated
   a. by whom
   b. to whom
   c. whose
   d. with whom

8. In line 275, *-que* connects
   a. *regnum* and *tellus* (line 275)
   b. *Romana* and *tellus* (line 275)
   c. *cui* and *Romana* (line 275)
   d. *Italiae* and *Romana* (line 275)

9. In line 276, *Cyllenius* refers to
   a. Ascanius
   b. Mercury
   c. Italy
   d. Jupiter

10. The metrical pattern of the first four feet of line 280 is
    a. spondee-dactyl-dactyl-dactyl
    b. spondee-dactyl-spondee-dactyl
    c. spondee-spondee-dactyl-spondee
    d. spondee-spondee-dactyl-dactyl

11. In line 282, *monitu* is a(n)
    a. supine
    b. accusative singular noun
    c. ablative singular noun
    d. adverb

12. We learn from lines 285–286 (*atque . . . versat*)
    a. Jupiter's command involved several parts
    b. Aeneas divided the work among his men
    c. Aeneas wanted Jupiter's command completed swiftly
    d. Aeneas had mixed feelings about what he had to do

13. In line 287, *alternanti* is best translated
    a. to him wavering
    b. for her changing
    c. of him alternating
    d. to her alternating

14. In line 289, *aptent* is present subjunctive in an implied
    a. indirect command
    b. result clause
    c. indirect question
    d. future less vivid condition

15. The case and form of *novandis* (line 290) are
    a. ablative gerund
    b. dative gerund
    c. ablative gerundive
    d. dative gerundive

16. In line 291, *sese* refers to
    a. Dido
    b. Aeneas
    c. Serestus
    d. *amores* (line 292)

17. The case and use of *sese* (line 291) are
    a. ablative of means with *rumpi* (line 292)
    b. accusative object of *temptaturum* (line 293)
    c. accusative subject of of *temptaturum* (line 293)
    d. accusative object of *nesciat* (line 292)

18. In line 294, *ocius* is
    a. comparative adjective, accusative singular neuter
    b. positive adverb
    c. positive adjective, nominative singular masculine
    d. comparative adverb

19. From lines 296–298 (*At . . . timens*) we learn that Dido
    a. sensed everything ahead of time
    b. **feared even those things she did not need to**
    c. had planned to deceive her lover first
    d. was fearful of any future movements

20. *eadem* (line 298) modifies
    a. *prima* (line 297)
    b. *omnia* (line 298)
    c. ***Fama* (line 298)**
    d. *classem* (line 299)

Translation *Suggested time: 20 minutes*

Translate the following passage as literally as possible.

> Continuo invadit: 'Tu nunc Karthaginis altae
> fundamenta locas pulchramque uxorius urbem
> exstruis? Heu, regni rerumque oblite tuarum!
> Ipse deum tibi me claro demittit Olympo
> 5   regnator, caelum et terras qui numine torquet,
> ipse haec ferre iubet celeres mandata per auras:
> quid struis? Aut qua spe Libycis teris otia terris?

Literal Translation:
Straightaway he addresses [him]: 'Are you now laying the foundations of lofty Carthage and, wife-ruled, do you build up a lovely city? Alas, [you], having forgotten the kingdom and your affairs! The ruler himself of the gods, who turns the heaven and lands with [his] power, sends me to you from bright Olympus; he himself orders [me] to bear these commands through the swift breezes: What are you planning? Or with what expectation do you waste times in idleness in Libyan lands?

The sections into which a passage is divided are flexible, as are the possible acceptable meanings for any given word. Teachers may prefer a different scheme of "chunking" and range of meanings; what is given below is just one option. Since students must prove to the reader that they understand the grammar of the passage, loose translations are not acceptable, and students should clearly demonstrate the information given under "notes."

18 units
Range of possible meanings followed by notes on grammar and syntax:

continuo invadit	immediately/at once he attacks/addresses
tu uxorius	you wife ruled/uxorious/hen-pecked
nunc Karthaginis altae fundamenta locas	are now placing/establishing/laying/locating the foundations/bases of lofty/high/tall Carthage?
pulchramque urbem exstruis?	and you are building/rearing/constructing a beautiful/handsome/noble/splendid/illustrious city/town?

heu, oblite	alas!/ah!/ah me!, [you] forgetful of/having forgotten (*oblite* is vocative [not imperative])
regni rerumque tuarum	[of] your kingdom/realm/royal power/sovereignty and [of] your affairs/situation/things (genitive with *oblite*)
ipse deum regnator	the ruler/guider/lord/director of the gods himself (*deum* is genitive)
tibi me demittit	sends down/sends me to you
claro Olympo	from clear/bright/shining/illustrious Olympus (ablative of separation)
caelum et terras qui torquet	[the ruler] who twists/hurls/sways the sky/heaven and earth(s)/lands (antecedent of *qui* is *regnator*)
numine	with [his] power/divinity/godhead
ipse ferre iubet	he himself orders [me] to carry/bring (understood *me* as object of *iubet*)
haec mandata	these commands/orders/mandates (object of *ferre*)
celeres per auras	through the swift/speedy breezes/air(s)
quid struis?	what are you building/contriving?
aut qua spe	or with what hope/intention
otia teris	do you wear away/waste [your] leisure/idleness/quiet (*otia* is direct object of *teris*)
Libycis terris?	in the Libyan lands

Short Answer Questions

Matching from lines 259–278

1. **E** *oblite* (line 267)
2. **I** *deum* (line 268)
3. **B** *quid* (line 271)
4. **G** *discreverat* (line 264)
5. **J** *continuo* (line 265)
6. **H** *erat* (line 262)
7. **C** *visus* (line 277)
8. **F** contains two present participles
9. **A** contains two prepositional phrases
10. **D** contains an imperative

a. line 278
b. interrogative pronoun
c. accusative noun
d. line 275
e. participle in the vocative
f. line 260
g. pluperfect indicative verb
h. imperfect indicative verb
i. second declension genitive in *-um*
j. adverb

Matching from lines 279–299

#				
1.	**C**	accusative neuter plural	a.	*vero* (line 279)
2.	**E**	ablative of means	b.	*relinquere* (line 281)
3.	**D**	ablative of manner	c.	*iussa* (line 295)
4.	**F**	accusative plural masculine	d.	*fuga* (line 281)
5.	**A**	adverb	e.	*imperio* (line 282)
6.	**B**	complementary infinitive	f.	*motus* (line 297)
7.	**I**	gerund	g.	*modus* (line 294)
8.	**H**	gerundive	h.	*novandis* (line 290)
9.	**J**	infinitive in indirect statement	i.	*fandi* (line 293)
10.	**G**	nominative singular masculine	j.	*armari* (line 299)

Essay *Suggested time: 20 minutes*

In lines 279–294, Aeneas reacts to Mercury's message from Jupiter. How does he react? What does this say about his character? Present your response in a well-organized essay.

Support your assertions with references drawn from throughout this passage (lines 279–294 only). All Latin words must be copied or their line numbers provided, AND they must be translated or paraphrased closely enough so that it is clear you understand the Latin. It is your responsibility to convince your reader that you are basing your conclusions on the Latin text and not merely on a general recollection of the passage. Direct your answer to the question; do not merely summarize the passage. Please write your essay on a separate piece of paper.

Students will respond to essay topics in various ways, and different essays, with quite different approaches, may be of equal quality. The following are some possible points students may make; it is not a sample essay.

This essay expects students to draw a conclusion about Aeneas's character based on his reaction to Mercury's message from Jupiter in lines 279–294. Students should be sure to write a thesis statement and then support it. Ideas and phrases, <u>all of which must be translated</u> in student essays, may include the following. Aeneas is at first stunned by what he has seen and heard (lines 279–280), and immediately wants to leave Carthage (line 281), struck by the magnitude of the gods' warning and command (line 282). Aeneas then expresses self-doubt about how to approach Dido, through a series of deliberative subjunctives (lines 283–284), and an inability to settle on a course of action (lines 285–286). When he does decide what makes better sense to him (line 287), he orders his men to prepare to leave Carthage but tells them to conceal their actions (lines 288–290). He says that he will figure out the best time and method for speaking with Dido (lines 290–294). Students may use any of this argument to argue a particular aspect or aspects of Aeneas's character: that he is thoughtful or not; that he is trying to be kind, or not; that he is obedient to the gods; that he is deceitful; that he is thinking of his people and their future; or that he is indecisive, are among the characteristics that students may address.

See the Scoring Guidelines on pp. xvii–xviii.

Scansion

Indicate whether or not each line is scanned properly. In the line provided, mark a "Y" for yes or an "N" for no as appropriate. NB: These are not consecutive lines but four discrete selections.

1. **Y**   ūt prī|m(um) ālā|tīs tĕtĭ|gīt mā|gālĭă |plāntīs

2. **Y**   Āenē|ān fūn|dānt(em) ār|cēs āc| tēctă nŏv|āntēm

3. **N**   ēt prŏcŭl| īn tĕnu(em) ĕx| ōcŭlĭs| ēvā|nūĭt ă|ūrăm

4. **N**   ārrēc|taequĕ hŏr|rōrĕ cŏ|m(ae) ēt vōx| fāucĭbŭs| haesīt

LESSON 15: BOOK 4.300–361

300 Saevit inops animi totamque incensa per urbem
     bacchatur, qualis commotis excita sacris
     Thyias, ubi audito stimulant trieterica Baccho
     orgia nocturnusque vocat clamore Cithaeron.
     Tandem his Aenean compellat vocibus ultro:
305 'Dissimulare etiam sperasti, perfide, tantum
     posse nefas tacitusque mea decedere terra?
     Nec te noster amor nec te data dextera quondam
     nec moritura tenet crudeli funere Dido?
     Quin etiam hiberno moliri sidere classem
310 et mediis properas Aquilonibus ire per altum,
     crudelis? Quid, si non arva aliena domosque
     ignotas peteres, et Troia antiqua maneret,
     Troia per undosum peteretur classibus aequor?
     Mene fugis? Per ego has lacrimas dextramque tuam te
315 (quando aliud mihi iam miserae nihil ipsa reliqui),
     per conubia nostra, per inceptos hymenaeos,
     si bene quid de te merui, fuit aut tibi quicquam
     dulce meum, miserere domus labentis et istam,
     oro, si quis adhuc precibus locus, exue mentem.
320 Te propter Libycae gentes Nomadumque tyranni
     odere, infensi Tyrii; te propter eundem
     exstinctus pudor et, qua sola sidera adibam,
     fama prior. Cui me moribundam deseris hospes
     (hoc solum nomen quoniam de coniuge restat)?
325 Quid moror? An mea Pygmalion dum moenia frater
     destruat aut captam ducat Gaetulus Iarbas?
     Saltem si qua mihi de te suscepta fuisset
     ante fugam suboles, si quis mihi parvulus aula
     luderet Aeneas, qui te tamen ore referret,
330 non equidem omnino capta ac deserta viderer.'
     Dixerat. Ille Iouis monitis immota tenebat
     lumina et obnixus curam sub corde premebat.
     Tandem pauca refert: 'Ego te, quae plurima fando
     enumerare vales, numquam, regina, negabo
335 promeritam, nec me meminisse pigebit Elissae
     dum memor ipse mei, dum spiritus hos regit artus.
     Pro re pauca loquar. Neque ego hanc abscondere furto
     speravi (ne finge) fugam, nec coniugis umquam
     praetendi taedas aut haec in foedera veni.
340 Me si fata meis paterentur ducere vitam
     auspiciis et sponte mea componere curas,

urbem Troianam primum dulcesque meorum
reliquias colerem, Priami tecta alta manerent,
et recidiva manu posuissem Pergama victis.
345　Sed nunc Italiam magnam Gryneus Apollo,
Italiam Lyciae iussere capessere sortes;
hic amor, haec patria est. Si te Karthaginis arces
Phoenissam Libycaeque aspectus detinet urbis,
quae tandem Ausonia Teucros considere terra
350　invidia est? Et nos fas extera quaerere regna.
Me patris Anchisae, quotiens umentibus umbris
nox operit terras, quotiens astra ignea surgunt,
admonet in somnis et turbida terret imago;
me puer Ascanius capitisque iniuria cari,
355　quem regno Hesperiae fraudo et fatalibus arvis.
Nunc etiam interpres divum Iove missus ab ipso
(testor utrumque caput) celeres mandata per auras
detulit: ipse deum manifesto in lumine vidi
intrantem muros vocemque his auribus hausi.
360　Desine meque tuis incendere teque querelis;
Italiam non sponte sequor.'

Comprehension Questions

1. Why does Vergil compare Dido to a Bacchante (lines 301–303)? **Bacchantes were conceived as senseless and raving, possessed as they were by the god Bacchus. Like a Bacchante, Dido has no control over her feelings of rage, and, furthermore, she openly displays them.**

2. In her speech (lines 305–330) Dido begs Aeneas in several different ways not to leave. Paraphrase at least three of the reasons why she does not want him to depart.

    Among her rather unconnected list of reasons, Dido mentions their love and pledge to one another (*amor*; *data dextera*, line 307) and the wintry weather, unsuitable for sailing (*hiberno sidere*, line 309; *mediis Aquilonibus*, line 310; *undosum aequor*, line 313). She begs him to think of their marriage (line 316) and the pleasure she has given him (*quicquam dulce*, lines 317–318). She says that the neighboring tribes and even her own people now hate her (lines 320–321); that she still fears retribution from her brother (line 325) and Iarbas (line 326). Finally, she wishes that she at least had a child by Aeneas who could be a companion and a reminder of Aeneas's love (lines 328–330).

3. In response to Dido's distraught pleadings, Aeneas gives a remarkably logical list of reasons why he must do what he is doing. Paraphrase at least four of his points.

    Aeneas explains his side of the case by saying that he will always think fondly of Dido (line 335); that he never married her (lines 338–339); that if it were up to him, he would be in Troy, which would still be standing (lines 340–344); that it is his fate to seek Italy (lines 345–346). He reasons that Dido sought her own country, so he should be able to do likewise (lines 347–350). The memory of his father (lines 351–353) and the thought of his son's future (lines 354–355) compel him to go. Finally, he states that he has been commanded by Jupiter himself to depart, so he must (lines 356–359).

Multiple Choice Questions *Suggested time: 35 minutes*

1. The metrical pattern of the first four feet of line 302 is
   a. dactyl-spondee-dactyl-dactyl
   b. spondee-dactyl-dactyl-dactyl
   c. dactyl-dactyl-dactyl-dactyl
   d. spondee-spondee-dactyl-dactyl

2. In line 302, *Thyias* is a name for
   a. Bacchus
   b. a worshipper of Bacchus
   c. a place where Bacchus is worshipped
   d. Bacchus's mother

3. Lines 305–306 (*dissimulare . . . terra*) are best translated
   a. did you also hope to conceal treacherously so great a crime and be able to depart my land in silence
   b. did not I also hope to conceal, treacherous one, such a great crime and that you would be able to depart my land silently
   c. did I even hope that you would be able to conceal such a great wrongdoing, treacherous one, and depart, silent, from my land
   d. did you even hope that you, treacherous one, were able to conceal such a great wrongdoing and to depart from my land silently

4. Lines 307–308 contain an example of
   a. aposiopesis
   b. anastrophe
   c. apostrophe
   d. anaphora

5. The future participle *moritura* (line 308) modifies
   a. *te* (line 307)
   b. *dextera* (line 307)
   c. *funere* (line 308)
   d. *Dido* (line 308)

6. In line 309, *sidere* is
   a. ablative
   b. adverb
   c. present imperative
   d. present infinitive

7. In lines 311–313 (*quid . . . aequor*) Dido argues that
   a. Aeneas should not seek unknown lands
   b. if Troy still stood, Aeneas would not seek foreign lands
   c. Aeneas would not sail through stormy waters even if he were going back to Troy
   d. by sailing to foreign lands, Aeneas is endangering his fleet

8. The best translation of *peteres* (line 312) is
   a. you were seeking
   b. you should seek
   c. you had sought
   d. you seek

9. In line 317, *quicquam* is
    a. accusative singular feminine
    c. accusative singular neuter
    b. nominative singular neuter
    d. dative singular masculine

10. Line 321 contains an example of
    a. anastrophe
    c. synchysis
    b. chiasmus
    d. hendiadys

11. In lines 320–321 (*te . . . Tyrii*) Dido claims that because of Aeneas
    a. the surrounding tribes and her own people hate her
    c. her own people are defenseless
    b. the Libyans are tyrants
    d. the Libyans hate the Nomads and the Tyrians hate Dido

12. In line 322, *sola* is
    a. ablative singular feminine
    c. accusative plural neuter
    b. nominative singular feminine
    d. nominative plural neuter

13. Dido in lines 323–324 (*cui . . . restat*) says that
    a. only her name is left to her
    c. she will now die because Aeneas is her enemy
    b. Aeneas is now no longer her husband but an enemy
    d. she can now call Aeneas only a guest and not a husband

14. In line 325, *dum* is translated
    a. when
    c. until
    b. as long as
    d. while

15. The antecedent of *qui* (line 329) is
    a. *ego* (understood)
    c. Aeneas (line 329)
    b. *mihi* (line 328)
    d. *parvulus* (line 328)

16. From lines 334–336 (*numquam . . . artus*), we learn that
    a. Aeneas will find Dido deserving when the spirit moves him
    c. as long as Aeneas is mindful, Dido will not control his feelings
    b. as long as he is alive, Aeneas will find pleasure in remembering Dido
    d. Aeneas will deny that he owes Dido anything as long as he is alive

17. *Elissae* (line 335) is
    a. dative with *promeritam* (line 335)
    c. genitive with *pigebit* (line 335)
    b. genitive with *meminisse* (line 335)
    d. dative with *pigebit* (line 335)

18. In line 343, *colerem* is subjunctive in
    a. an implied result clause
    b. the protasis ("if clause") of a present contrary to fact condition
    c. the apodosis ("then clause") of a present contrary-to-fact condition
    d. the apodosis ("then clause") of a past contrary to fact condition

19. Another name for *Pergama* (line 344) is
    a. Crete
    b. Rome
    c. Tyre
    d. Troy

20. In line 346, *sortes* is
    a. second person singular present active indicative
    b. nominative plural feminine
    c. second person singular present active subjunctive
    d. accusative singular neuter

21. Lines 347–348 (*si te . . . urbis*) are best translated
    a. if the view of Carthage and the Libyan city keep you at its citadel, a Phoenician one
    b. if the citadels of Carthage and the view of the Libyan city keep you, a Phoenician
    c. if the citadels keep you at Carthage and Libya and the views of the city, Phoenicia
    d. if the view of the Carthaginian citadels and of the city of Libya detain you, a Phoenician

22. *Ausonia terra* (line 349) is
    a. Tyre
    b. Italy
    c. Libya
    d. Greece

23. In line 349, *quae* modifies
    a. *urbis* (line 348)
    b. *Ausonia* (line 349)
    c. *terra* (line 349)
    d. *invidia* (line 350)

24. In line 354, *-que* connects
    a. *Ascanius* and *capitis* (line 354)
    b. *Ascanius* and *cari* (line 354)
    c. *puer* and *iniuria* (line 354)
    d. *puer* and *cari* (line 354)

25. Line 354 contains an example of
    a. polysyndeton
    b. synecdoche
    c. litotes
    d. enallage

26. In line 355, *fraudo* is
    a. ablative singular neuter
    b. first singular present active indicative
    c. dative singular neuter
    d. positive adverb

27. The number of elisions in line 355 is
    a. zero
    b. one
    c. two
    d. three

28. Aeneas says *testor utrumque caput* (line 357) because
    a. otherwise he will not have a witness
    b. Mercury was a witness
    c. he fears for his and his son's life
    d. he thinks Dido may not believe him

29. In line 358, *ipse* modifies
    a. *manifesto* (line 358)
    b. *lumine* (line 358)
    c. *ego* (understood)
    d. *celeres* (line 357)

Translation *Suggested time: 25 minutes*

Translate the following passage as literally as possible.

> Pro re pauca loquar. Neque ego hanc abscondere furto
> speravi (ne finge) fugam, nec coniugis umquam
> praetendi taedas aut haec in foedera veni.
> Me si fata meis paterentur ducere vitam
> 5   auspiciis et sponte mea componere curas,
> urbem Troianam primum dulcesque meorum
> reliquias colerem, Priami tecta alta manerent,
> et recidiva manu posuissem Pergama victis.

Literal Translation
I shall say a few things on behalf of [my] case. I neither expected—don't imagine [this]—to hide this escape by stealth, nor did I ever hold out the marriage torches of a husband or come into these agreements. If the fates permitted me to lead a life by my own authority and to calm [my] cares of my own accord, I would [dwell in] the city [of] Troy first of all and would cherish the sweet remnants of my [people], [and] the lofty walls of Priam would remain, and I would have established by [my own] hand a reborn Troy for the conquered.

The sections into which a passage is divided are flexible, as are the possible acceptable meanings for any given word. Teachers may prefer a different scheme of "chunking" and range of meanings; what is given below is just one option. Since students must prove to the reader that they understand the grammar of the passage, loose translations are not acceptable, and students should clearly demonstrate the information given under "notes."

18 units
Range of possible meanings followed by notes on grammar and syntax:

pro re	in defense of/on behalf of/for [my] situation/case/matter/course of action/deed

pauca loquar	I shall/will speak/say a few things/words
neque ego hanc abscondere speravi fugam	I did not/neither did I hope/expect/suppose to hide/conceal this flight/departure
furto	with/in stealth/trickery/theft
(ne finge)	do not imagine/fashion/pretend/form/mold [it] (imperative)
nec umquam praetendi	nor did I/and I did not ever hold forth/hold before/offer
coniugis taedas	the torches/wedding torches of marriage/wedlock
aut veni	or/nor did I come
haec in foedera	into these agreements/treaties/pacts
me si fata paterentur	if the/my fates were to allow/suffer/endure (or, allowed/suffered/endured) me (present contrary to fact protasis)
meis ducere vitam auspiciis	to lead/conduct [my] life by/with/under my [own] auspices/authority
et sponte mea componere curas	and to settle/put together/calm/quiet worries/anxieties/cares by/with my own will/wish/desire
primum colerem	first I would be cultivating/cherishing/honoring (present contrary to fact apodosis)
urbem Troianam	the Trojan city/town
dulcesque meorum reliquias	and the sweet/dear/fond remains/remnants/relics/leavings of my people/companions
Priami tecta alta manerent	the tall/lofty/high roofs/buildings/homes/dwellings of Priam would remain/stay (present contrary to fact apodosis)
et recidiva manu posuissem Pergama	and I would have established/placed/put a revived/renewed Troy/Pergamum/Trojan citadel (past contrary to fact apodosis)
victis	for the [having been] conquered/vanquished (dative of reference)

Short Answer Questions

Matching from lines 300–319

1. **E**   *audito* (line 302)
2. **A**   *data* (line 307)
3. **J**   *decedere* (line 306)
4. **D**   *dulce* (line 318)
5. **F**   *hiberno* (line 309)
6. **G**   *inceptos* (line 316)
7. **I**   *labentis* (line 318)
8. **B**   *miserere* (line 318)
9. **C**   *perfide* (line 305)
10. **H**   *ultro* (line 304)

a. participle modifying a subject
b. imperative
c. vocative
d. nominative adjective
e. participle in an ablative absolute
f. ablative
g. participle modifying the object of a preposition
h. adverb
i. participle modifying a genitive object
j. complementary infinitive

Matching from lines 320–339

1. **F**   first person singular
2. **E**   second person singular
3. **J**   third person plural
4. **A**   ablative
5. **C**   accusative
6. **I**   dative
7. **G**   genitive
8. **H**   infinitive
9. **B**   nominative
10. **D**   vocative

a. *aula* (line 328)
b. *suboles* (line 328)
c. *artus* (line 336)
d. *regina* (line 334)
e. *deseris* (line 323)
f. *praetendi* (line 339)
g. *mei* (line 336)
h. *abscondere* (line 337)
i. *cui* (line 323)
j. *odere* (line 321)

Matching from lines 340–361

1. **G** *iussere* (line 346)
2. **I** *capessere* (line 346)
3. **F** *incendere* (line 360)
4. **A** *tecta* (line 343)
5. **C** *mandata* (line 357)
6. **B** *divum* (line 356)
7. **H** *utrumque* (line 357)
8. **D** *posuissem* (line 344)
9. **E** *imago* (line 353)
10. **J** *Anchisae* (line 351)

a. nominative plural
b. genitive plural
c. accusative plural
d. first person singular
e. nominative singular
f. complementary infinitive
g. third person plural
h. accusative singular
i. objective infinitive
j. genitive singular

Essay *Suggested time: 40 minutes*

Dido's speech in lines 305–330 is in contrast, both in tone and content, with Aeneas's speech in lines 333–361. Which one is more effective, and why? Present your response in a well-organized essay using specific examples from throughout both speeches to support the points you make.

Support your assertions with references drawn from throughout the two passages (lines 305–330 and 333–361). All Latin words must be copied or their line numbers provided, AND they must be translated or paraphrased closely enough so that it is clear you understand the Latin. It is your responsibility to convince your reader that you are basing your conclusions on the Latin text and not merely on a general recollection of the passage. Direct your answer to the question; do not merely summarize the passage. Please write your essay on a separate piece of paper.

(See Lesson 16 for an additional essay on this passage.)

Students will respond to essay topics in various ways, and different essays, with quite different approaches, may be of equal quality. The following are some possible points students may make; it is not a sample essay.

The essay asks students to compare the two speeches and to argue for the greater effectiveness of one. Students should be sure to write a thesis statement and then support it. Ideas and phrases, <u>all of which must be translated</u> in student essays, may include the following. The emotional character of Dido's speech (rhetorical questions, focus on love and betrayal, her sense of abandonment and her desire for a *parvulus Aeneas*, lines 328–329) may be contrasted with the logical nature of Aeneas's (statement of facts, refutation of her assertions, demands of destiny, and sense of obligation to his father and son). This essay provides students with a good opportunity for supporting their arguments with citations from the text since there are many words, phrases, and figures of speech with which to do so.

See the Scoring Guidelines on pp. xvii–xviii.

Scansion

Scan the following lines.

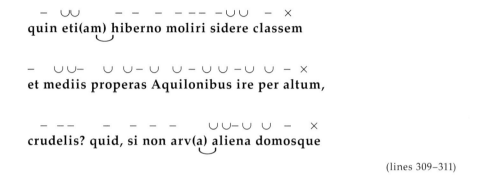

(lines 309–311)

LESSON 16: BOOK 4.659–705

Dixit, et os impressa toro 'Moriemur inultae,
660 sed moriamur' ait. 'Sic, sic iuvat ire sub umbras.
Hauriat hunc oculis ignem crudelis ab alto
Dardanus, et nostrae secum ferat omina mortis.'
Dixerat, atque illam media inter talia ferro
conlapsam aspiciunt comites, ensemque cruore
665 spumantem sparsasque manus. It clamor ad alta
atria: concussam bacchatur Fama per urbem.
Lamentis gemituque et femineo ululatu
tecta fremunt, resonat magnis plangoribus aether,
non aliter quam si immissis ruat hostibus omnis
670 Karthago aut antiqua Tyros, flammaeque furentes
culmina perque hominum volvantur perque deorum.
Audiit exanimis trepidoque exterrita cursu
unguibus ora soror foedans et pectora pugnis
per medios ruit, ac morientem nomine clamat:
675 'Hoc illud, germana, fuit? Me fraude petebas?
Hoc rogus iste mihi, hoc ignes araeque parabant?
Quid primum deserta querar? Comitemne sororem
sprevisti moriens? Eadem me ad fata vocasses:
idem ambas ferro dolor atque eadem hora tulisset.
680 His etiam struxi manibus patriosque vocavi
voce deos, sic te ut posita, crudelis, abessem?
Exstinxti te meque, soror, populumque patresque
Sidonios urbemque tuam. Date, vulnera lymphis
abluam et, extremus si quis super halitus errat,
685 ore legam.' Sic fata gradus evaserat altos,
semianimemque sinu germanam amplexa fovebat
cum gemitu atque atros siccabat veste cruores.
Illa graves oculos conata attollere rursus
deficit; infixum stridit sub pectore vulnus.
690 Ter sese attollens cubitoque adnixa levavit,
ter revoluta toro est oculisque errantibus alto
quaesivit caelo lucem ingemuitque reperta.
Tum Iuno omnipotens longum miserata dolorem
difficilesque obitus Irim demisit Olympo
695 quae luctantem animam nexosque resolveret artus.
Nam quia nec fato merita nec morte peribat,
sed misera ante diem subitoque accensa furore,
nondum illi flavum Proserpina vertice crinem
abstulerat Stygioque caput damnaverat Orco.

700 Ergo Iris croceis per caelum roscida pennis
mille trahens varios adverso sole colores
deuolat et supra caput astitit. 'Hunc ego Diti
sacrum iussa fero teque isto corpore solvo':
sic ait et dextra crinem secat, omnis et una
705 dilapsus calor atque in ventos vita recessit.

Comprehension Questions

1. For what does Dido wish (lines 660–662) just before she kills herself? **She hopes that from the sea Aeneas will see her funeral pyre burning and will carry the omen of her death with him.**

2. How do lines 667–671 recall the events of Book 2? **The grief that is shown at Dido's death is as great as if the city were being destroyed by an enemy; in Book 2, the city was indeed being destroyed by the enemy.**

3. Anna expresses different emotions in her speech in lines 675–685. What are two of them? Support your answer with words or phrases from her speech and provide line references in parentheses.

    Anna feels deceived (*fraude*, line 675), deserted (*deserta*, line 677), that Dido should have allowed Anna to die with her (*eadem me ad fata vocasses*, line 678), that Dido has been cruel (*crudelis*, line 681). Nevertheless, Anna wants to perform the last rites (*abluam*, line 685; *legam*, line 685).

4. How does Vergil show that Dido's death is slow and painful? **Vergil uses anaphora to show that Dido struggled three times to raise herself, but was unable (*ter*, lines 690 and 691). He also says that Juno pitied Dido's long suffering (*longum dolorem*, line 693).**

5. Why does Juno send Iris to Dido? **Juno sends Iris to cut a lock of Dido's hair so that Dido can finally die and be transported to the underworld.**

6. Why, do you think, does Vergil stop, at this point in the poem, to give a description of Iris, the rainbow?

    It reminds us of Juno's involvement in Dido's demise, and, with its beautiful imagery, brings the tumultuous events of the book to a disconcertingly peaceful close.

Multiple Choice Questions

1. *se* (line 662) refers to
   a. **Aeneas**
   b. Dido

2. *conlapsam* (line 664) indicates that Dido has
   a. **stabbed herself**
   b. slipped

3. *sparsas* (line 665) is translated
   a. sparse
   b. **spattered**

4. How many elisions are in line 667?
   a. **one**
   b. two

5. *ruat* (line 669) is in a
   a. **future-less-vivid ("should/would") condition**
   b. present contrary to fact condition

6. *-que* (line 672) connects
   a. *exanimis* and *trepido* (line 672)
   b. ***exanimis* and *exterrita* (line 672)**

7. *pectora* (line 673) is the object of
   a. ***foedans* (line 673)**
   b. *ruit* (line 674)

8. *eadem* (line 678) modifies
   a. *me* (line 678)
   b. ***fata* (line 678)**

9. The form *tulisset* (line 679) indicates that
   a. something happened before the action of the main verb
   b. **something had been desired but not received**

10. *exstinxti* (line 682) is
    a. first person
    b. **second person**

11. *quis* (line 684) is translated
    a. who
    b. **any**

12. *illa* (line 688) refers to
    a. Anna
    b. **Dido**

13. *-que* (line 690) connects
    a. ***attollens* and *adnixa* (line 690)**
    b. *sese* and *cubito* (line 690)

14. *-que* (line 694) connects
    a. ***dolorem* (line 693) and *obitus* (line 694)**
    b. *miserata* (line 693) and *difficiles* (line 694)

15. Line 693 contains an example of
    a. chiasmus
    b. **synchysis**

16. *resolveret* (line 695) is in a
    a. clause of characteristic
    b. **purpose clause**

17. *illi* (line 698) refers to
    a. Iris
    b. **Dido**

18. Line 701 contains an example of
    a. **chiasmus**
    b. synchysis

19. *iussa* (line 703) is
    a. **accusative plural neuter**
    b. nominative singular feminine

20. *una* (line 704) here is an
    a. **adverb**
    b. adjective

Translation *Suggested time: 20 minutes*

Translate the following passage as literally as possible.

> Tum Iuno omnipotens longum miserata dolorem
> diffcilesque obitus Irim demisit Olympo
> quae luctantem animam nexosque resolveret artus.
> Nam quia nec fato merita nec morte peribat,
> 5 sed misera ante diem subitoque accensa furore,
> nondum illi flavum Proserpina vertice crinem
> abstulerat Stygioque caput damnaverat Orco.

Literal Translation
Then all-powerful Juno, pitying the long grief and the difficult death(s), sent down Iris from Olympus to loose the struggling spirit and the bound limbs. For because she was dying neither deserved by fate nor by death, but wretched before her time and inflamed by sudden passion, not yet had Proserpina stolen a tawny lock from her head and condemned her life to Stygian Orcus.

The sections into which a passage is divided are flexible, as are the possible acceptable meanings for any given word. Teachers may prefer a different scheme of "chunking" and range of meanings; what is given below is just one option. Since students must prove to the reader that they understand the grammar of the passage, loose translations are not acceptable, and students should clearly demonstrate the information given under "notes."

17 units
Range of possible meanings followed by notes on grammar and syntax:

Tum Iuno omnipotens	Then all-powerful/omnipotent Juno
miserata	pitying/having pitied (deponent; must be translated actively)
longum dolorem	the long/lengthy grief/pain/passion/anger/suffering (object of *miserata*)
difficilesque obitus	and the difficult/hard/painful death/downfall/ruin(s)
Irim demisit Olympo	sent down/let go/lowered Iris from Olympus
quae resolveret	to/in order to/ who was to loosen/free (must be rendered as showing purpose)
luctantem animam	the struggling/wrestling spirit/soul/shade
nexosque artus	and the woven/fastened/bound joints/limbs/members
Nam quia peribat	For because she was perishing/dying
nec fato merita nec morte	[having] deserved/earned/merited by neither fate/destiny nor death (*merita*, nominative)
sed misera ante diem	but wretched/unhappy/miserable before [her] day
subitoque accensa furore	and inflamed by sudden/unexpected rage/madness/frenzy/passion/fury (*accensa*, nominative)

nondum Proserpina abstulerat vertice	Proserpina had not yet taken away from the/her head
flavum crinem	the yellow/tawny/blond hair/locks/tresses
illi	for her/of hers/her (dative of reference)
Stygioque Orco	and to Stygian Orcus
caput damnaverat	had [not] condemned/sentenced her life/head

Essay *Suggested time: 40 minutes*

```
305   'Dissimulare etiam sperasti, perfide, tantum
      posse nefas tacitusque mea decedere terra?
      Nec te noster amor nec te data dextera quondam
      nec moritura tenet crudeli funere Dido?
      Quin etiam hiberno moliri sidere classem
310   et mediis properas Aquilonibus ire per altum,
      crudelis? Quid, si non arva aliena domosque
      ignotas peteres, et Troia antiqua maneret,
      Troia per undosum peteretur classibus aequor?
      Mene fugis? Per ego has lacrimas dextramque tuam te
315    (quando aliud mihi iam miserae nihil ipsa reliqui),
      per conubia nostra, per inceptos hymenaeos,
      si bene quid de te merui, fuit aut tibi quicquam
      dulce meum, miserere domus labentis et istam,
      oro, si quis adhuc precibus locus, exue mentem.
320   Te propter Libycae gentes Nomadumque tyranni
      odere, infensi Tyrii; te propter eundem
      exstinctus pudor et, qua sola sidera adibam,
      fama prior. Cui me moribundam deseris hospes
       (hoc solum nomen quoniam de coniuge restat)?
325   Quid moror? An mea Pygmalion dum moenia frater
      destruat aut captam ducat Gaetulus Iarbas?
      Saltem si qua mihi de te suscepta fuisset
      ante fugam suboles, si quis mihi parvulus aula
      luderet Aeneas, qui te tamen ore referret,
330   non equidem omnino capta ac deserta viderer.'
                                        (Book 4.305–330)


      Audiit exanimis trepidoque exterrita cursu
      unguibus ora soror foedans et pectora pugnis
      per medios ruit, ac morientem nomine clamat:
675   'Hoc illud, germana, fuit? Me fraude petebas?
      Hoc rogus iste mihi, hoc ignes araeque parabant?
      Quid primum deserta querar? Comitemne sororem
      sprevisti moriens? Eadem me ad fata vocasses:
      idem ambas ferro dolor atque eadem hora tulisset.
```

> 680 His etiam struxi manibus patriosque vocavi
>   voce deos, sic te ut posita, crudelis, abessem?
>   Exstinxti te meque, soror, populumque patresque
>   Sidonios urbemque tuam. Date, vulnera lymphis
>   abluam et, extremus si quis super halitus errat,
> 685 ore legam.' Sic fata gradus evaserat altos,
>   semianimemque sinu germanam amplexa fovebat
>   cum gemitu atque atros siccabat veste cruores.
>
>   (Book 4.672–687)

Compare the feeling of betrayal that each speaker expresses. In your opinion, which of the speakers is more fully justified in her feeling of betrayal? Use specific details from both passages to support your position.

Support your assertions with references drawn from throughout both passages. All Latin words must be copied or their line numbers provided, AND they must be translated or paraphrased closely enough so that it is clear you understand the Latin. It is your responsibility to convince your reader that you are basing your conclusions on the Latin text and not merely on a general recollection of the passages. Direct your answer to the question; do not merely summarize the passages. Please write your essays on a separate piece of paper.

This question has two dimensions. First, it asks students to show their comprehension of both passages, by requiring them to identify the speakers and addresses of both passages (Dido to Aeneas in the first, and Anna to Dido in the second) and to explain the context for their reproaches. In the first passage, Dido begins by emphasizing feelings of treachery/deceit (*dissimulare*, line 305; *tantum nefas*, lines 305–306) and then emphasizes feelings of abandonment (*mea decedere terra*, line 306; *mene fugis*, line 314; *deseris*, line 323; *capta ac deserta*, line 330); she also hints repeatedly that this will be the cause of her death, though it is not yet clear how literally she means this (*moritura crudeli funere Dido*, line 308; *domus labentis*, line 318; *me moribundam*, line 323). In the second passage, Anna expresses a similar sequence of ideas, beginning with treachery/deceit (*fraude*, line 675; *comitemne sororem sprevisti*, lines 677–678), moving to abandonment (*deserta*, line 677; *ut abessem*, line 681), and then death, first wishing that she could have shared in Dido's death (lines 678–679) and then declaring her own virtual death as a result of Dido's suicide (lines 682–683).

Secondly, the question invites students to make a case for one or the other speaker as more fully justified in her complaint, and thus gives them the opportunity to present a well-argued and thoughtful opinion based on specific details in the two passages. Neither option in itself is better or more correct than the other; rather, this aspect of the question expects students to demonstrate their overall understanding of the events of Book 4 (and of the *Aeneid* as a whole) and their thoughtful appreciation of each character's perspective on those events.

See the Scoring Guidelines on pp. xvii–xviii.

Scansion

Indicate whether each line is scanned correctly or not. In the line provided, mark a "Y" for yes or an "N" for no as appropriate.
NB: These are not consecutive lines but four discrete selections.

1. **Y**   lāmēn|tīs gĕmĭ|tūqu(e) ēt |fēmĭnĕ|ō ŭlŭ|lātū

2. **Y**   cūlmĭnă| pērqu(e) hŏmĭ|nūm vōl|vāntūr |pērquĕ dĕ|lōrŭm

3. **N**   sēmĭă|nīmĕmquĕ| sīnŭ gĕr|mān(am) ām|plēxă fŏv|ēbāt

4. **Y**   sēd mĭsĕr(a) |āntĕ dĭ|ēm sŭbĭt|ōqu(e) āc|cēnsă fŭ|rōrĕ

LESSON 17: BOOK 6.295-332

295 Hinc via Tartarei quae fert Acherontis ad undas.
    Turbidus hic caeno vastaque voragine gurges
    aestuat atque omnem Cocyto eructat harenam.
    Portitor has horrendus aquas et flumina servat
    terribili squalore Charon, cui plurima mento
300 canities inculta iacet, stant lumina flamma,
    sordidus ex umeris nodo dependet amictus.
    Ipse ratem conto subigit velisque ministrat
    et ferruginea subvectat corpora cumba,
    iam senior, sed cruda deo viridisque senectus.
305 Huc omnis turba ad ripas effusa ruebat,
    matres atque viri defunctaque corpora vita
    magnanimum heroum, pueri innuptaeque puellae,
    impositique rogis iuvenes ante ora parentum:
    quam multa in silvis autumni frigore primo
310 lapsa cadunt folia, aut ad terram gurgite ab alto
    quam multae glomerantur aves, ubi frigidus annus
    trans pontum fugat et terris immittit apricis.
    Stabant orantes primi transmittere cursum
    tendebantque manus ripae ulterioris amore.
315 Navita sed tristis nunc hos nunc accipit illos,
    ast alios longe summotos arcet harena.
    Aeneas miratus enim motusque tumultu
    'Dic,' ait, 'o virgo, quid vult concursus ad amnem?
    Quidve petunt animae? Vel quo discrimine ripas
320 hae linquunt, illae remis vada livida verrunt?'
    Olli sic breviter fata est longaeva sacerdos:
    'Anchisa generate, deum certissima proles,
    Cocyti stagna alta vides Stygiamque paludem,
    di cuius iurare timent et fallere numen.
325 Haec omnis, quam cernis, inops inhumataque turba est;
    portitor ille Charon; hi, quos vehit unda, sepulti.
    Nec ripas datur horrendas et rauca fluenta
    transportare prius quam sedibus ossa quierunt.
    Centum errant annos volitantque haec litora circum;
330 tum demum admissi stagna exoptata revisunt.'
    Constitit Anchisa satus et vestigia pressit
    multa putans sortemque animo miseratus iniquam.

Comprehension Questions

1. How does the description of Acheron contribute a sense of foreboding to the passage?

   The description creates a sense of foreboding and danger because the Acheron is a swollen whirlpool (*turbidus gurges*, line 296) with mud and much whirling water (*caeno vastaque voragine*, line 296), and it is seething (*aestuat*, line 297) and belching forth sand (*eructat harenam*, line 297).

2. How is Charon described? Why do you think Vergil portrays him in this way?

   Charon is fearsome (*horrendus*, line 298), disheveled (*terribili squalore*, line 299), with a long, white, untrimmed beard (*plurima mento canities inculta*, lines 299–300) and with fiery eyes (*stant lumina flamma*, line 300). His cloak is dirty (*sordidus amictus*, line 301). Despite all this, he is vigorous in his old age (*cruda deo viridisque senectus*, line 304). Vergil portrays him as intimidating to show how much power Charon wields, and as vigorous in contrast to the shades by which he is surrounded.

3. Whom does Vergil specify among the shades in lines 305–308? **Mothers and husbands/men (*matres atque viri*, line 306), the bodies of great-hearted heroes (*corpora magnanimum heroum*, lines 306–307), boys and unmarried girls (*pueri innuptaeque puellae*, line 307), and young people who have died in the sight of their parents (*iuvenes ante ora parentum*, line 308).**

4. What do the similes in lines 309–312 emphasize? **The very large number of shades clamoring to cross.**

5. What is the Sibyl's explanation (lines 325–326) of the difference between those souls Charon ferries across and those he leaves behind?

   The poor and unburied (*inops inhumataque*, line 325) are not allowed to cross but must wander one hundred years (*centum errant annos*, line 329) on the shore while the buried are carried across (*hi quos vehit unda sepulti*, line 326).

6. What can we tell about Aeneas's character from his reaction (lines 331–332) to the Sibyl's explanation?

   He is thoughtful (*multa putans*, line 332) and compassionate (*sortemque animo miseratus iniquam*, line 332).

Multiple Choice Questions *Suggested time: 30 minutes*

1. In line 296, *turbidus* modifies
   a. *hic* (line 296)
   b. *caeno* (line 296)
   c. *voragine* (line 296)
   d. ***gurges* (line 296)**

2. Line 298 contains an example of
   a. chiasmus
   b. **synchysis**
   c. prolepsis
   d. anaphora

3. The case of *terribili* (line 299) is
    a. **ablative**
    b. dative
    c. nominative
    d. genitive

4. In line 299, *plurima* modifies
    a. *squalore* (line 299)
    b. *flamma* (line 300)
    c. ***canities* (line 300)**
    d. *lumina* (line 300)

5. Line 300 (*canities . . . flamma*) contains an example of
    a. tmesis
    b. anastrophe
    c. hiatus
    d. **chiasmus**

6. In line 302, *ipse* refers to
    a. *canities* (line 300)
    b. *amictus* (line 301)
    c. ***Charon* (line 299)**
    d. *corpora* (line 303)

7. In line 302, *-que* connects
    a. *subigit* and *velis* (line 302)
    b. ***subigit* and *ministrat* (line 302)**
    c. *velis* and *ministrat* (line 302)
    d. *conto* and *ministrat* (line 302)

8. In line 303, *cumba*
    a. is nominative subject
    b. modifies *corpora* (line 303)
    c. is an adverb
    d. **is an ablative of means**

9. In line 304, the case and use of *deo* are
    a. **dative of possession**
    b. dative of agent
    c. ablative of agent
    d. ablative of place where

10. Line 305 (*Huc . . . ruebat*) is best translated
    a. Poured forth from here, the throng rushed to each bank
    b. To here the whole throng rushed toward the overflowing banks
    c. **To here the whole throng rushed, poured forth to the banks**
    d. Here every throng rushed near the banks having overflowed

11. In line 306, how many words are in the nominative?
    a. one
    b. two
    c. three
    d. **four**

12. In lines 307–308 (*pueri . . . parentum*), Vergil focuses on
    a. the importance of funeral rites
    b. **the loss of young people**
    c. the appearance of parents
    d. the role of marriage

13. Lines 309–310 (*quam . . . folia*) are best translated
    a. which leaves, having slipped, the autumns cause to fall in the woods in the first chill
    b. **as many as the leaves, having slipped, fall in the woods at the first chill of autumn**
    c. how, in the great first chill of autumn, the leaves, having slipped, fall in the woods
    d. as many as leaves fall in the woods, with the first chill of autumn having slipped in

14. In line 311, *quam* is best translated
    a. which
    b. how
    c. than
    d. **as**

15. The metrical pattern of the first four feet of line 313 is
    a. **spondee-spondee-spondee-spondee**
    b. dactyl-spondee-dactyl-spondee
    c. dactyl-dactyl-spondee-spondee
    d. spondee-dactyl-spondee-dactyl

16. In line 314, *ripae* is
    a. dative indirect object
    b. dative of direction
    c. **objective genitive**
    d. genitive with *tendebant* (line 314)

17. In line 316, *harena* is
    a. ablative of means
    b. **ablative of separation**
    c. nominative subject
    d. predicate nominative

18. Line 320 (*hae . . . verrunt*) contains an example of
    a. anaphora
    b. hendiadys
    c. polysyndeton
    d. **asyndeton**

19. In line 322, *generate* is
    a. **vocative of a perfect passive participle**
    b. singular positive imperative
    c. ablative of a perfect passive participle
    d. nominative singular adjective

20. In line 323, *-que* connects
    a. *vides* and *Stygiam* (line 323)
    b. *Stygiam* and *paludem* (line 323)
    c. ***stagna* and *paludem* (line 323)**
    d. *alta* and *Stygiam* (line 323)

21. The antecedent of *cuius* (line 324) is
    a. *di* (line 324)
    b. *Cocyti* (line 323)
    c. ***paludem* (line 323)**
    d. *numen* (line 324)

134 • VERGIL

22. Line 326 (*portitor . . . sepulti*) is best translated
    a. **that ferryman is Charon; these whom the wave carries have been buried**
    b. I am that ferryman Charon; these who are carried by the wave have been buried
    c. I am carried by that Charon; these, having been buried, are carried by the wave
    d. that Charon will be the ferryman; having been buried by the wave, they carry themselves

23. How many elisions does line 329 contain?
    a. zero
    b. one
    c. **two**
    d. three

24. In line 332, *miseratus* modifies
    a. **Anchisa (line 331)**
    b. the same one(s) as *satus* (line 331)
    c. *Charon* (understood)
    d. the same one(s) as *admissi* (line 330)

Translation *Suggested time: 20 minutes*

Translate the following passage as literally as possible.

>   'Quidve petunt animae? Vel quo discrimine ripas
>   hae linquunt, illae remis vada livida verrunt?'
>   Olli sic breviter fata est longaeva sacerdos:
>   'Anchisa generate, deum certissima proles,
> 5   Cocyti stagna alta vides Stygiamque paludem,
>   di cuius iurare timent et fallere numen.'

Literal Translation
"Or what do the souls seek? Or by what distinction do these leave the shores, [but] those sweep over the dark shallows with oars?" To him the aged priestess spoke briefly thus: "Sprung from Anchises, most sure offspring of the gods, you see the deep pools of Cocytus and the Stygian swamp, [by] whose divine power the gods fear to take an oath and to deceive."

The sections into which a passage is divided are flexible, as are the possible acceptable meanings for any given word. Teachers may prefer a different scheme of "chunking" and range of meanings; what is given below is just one option. Since students must prove to the reader that they understand the grammar of the passage, loose translations are not acceptable, and students should clearly demonstrate the syntactical information provided in parentheses in the column below with the English range of meanings.

15 units
Range of possible meanings followed by notes on grammar and syntax:

Quidve petunt animae?	Or what do the shades/spirits/ghosts/souls seek/look for (*quid* object of *petunt*)
Vel quo discrimine	Or with/by what distinction

hae linquunt ripas	do these leave/leave behind the banks/shores
illae verrunt remis	[and/but] those sweep/sweep over with/by oars
vada livida	the blue/dark/livid shallows/shoals/depths
longaeva sacerdos	the aged/very old priestess
sic breviter fata est	thus briefly spoke/said
Olli	to him/that one
Anchisa generate	born/begotten from Anchises (*generate*, vocative)
certissima proles deum	most sure/certain offspring of the gods
stagna alta vides Cocyti	you see the deep pools/depths/still waters of Cocytus
Stygiamque paludem	and the Stygian swamp/swamp of the Styx
cuius numen	whose divinity/divine power (antecedent of *cuius* is *Stygiam numen*)
di timent	the gods fear
iurare et fallere	to swear [by] and to deceive

Short Answer Questions

Matching

1. **G** present participle
2. **J** ablative of means
3. **H** adverb
4. **F** perfect passive participle
5. **D** genitive plural
6. **I** ablative of time when
7. **C** accusative, plural, feminine
8. **B** accusative, plural, neuter
9. **E** superlative adjective
10. **A** dative singular

a. *cui* (line 299)
b. *flumina* (line 298)
c. *manus* (line 314)
d. *magnanimum* (line 307)
e. *plurima* (line 299)
f. *impositi* (line 308)
g. *orantes* (line 313)
h. *hic* (line 296)
i. *frigore* (line 309)
j. *cumba* (line 303)

1.	**C**	*harena* (line 316)	a. perfect passive participle
2.	**I**	*longe* (line 316)	b. present participle
3.	**G**	*Dic* (line 318)	c. ablative of separation
4.	**H**	*Olli* (line 321)	d. vocative
5.	**D**	*certissima* (line 322)	e. nominative, singular subject
6.	**E**	*unda* (line 326)	f. accusative, neuter, plural
7.	**J**	*annos* (line 329)	g. imperative
8.	**F**	*haec* (line 329)	h. dative singular
9.	**A**	*admissi* (line 330)	i. adverb
10.	**B**	*putans* (line 332)	j. accusative of extent of time

Essay *Suggested time: 20 minutes*

Although lines 295–332 do not contain much narrative action, Vergil shows movement throughout the passage. How does he do this? Why would Vergil emphasize this movement at this point in the poem? Present your response in a well-organized essay.

Support your assertions with references drawn from throughout this passage (lines 295–332 only). All Latin words must be copied or their line numbers provided, AND they must be translated or paraphrased closely enough so that it is clear you understand the Latin. It is your responsibility to convince your reader that you are basing your conclusions on the Latin text and not merely on a general recollection of the passage. Direct your answer to the question; do not merely summarize the passage. Please write your essay on a separate piece of paper.

Students will respond to essay topics in various ways, and different essays, with quite different approaches, may be of equal quality. The following are some possible points students may make; this is not a sample essay.
  The essay asks students to identify and describe the difference between what actually happens in the passage and the effects of Vergil's description, and to consider possible reasons for Vergil's emphasis on movement in this passage. Students should be sure to write a thesis statement and then support it. Ideas and phrases, <u>all of which must be translated</u> in student essays, may include the following: the landscape of the underworld (including the constant movement of water and sand, and Charon's boat repeatedly crossing the river); the presence of the shades of the dead (crowding the river's bank, desiring to cross); and Aeneas's careful observation of their behavior. Vergil's use of similes comparing the shades in the underworld to leaves or birds affected by seasonal change and his detailed description of Charon's appearance give students a good opportunity to discuss Vergilian imagery, and the Sibyl's explanation of what is happening invites consideration of the scene's importance to Aeneas. This essay provides students with a good opportunity for supporting their arguments with citations from throughout the entire passage, since there are many words, phrases, and figures of speech that support the question.

See the Scoring Guidelines on pp. xvii–xviii.

Scansion

Scan the following lines. NB: These are not consecutive lines but four discrete selections.

```
 −  ∪∪  −      −     −    − −    − −  ∪   ∪  − ×
```
aestuat atqu(e) omnem Cocyt(o) eructat harenam (line 297)

```
 −   − −∪∪−    −    − −    − ∪∪   −   ×
```
et ferruginea subvectat corpora cumba (line 303)

How does scansion show that *ferruginea* cannot modify *corpora*? **The final -a of *ferruginea* scans long, so it must modify the ablative *cumba* rather than *corpora*, which is neuter plural and therefore ends with a short -a.**

```
 − ∪ ∪  −     ∪∪     −    −   − −    − ∪   ∪   − ×
```
lapsa cadunt foli(a,) aut ad terram gurgit(e) ab alto (line 310)

How does scansion show that *lapsa* must modify *folia*? **The final -a of *lapsa* scans short, so it must modify the neuter plural *folia*.**

```
 −       − −    −   −  ∪∪−      −     − ∪∪   − ×
```
Cent(um) errant annos volitantqu(e) haec litora circum (line 329)

LESSON 18: BOOK 6.384-425

Ergo iter inceptum peragunt fluvioque propinquant.
385 Navita quos iam inde ut Stygia prospexit ab unda
per tacitum nemus ire pedemque advertere ripae,
sic prior adgreditur dictis atque increpat ultro:
'Quisquis es, armatus qui nostra ad flumina tendis,
fare age, quid venias, iam istinc et comprime gressum.
390 Umbrarum hic locus est, somni noctisque soporae:
corpora viva nefas Stygia vectare carina.
Nec vero Alciden me sum laetatus euntem
accepisse lacu, nec Thesea Pirithoümque,
dis quamquam geniti atque invicti viribus essent.
395 Tartareum ille manu custodem in vincla petivit
ipsius a solio regis traxitque trementem;
hi dominam Ditis thalamo deducere adorti.'
Quae contra breviter fata est Amphrysia vates:
'Nullae hic insidiae tales (absiste moveri),
400 nec vim tela ferunt; licet ingens ianitor antro
aeternum latrans exsangues terreat umbras,
casta licet patrui servet Proserpina limen.
Troius Aeneas, pietate insignis et armis,
ad genitorem imas Erebi descendit ad umbras.
405 Si te nulla movet tantae pietatis imago,
at ramum hunc' (aperit ramum qui veste latebat)
'agnoscas.' Tumida ex ira tum corda residunt;
nec plura his. Ille admirans venerabile donum
fatalis virgae longo post tempore visum
410 caeruleam advertit puppim ripaeque propinquat.
Inde alias animas, quae per iuga longa sedebant,
deturbat laxatque foros; simul accipit alveo
ingentem Aenean. Gemuit sub pondere cumba
sutilis et multam accepit rimosa paludem.
415 Tandem trans fluvium incolumes vatemque virumque
informi limo glaucaque exponit in ulva.
Cerberus haec ingens latratu regna trifauci
personat adverso recubans immanis in antro.
Cui vates horrere videns iam colla colubris
420 melle soporatam et medicatis frugibus offam
obicit. Ille fame rabida tria guttura pandens
corripit obiectam, atque immania terga resolvit
fusus humi totoque ingens extenditur antro.
Occupat Aeneas aditum custode sepulto
425 evaditque celer ripam inremeabilis undae.

Comprehension Questions

1. Why does Charon mention *Alciden* (line 392) and *Thesea Pirithoümque* (line 393)? To what story about each is he alluding?

   Hercules (*Alciden*) in one of his twelve labors descended to the underworld to carry off Cerberus; Theseus and Perithoüs went to carry off Proserpina. Here in Book 6, Charon fears that Aeneas is trying to cross the river in order to attempt some equally violent act.

2. How does the Sibyl reassure Charon in lines 399–404? **She says that their weapons do not bring violence (*nec vim tela ferunt*, line 400), and that Cerberus may continue to terrify the shades (*terreat umbras*, line 401) and Proserpina may continue to protect her uncle's threshold/realm (*servet Proserpina limen*, line 402).**

3. What talisman does the Sibyl show Charon that assures Aeneas's crossing of the river?

   She shows him the branch (the golden one that Aeneas found earlier in Book 6 with the help of his mother's birds).

4. What detail does Vergil give in lines 413–414 that emphasizes Aeneas's vitality, in contrast to the shades around him?

   Charon's boat is accustomed to carrying weightless shades, so when Aeneas, a living human with flesh and blood, gets into it, it groans with the weight (*gemuit sub pondere*) and takes on water as it sinks lower into the river (*multam accepit . . . paludem*).

5. How does the Sibyl control Cerberus in lines 419–425? **She feeds him a drugged cake (*soporatam offam*, line 420) so he will fall asleep.**

Short Answer Questions

Complete the statement or answer the question.

1. The case and use of *fluvio* (line 384) is **dative of direction or dative with *propinquo*.**
2. In line 385, *quos* is best translated **them.**
3. *quos* (line 385) is accusative because **it is the subject of the infinitive in indirect statement.**
4. *ut* (line 385) is best translated **as/when.**
5. The case and use of *nemus* (line 386) is **accusative with preposition *per*.**
6. Is *pedem* (line 386) the subject or object of *advertere*? **object.**
7. The adjective *prior* (line 387) modifies **navita (line 385).**
8. The part of speech of *ultro* (line 387) is **adverb.**
9. The participle *armatus* (line 388) modifies **qui.**
10. The form of *fare* (line 389) is **present imperative.**

11. *Venias* (line 389) is subjunctive because **it is in an indirect question.**
12. The part of speech of *viva* (line 391) is **adjective.**
13. The case and use of *carina* (line 391) is **ablative of means/instrument.**
14. The use of *Alciden* (line 392) for Hercules is an example of a **patronymic.**
15. *Alciden* (line 392) is modified by the word **euntem (line 392).**
16. The subject of the infinitive *accepisse* (line 393) is **me (line 392).**
17. The understood subjects of *geniti [essent]* and *invicti essent* (line 394) are **Hercules, Theseus, and Pirithoüs.**
18. *ille* in line 395 refers to **Hercules.**
19. *custodem* in line 395 refers to **Cerberus.**
20. *regis* in line 396 refers to **Pluto/Hades/Dis.**
21. *hi* in line 397 refers to **Theseus and Pirithoüs.**
22. The case of *Ditis* (line 397) is **genitive.**
23. The case, number, and gender of *quae* (line 398) are **accusative neuter plural.**
24. The form of *moveri* (line 399) is **present passive infinitive.**
25. *aeternum* in line 401 is best translated **eternally/forever/without end.**
26. *Latrans* (line 401) modifies **ianitor (line 400).**
27. *patrui* in line 402 refers to **Pluto/Hades/Dis.**
28. *et* in line 403 connects __ and __. **pietate, armis.**
29. The antecedent of *qui* (line 406) is **ramum.**
30. *Agnoscas* (line 407) is subjunctive because **it is in a polite command/jussive.**
31. *His* (line 408) is what use of the ablative? **comparison.**
32. *Venerabile* (line 408) modifies **donum.**
33. The subject of *laxat* (line 412) is **Charon (understood) or Ille (line 408).**
34. *Sutilis* (line 414) modifies **cumba (line 413).**
35. *incolumes* in line 415 modifies **vatemque virumque (line 415).**
36. *Informi* (line 416) modifies **limo (line 416).**
37. The three words in lines 417–418 that modify *Cerberus* (line 417) are **ingens, recubans, and immanis.**
38. *Colla* (line 419) is in the accusative because **it is the subject of the infinitive *horrere* in indirect statement.**

39. The case of *melle* (line 420) is **ablative.**
40. The direct object of *obicit* (line 421) is ***offam* (line 420).**
41. *Obiectam* (line 422) modifies ***offam* (line 420).**
42. The case of *humi* (line 423) is **locative.**
43. *Fusus* and *ingens* (line 423) modify ***Ille* (line 421).**
44. *Custode* (line 424) is ablative because **it is in an ablative absolute.**
45. *Celer* (line 425) modifies ***Aeneas* (line 424).**

Translation *Suggested time: 25 minutes*

Translate the following passage as literally as possible.

> 'Nullae hic insidiae tales (absiste moveri),
> nec vim tela ferunt; licet ingens ianitor antro
> aeternum latrans exsangues terreat umbras,
> casta licet patrui servet Proserpina limen.
> 5   Troius Aeneas, pietate insignis et armis,
> ad genitorem imas Erebi descendit ad umbras.
> Si te nulla movet tantae pietatis imago,
> at ramum hunc' (aperit ramum qui veste latebat)
> 'agnoscas.'

Literal Translation
'No such plots are here (cease to be moved), nor do [our] weapons bring violence; it is permitted that the huge doorkeeper barking eternally in [his] cave terrify the bloodless shades, it is permitted that chaste Proserpina protect the threshold of her uncle. Trojan Aeneas, outstanding because of his devotion and weapons, descends to the deepest shades of Erebus to his father. If no image of such great devotion moves you, at least' (she reveals the bough that was lying hidden in [her] robe) 'recognize this bough.'

The sections into which a passage is divided are flexible, as are the possible acceptable meanings for any given word. Teachers may prefer a different scheme of "chunking" and range of meanings; what is given below is just one option. Since students must prove to the reader that they understand the grammar of the passage, loose translations are not acceptable, and students should clearly demonstrate the syntactical information provided in parentheses in the column below with the English range of meanings.

15 units
Range of possible meanings followed by notes on grammar and syntax:

Nullae hic insidiae tales	No such plots/snare/ambush/treachery [are] here
absiste moveri	cease/stop to be moved/upset

nec vim tela ferunt	nor do our/the weapons bring/carry/bear force/violence
ingens ianitor	the huge/immense/mighty/enormous doorkeeper/guard (also permissible construction: let the huge doorkeeper)
aeternum latrans antro	barking eternally/for an eternity in a/his cave (*latrans* must modify *ianitor*)
licet exsangues terreat umbras	it is permitted that frighten/terrify the bloodless/lifeless/pale shades/ghosts/shadows (*ianitor* must be subject of *terreat*)
casta Proserpina	chaste/pure/holy Proserpina (also permissible construction: let chaste Proserpina)
licet patrui servet limen	it is permitted that protect/save/watch/guard the threshold/home/palace/realm of her uncle/paternal uncle (*Proserpina* must be subject of *servet*)
Troius Aeneas descendit ad genitorem	Trojan Aeneas descends/is descending to [his] father
pietate insignis et armis	known/famous/noted/marked/distinguished/splendid because of/for/by [his] devotion/loyalty/piety/sense of duty and weapons/arms (*insignis* must modify *Aeneas*)
imas Erebi ad umbras	to the lowest/deepest shades/shadows/ghosts of Erebus
Si te nulla movet tantae pietatis imago	If no image/likeness/ghost/soul/form of such great/so great devotion/loyalty/piety/sense of duty (dependent on *imago*) moves you
at ramum hunc agnoscas	but/at least recognize/you may recognize this branch/bough
aperit ramum	she reveals/discloses the branch/bough
qui veste latebat	that was hiding/lying hidden/lurking/escaping notice in her robe/clothing

Translation and Analysis Questions

Translate the Latin used in the question and answer the question.

1. By recalling that, '*Tartareum ille manu custodem in vincla petivit / ipsius a solio regis traxitque trementem; / hi dominam Ditis thalamo deducere adorti*' (lines 395–397), what does Charon imply may be Aeneas's reasons for wanting to visit the underworld?

    When Charon relates that, "The former (*i.e.*, Hercules) sought to to put with his hand the Tartarean guard into chains and dragged him, trembling, from the throne of the king himself; the latter (*i.e.*, Theseus and Pirithous) attempted to lead away the wife of Dis from her bedchamber," he implies that Aeneas may be coming to attempt a kidnapping or some other form of violence.

2. How might the words *licet ingens ianitor antro / aeternum latrans exsangues terreat umbras, / casta licet patrui servet Proserpina limen* (lines 400–402), while reassuring to Charon, be considered ominous by the reader?

   The lines, "The huge doorkeeper, barking endlessly in his cave, may terrify the bloodless shades, chaste Proserpina may keep watch over the threshold of her paternal uncle," reassure Charon that the Sibyl and Aeneas are not coming to do any harm to Cerberus or Proserpina. On the other hand, Cerberus's endless barking and his terrifying of the shades sets a frightening tone. The adjective *casta* to describe Proserpina and the reminder that she is the wife of her uncle remind the reader of the violent manner in which she was made the queen of the underworld.

3. What aspects of Aeneas's character does the Sybil highlight with the phrase *pietate insignis et armis* (line 403)?

   The Sibyl emphasizes Aeneas's sense of duty or devotion, and his skill in arms/warfare.

4. The lines *Ille admirans venerabile donum / fatalis virgae longo post tempore visum / caeruleam advertit puppim ripaeque propinquat* (lines 408–410) show Charon's response to the branch. What is his reaction?

   "He, admiring the awe-inspiring gift of the fateful branch, [a gift] seen after a long time, turns his dark ship and approaches the bank," shows how important the branch is. Charon admires it and immediately changes his attitude from one of brusqueness and defensiveness to one of compliance.

5. Why is Aeneas described as *ingentem* (line 413)?

   Compared to the weightless shades, Aeneas is very heavy/huge.

6. Various forms of *gemuit* (line 413) occur throughout the *Aeneid*, but the subject is usually a person in grief or despair. What makes this occurence different? How is its use here somewhat ironic?

   Here it is the boat (*cumba*) that groans with the weight of Aeneas. It is ironic that in the underworld, full of shades who are being grieved for, it is the living person who causes the lament.

7. What does Vergil call to the reader's attention by the use of *ingens* (line 417), *immanis* (line 418), *immania* (line 422), and *ingens* (line 423)?

   The repetition of words that mean "huge," "immense" or "monstrous" to describe Cerberus or parts of Cerberus emphasize his size and therefore his frightening appearance.

8. In Book 2, Vergil writes of the Greeks, *Invadunt urbem somno vinoque sepultam* (line 265, "They invade the city overcome/buried in sleep and wine"). Here Vergil describes Cerberus as a *custode sepulto* (line 424). In both places, the participle of *sepelio* has multiple layers of meaning. How do the different meanings of *sepelio* add depth to the line here in Book 6?

   While the reader knows that "With the guard [having been] buried" means that Cerberus is asleep, the word *sepultam* connotes being buried in death, a connotation that is interesting given that Cerberus is surrounded by the dead, some of whom are buried and some not.

Essay *Suggested time: 20 minutes*

How does this passage (lines 384–425) contribute to the characterization of Aeneas? How does this characterization link Aeneas to his ancestors and descendants?

Support your assertions with references drawn from throughout this passage (lines 384–425). All Latin words must be copied or their line numbers provided, AND they must be translated or paraphrased closely enough so that it is clear you understand the Latin. It is your responsibility to convince your reader that you are basing your conclusions on the Latin text and not merely on a general recollection of the passage. Direct your answer to the question; do not merely summarize the passage. Please write your essay on a separate piece of paper.

(See Lesson 20 for an additional essay on this passage.)

Students will respond to essay topics in various ways, and different essays, with quite different approaches, may be of equal quality. The following are some possible points students may make; this is not a sample essay.

The essay asks students to reflect on Vergil's continuing characterization of Aeneas by looking carefully at both the descriptive language used throughout the entire passage and the actions and reactions described; the result is a combined emphasis on Aeneas's heroic stature, his *pietas*, and the divine assistance he merits. Students should be sure to write a thesis statement and then support it. Supporting ideas and phrases, <u>all of which must be translated</u> in student essays, may include the following: Charon has no idea who Aeneas is, but notes immediately that he is armed (line 288) and suggests that he is to be compared to the Greek heroes Hercules and Theseus, who treated Charon in a violent manner (lines 392–397). The Sybil answers for Aeneas, and explains that the Trojan is armed but not violent (lines 399–404); she also emphasizes that he is motivated by *pietas* to visit the underworld (lines 403–405), and shows Charon the golden bough to prove that Aeneas has divine authority to proceed (lines 406–407). Aeneas is great in size, but Charon's small boat carries him and the Sibyl across the Styx successfully (lines 412–416); with the Sibyl's help Aeneas avoids Cerberus and lands on the other side (lines 417–425).

Scansion

Scan the following lines. NB: These are not consecutive lines but four discrete selections.

```
 −    −    −    −    −   − −    ∪ ∪ −∪ ∪  −  ×
```
nec plur(a) his. Ill(e) admirans venerabile donum (line 408)

```
 − ∪ ∪    −    − −  −   −   − −   ∪   ∪   −  ×
```
caerule(am) advertit puppim ripaeque propinquat. (line 410)

```
 −  −      −   − −    ∪  ∪−  −    −  ∪ ∪  −  ×
```
ingent(em) Aenean. Gemuit sub pondere cumba (line 413)

```
 −  −  − −    − −        −   −  ∪ ∪  − ×
```
informi limo glaucaqu(e) exponit in ulva. (line 416)

LESSON 19: BOOK 6.450–476

450 Inter quas Phoenissa recens a vulnere Dido
errabat silva in magna; quam Troius heros
ut primum iuxta stetit agnovitque per umbras
obscuram, qualem primo qui surgere mense
aut videt aut vidisse putat per nubila lunam,
455 demisit lacrimas dulcique adfatus amore est:
'Infelix Dido, verus mihi nuntius ergo
venerat exstinctam ferroque extrema secutam?
Funeris heu tibi causa fui? Per sidera iuro,
per superos et si qua fides tellure sub ima est,
460 invitus, regina, tuo de litore cessi.
Sed me iussa deum, quae nunc has ire per umbras,
per loca senta situ cogunt noctemque profundam,
imperiis egere suis; nec credere quivi
hunc tantum tibi me discessu ferre dolorem.
465 Siste gradum teque aspectu ne subtrahe nostro.
Quem fugis? Extremum fato quod te adloquor hoc est.'
Talibus Aeneas ardentem et torva tuentem
lenibat dictis animum lacrimasque ciebat.
Illa solo fixos oculos aversa tenebat
470 nec magis incepto vultum sermone movetur
quam si dura silex aut stet Marpesia cautes.
Tandem corripuit sese atque inimica refugit
in nemus umbriferum, coniunx ubi pristinus illi
respondet curis aequatque Sychaeus amorem.
475 Nec minus Aeneas casu percussus iniquo
prosequitur lacrimis longe et miseratur euntem.

Comprehension Questions

1. What literal wound (line 450) is Dido bearing? What figurative one? **Dido is bearing the literal wound from stabbing herself to death and the figurative one of having been betrayed by Aeneas.**

2. From the simile in lines 453–454, how are we supposed to imagine Dido? How does this image differ from the one in the simile in Book 1.498–502 with which Vergil introduced her to us?

   Dido here is a shadowy, almost transparent figure, like a new moon with clouds passing before it. In Book 1, she was compared to Diana leading her chorus through the mountains and surpassing them all.

3. What different feelings does Aeneas have in lines 458–466? **Aeneas feels taken aback or surprised that his departure caused Dido such pain that she died, and so, he feels he must explain or excuse himself. He shows his care for her and at the same time his feelings of obligation to follow his sense of duty. He also longs for her to stop and speak with him.**

4. In lines 467–471, how does Dido appear as Aeneas speaks to her? **Dido is watching him grimly (*torva tuentem*, line 467). She is turned away from him (*aversa*, line 469) and keeps her eyes fixed on the ground (*solo fixos oculos tenebat*, line 469). Further, Dido is not moved by Aeneas's reaching out to her (*nec vultum sermone movetur*, line 470). The simile Vergil uses comparing Dido to "hard flint or a Marpesian crag" (line 471) emphasizes the lack of effectiveness in Aeneas's attempt to move her emotionally.**

5. Why is Aeneas crying in line 476? **He either feels his own situation seems unfair—he could not have stayed with Dido nor have departed without causing her death—or he feels that her situation is worthy of sympathy.**

Multiple Choice Questions *Suggested time: 12 minutes*

1. The best translation of *ut primum* (line 452) is
   a. in order that at first
   b. with the result that at first
   c. as soon as
   d. as at first

2. *qualem* in line 453 modifies
   a. *Dido* (line 450)
   b. *qui* (line 453)
   c. *mense* (line 453)
   d. *lunam* (line 454)

3. The best translation of *ferroque extrema secutam* (line 457) is
   a. [and that you] had sought your death with a sword
   b. [and that you] would see your death with a sword
   c. [and you] having followed the final things with a sword
   d. [and that you] in your death pursued it with a sword

4. *qua* in line 459 modifies
   a. *sidera* (line 458)
   b. *fides* (line 459)
   c. *tellure* (line 459)
   d. *ima* (line 459)

5. The antecedent of *quae* (line 461) is
   a. *me* (line 461)
   b. ***iussa* (line 461)**
   c. *deum* (line 461)
   d. *loca* (line 462)

6. The form of *discessu* (line 464) is
   a. supine
   b. ablative participle
   c. **ablative noun**
   d. adverb

7. In line 464, *ferre* is a(n)
   a. **infinitive in indirect statement**
   b. objective infinitive
   c. historical infinitive
   d. complementary infinitive

8. In line 468, *lenibat* is best translated
   a. was soothing
   b. used to soothe
   c. **was trying to soothe**
   d. began to soothe

9. The best translation of *solo* (line 469) is
   a. alone
   b. **on the ground**
   c. towards him alone
   d. from the ground

10. The Latin word *pristinus* (line 473) means
    a. **former**
    b. pristine
    c. untouched
    d. outstanding

Translation *Suggested time: 25 minutes*

Translate the following passage as literally as possible.

>   Illa solo fixos oculos aversa tenebat
>   nec magis incepto vultum sermone movetur
>   quam si dura silex aut stet Marpesia cautes.
>   Tandem corripuit sese atque inimica refugit
> 5   in nemus umbriferum, coniunx ubi pristinus illi
>   respondet curis aequatque Sychaeus amorem.
>   Nec minus Aeneas casu percussus iniquo
>   prosequitur lacrimis longe et miseratur euntem.

18 units
Range of possible meanings followed by notes on grammar and syntax:

Illa ... aversa tenebat	That one/she [having] turned away/averted was holding
fixos oculos	[her] eyes fixed/fastened
solo	on the ground
nec magis ... movetur	nor is she moved more
vultum	in respect to/as to her face/expression (accusative of respect)
incepto ... sermone	by the speech/conversation [having been] undertaken/begun
quam si ... stet	than if she stood
dura silex aut Marpesia cautes	[as] hard flint/rock/crag or a Marpesian rock/cliff/crag
Tandem corripuit sese	at last she betook/snatched away herself
atque inimica refugit	and hostile/unfriendly she fled back/fled away
in nemus umbriferum	into the shadowy/shade-bearing grove/forest
coniunx ubi pristinus illi ... Sychaeus	where her former husband, Sychaeus (or: former husband to her) (*illi* dative of reference)
respondet curis	responds to/answers/sympathizes with [her] cares/worries/anxieties
aequatque ... amorem	and he equals/matches [her] love
Nec minus	no less
Aeneas casu percussus iniquo	Aeneas [having been] struck/astounded by [the/his/her] unjust/harsh/uneven chance/misfortune
prosequitur lacrimis longe	follows/attends [from] afar/at a distance with tears
et miseratur euntem	and he pities/commiserates with [her] going

Essays *(20 minutes for the first essay and 40 for the second)*

1. What emotions does Aeneas convey with his speech in lines 456–466? How effective is he? Provide your response in a well-organized essay.

Support your assertions with references drawn from throughout this passage (lines 456–466 only). All Latin words must be copied or their line numbers provided, AND they must be translated or paraphrased closely enough so that it is clear you understand the Latin. It is your responsibility to convince your reader that you are basing your conclusions on the Latin text and not merely on a general recollection of the passage. Direct your answer to the question; do not merely summarize the passage. Please write your essay on a separate piece of paper.

Students will respond to essay topics in various ways, and different essays, with quite different approaches, may be of equal quality. The following are some possible points students may make; it is not a sample essay.
   This essay asks students to evaluate the tone of Aeneas's speech and its effectiveness. Students should be sure to write a thesis statement and then support it. Ideas and phrases, <u>all of which must be translated</u> in student essays, may include the following: surprise and disbelief (expressed in initial questions; *nec credere quivi*, line 463), lack of choice (*invitus*, line 460; *iussa deum*, line 461; *imperiis*, line 463), desire for conversation with Dido (*ne subtrahe*, line 465).

```
     [Iamque adeo super unus eram, cum limina Vestae
     seruantem et tacitam secreta in sede latentem
     Tyndarida aspicio; dant claram incendia lucem
570  erranti passimque oculos per cuncta ferenti.
     Illa sibi infestos eversa ob Pergama Teucros
     et Danaum poenam et deserti coniugis iras
     praemetuens, Troiae et patriae communis Erinys,
     abdiderat sese atque aris invisa sedebat.
575  Exarsere ignes animo; subit ira cadentem
     ulcisci patriam et sceleratas sumere poenas.
                                        (Book 2.567–576)


450  Inter quas Phoenissa recens a vulnere Dido
     errabat silva in magna; quam Troius heros
     ut primum iuxta stetit agnovitque per umbras
     obscuram, qualem primo qui surgere mense
     aut videt aut vidisse putat per nubila lunam,
455  demisit lacrimas dulcique adfatus amore est:
                                        (Book 6.450–455)
```

2. In these two passages, Aeneas encounters a woman important for the events of the *Aeneid* and is emotionally moved. How do the lines depicting these women help us to understand his reaction? What does his reaction tell us about his psychology?

Support your assertions with references drawn from throughout both passages (Book 2.567–76 and Book 6.450–455 only). All Latin words must be copied or their line numbers provided, AND they must be translated or paraphrased closely enough so that it is clear you understand the Latin. It is your responsibility to convince your reader that you are basing your conclusions on the Latin text and not merely on a general recollection of the passages. Direct your answer to the question; do not merely summarize the passages. Please write your essay on a separate piece of paper.

Students will respond to essay topics in various ways, and different essays, with quite different approaches, may be of equal quality. The following are some possible points students may make; it is not a sample essay.

This essay asks students to identify Helen and Dido as the subjects of these two passages, and to consider the effect of their presence on Aeneas. Aeneas's sighting of Helen provokes anger and a desire for revenge (2.575–576), while his sighting of Dido provokes tears and stirs his love (6.455); students should be able to use the information that Helen has caused the destruction of his home while he has caused the destruction of Dido's home to explain the difference. But Vergil also suggests some ironic similarities between the two by noting that light makes them visible (2.569–570; 6.452–454) in a dark landscape.

This essay provides students with a good opportunity to compare two parallel episodes of manageable length. Students should support their arguments with citations from throughout both passages.

See the Scoring Guidelines on pp. xvii–xviii.

Scansion

Scan the following lines.

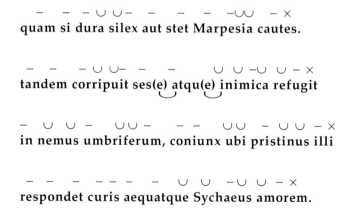

(lines 471–475)

LESSON 20: BOOK 6.847-899

'Excudent alii spirantia mollius aera
(credo equidem), vivos ducent de marmore vultus,
orabunt causas melius, caelique meatus
850 describent radio et surgentia sidera dicent:
tu regere imperio populos, Romane, memento
(hae tibi erunt artes), pacique imponere morem,
parcere subiectis et debellare superbos.'
Sic pater Anchises, atque haec mirantibus addit:
855 'Aspice, ut insignis spoliis Marcellus opimis
ingreditur victorque viros supereminet omnes.
Hic rem Romanam magno turbante tumultu
sistet eques, sternet Poenos Gallumque rebellem,
tertiaque arma patri suspendet capta Quirino.'
860 Atque hic Aeneas (una namque ire videbat
egregium forma iuvenem et fulgentibus armis,
sed frons laeta parum et deiecto lumina ultu)
'Quis, pater, ille, virum qui sic comitatur euntem?
Filius, anne aliquis magna de stirpe nepotum?
865 Qui strepitus circa comitum! Quantum instar in ipso!
Sed nox atra caput tristi circumvolat umbra.'
Tum pater Anchises lacrimis ingressus obortis:
'O gnate, ingentem luctum ne quaere tuorum;
ostendent terris hunc tantum fata nec ultra
870 esse sinent. Nimium vobis Romana propago
visa potens, superi, propria haec si dona fuissent.
Quantos ille virum magnam Mavortis ad urbem
campus aget gemitus! Vel quae, Tiberine, videbis
funera, cum tumulum praeterlabere recentem!
875 Nec puer Iliaca quisquam de gente Latinos
in tantum spe tollet avos, nec Romula quondam
ullo se tantum tellus iactabit alumno.
Heu pietas, heu prisca fides invictaque bello
dextera! Non illi se quisquam impune tulisset
880 obvius armato, seu cum pedes iret in hostem
seu spumantis equi foderet calcaribus armos.
Heu, miserande puer, si qua fata aspera rumpas—
tu Marcellus eris. Manibus date lilia plenis
purpureos spargam flores animamque nepotis
885 his saltem accumulem donis, et fungar inani
munere.' Sic tota passim regione vagantur
aeris in campis latis atque omnia lustrant.
Quae postquam Anchises natum per singula duxit

```
         incenditque animum famae venientis amore,
890      exim bella viro memorat quae deinde gerenda,
         Laurentesque docet populos urbemque Latini,
         et quo quemque modo fugiatque feratque laborem.
         Sunt geminae Somni portae, quarum altera fertur
         cornea, qua veris facilis datur exitus umbris,
895      altera candenti perfecta nitens elephanto,
         sed falsa ad caelum mittunt insomnia Manes.
         His ibi tum natum Anchises unaque Sibyllam
         prosequitur dictis portaque emittit eburna,
         ille viam secat ad naves sociosque revisit.
```

Comprehension Questions

NB: Some questions may have several possible correct responses; a sample is given.

1. In Anchises's prophecy about the accomplishments of the Greeks and Romans (lines 847–853), at what does he say the Greeks will be especially good? The Romans?

   The Greeks will be good at sculpture, in both bronze and marble, rhetoric, and astronomy. The Romans will be good at dominating and ruling.

2. Vergil has Anchises emphasize the elder Marcellus's military prowess. Why does Vergil do this?

   The older Marcellus, ancestor of the younger Marcellus, embodies the sort of career the younger Marcellus would have enjoyed if he had lived longer.

3. What can we infer about the younger Marcellus from Aeneas's questions and comments in lines 863–866?

   The younger Marcellus must have seemed similar to the older one, since Aeneas assumes that they are related. He is surrounded by many companions, so he must have been popular. He has, however, a shadow about him, foreshadowing his early demise.

4. What does Anchises say was the gods' reason for having Marcellus die so young?

   The Roman stock would have seemed too powerful if Marcellus had been allowed to live.

5. Marcellus died too young to achieve much in life. What would have been his strength, according to Anchises, if death had not come so early?

   Marcellus would have been an outstanding soldier like his ancestor.

6. Why does Anchises call his "duty" (*munere,* line 886) "useless" (*inani,* line 885)?

   Honoring the dead is useless in the sense that it does not bring them back to life.

7. How do lines 890–892 recall the role Anchises played in Book 3? **In Book 3, Anchises acted as a guide and interpreter just as he does here.**

8. Vergil describes the two gates of sleep, and says that Aeneas and the Sibyl left by the ivory one (lines 893–898). People have posited many reasons for this; what idea do you think Vergil was expressing with this detail?

   Perhaps he is calling into question Aeneas's understanding of what he has seen in the Underworld.

Multiple Choice Questions *Suggested time: 15 minutes*

Choose the better answer.

1. The *alii* in line 847 are
   a. **Greeks**
   b. Romans

2. The word *mollius* (line 847) is an
   a. adjective
   b. **adverb**

3. In line 849, *-que* connects
   a. *melius* and *meatus* (line 849)
   b. ***orabunt* (line 849) and *describent* (line 850)**

4. In line 853, *subiectis* is
   a. **dative**
   b. ablative

5. Marcellus (line 855) died
   a. **in the third century BCE**
   b. in the first century BCE

6. Marcellus acquired the *spolia opima* (cf. line 855) by
   a. leading skirmishes against the Carthaginian general Hannibal
   b. **killing the Gallic chief Viridomarus in hand-to-hand combat**

7. Marcellus defeated the *Poenos* (line 858) in the war against
   a. the Gallic invaders
   b. **the Carthaginians**

8. *Quirino* (line 859) is another name for
   a. **Romulus**
   b. Jupiter

9. The word *parum* (line 862) is an
   a. **adverb**
   b. adjective

10. In line 865 *circa* here is a(n)
    a. **adverb**
    b. preposition

11. The first four feet of line 868 scan
    a. dactyl-spondee-spondee-spondee
    b. **spondee-spondee-spondee-spondee**

12. The case of *propago* (line 870) is
    a. **nominative**
    b. ablative

13. The form of *esse* needed to complete the verb form *visa* (line 871) is
    a. sit
    b. **esset**

14. The word *fuissent* (line 871) is part of a
    a. **past contrary-to-fact condition**
    b. present contrary-to-fact condition

15. The form of *praeterlabere* (line 874) is
    a. **future indicative**
    b. imperative

16. In line 877, *tellus* is
    a. genitive
    b. **nominative**

17. In line 880, *armato* is
    a. ablative
    b. **dative**

18. In line 882, *qua* is
    a. **ablative feminine**
    b. accusative neuter

19. The form of *spargam* (line 884) is
    a. **present subjunctive**
    b. future indicative

20. The number of elisions in line 885 is
    a. zero
    b. **one**

21. In line 888, *quae* is
    a. **accusative plural neuter**
    b. nominative singular feminine

22. The form of *esse* needed to complete the verb form *gerenda* (line 890) is
    a. *erant*
    b. **sint**

23. In line 892, *ferat* is subjunctive in a(n)
    a. purpose clause
    b. **indirect question**

24. Line 894 contains an example of
    a. synecdoche
    b. **chiasmus**

Translation *Suggested time: 20 minutes*

Translate the following passage as literally as possible.

> Sunt geminae Somni portae, quarum altera fertur
> cornea, qua veris facilis datur exitus umbris,
> altera candenti perfecta nitens elephanto,
> sed falsa ad caelum mittunt insomnia Manes.
> 5   His ibi tum natum Anchises unaque Sibyllam
> prosequitur dictis portaque emittit eburna,
> ille viam secat ad naves sociosque revisit.

Literal Translation
There are twin doors of Sleep, one of which is said [to be] of horn, by which an easy exit is given to true shades, the other, shining, [is] made from gleaming ivory, but the souls of the dead send false dreams to the heavens. With these words then Anchises there escorts [his] son and the Sibyl together, and sends [them] out by the ivory gate, [and] that one [i.e., Aeneas] cuts a path to the ships and sees [his] comrades again.

The sections into which a passage is divided are flexible, as are the possible acceptable meanings for any given word. Teachers may prefer a different scheme of "chunking" and range of meanings; what is given below is just one option. Since students must prove to the reader that they understand the grammar of the passage, loose translations are not acceptable, and students should clearly demonstrate the syntactical information provided in parentheses in the column below with the English range of meanings.

18 units
Range of possible meanings followed by notes on grammar and syntax:

sunt geminae Somni portae	there are two/twin gates/portals/doors/entrances/exits of Sleep/Slumber
quarum	of which
altera fertur cornea	one is said [to be] of horn
qua	by which (ablative)
facilis datur exitus	[an] easy/ready/favorable exit/outlet/egress is given/granted

veris umbris	to true/real/genuine shades/shadows/ghosts (dative)
altera perfecta nitens	the other/the second [having been] made/completed/finished shining/gleaming/bright
candenti elephanto	by/with gleaming/shining/white ivory/elephant (ablative of material)
sed mittunt Manes	but the shades/souls of the dead/Hades send/send forth
falsa insomnia	false/unreal/deceitful/mock dreams/visions
ad caelum	to/toward heaven/the sky
ibi tum Anchises prosequitur	there/in that place then/at that time Anchises follows/escorts
natum unaque Sibyllam	[his] son and together/at the same time the Sibyl/prophetess (object of *prosequitur*)
his dictis	with these words
-que emittit	and he sends/sends forth [them]
porta eburna	by the ivory gate/portal/door/entrance/exit (ablative)
ille viam secat ad naves	that one/he/Aeneas cuts/cleaves/passes through the way/road/street to/toward the ships
sociosque revisit	and he revisits/sees again [his] comrades/allies/companions/followers

Essay *Suggested time: 40 minutes*

```
       nec plura his. Ille admirans venerabile donum
       fatalis virgae longo post tempore visum
410    caeruleam advertit puppim ripaeque propinquat.
       Inde alias animas, quae per iuga longa sedebant,
       deturbat laxatque foros; simul accipit alveo
       ingentem Aenean. Gemuit sub pondere cumba
       sutilis et multam accepit rimosa paludem.
415    Tandem trans fluvium incolumes vatemque virumque
       informi limo glaucaque exponit in ulva.
       Cerberus haec ingens latratu regna trifauci
       personat adverso recubans immanis in antro.
       Cui vates horrere videns iam colla colubris
420    melle soporatam et medicatis frugibus offam
       obicit. Ille fame rabida tria guttura pandens
       corripit obiectam, atque immania terga resolvit
       fusus humi totoque ingens extenditur antro.
       Occupat Aeneas aditum custode sepulto
425    evaditque celer ripam inremeabilis undae.
```
(Book 6.408–425)

> Quae postquam Anchises natum per singula duxit
> incenditque animum famae venientis amore,
> 890 exim bella viro memorat quae deinde gerenda,
> Laurentesque docet populos urbemque Latini,
> et quo quemque modo fugiatque feratque laborem.
> Sunt geminae Somni portae, quarum altera fertur
> cornea, qua veris facilis datur exitus umbris,
> 895 altera candenti perfecta nitens elephanto,
> sed falsa ad caelum mittunt insomnia Manes.
> His ibi tum natum Anchises unaque Sibyllam
> prosequitur dictis portaque emittit eburna,
> ille viam secat ad naves sociosque revisit.
>
> (Book 6.888–899)

These passages describe Aeneas's entrance into and departure from the Underworld. Does Vergil portray Aeneas as equally heroic in each passage? Use specific examples to support your analysis.

Support your assertions with references drawn from throughout both passages (Book 6.408–425 and Book 6.888–899 only). All Latin words must be copied or their line numbers provided, AND they must be translated or paraphrased closely enough so that it is clear you understand the Latin. It is your responsibility to convince your reader that you are basing your conclusions on the Latin text and not merely on a general recollection of the passages. Direct your answer to the question; do not merely summarize the passages. Please write your essay on a separate piece of paper.

Students will respond to essay topics in various ways, and different essays, with quite different approaches, may be of equal quality. The following are some possible points students may make; this is not a sample essay.

This essay asks students to compare the two scenes and the depiction of Aeneas in each of them and to characterize Aeneas's heroic nature. Students should be sure to write a thesis statement and then support it. Ideas and phrases, <u>all of which must be translated</u> in student essays, may include the following: Aeneas's interactions with others in each passage (inhabitants of the underworld and the Sibyl); nouns, adjectives, and verbs Vergil uses to describe Aeneas's appearance and behavior in each passage; the landscape in each passage. This essay provides students with a good opportunity to compare two parallel episodes of manageable length. Students should support their arguments with citations from throughout both passages.

See the Scoring Guidelines on pp. xvii–xviii.

Scansion

Scan the following lines.

$$- \ - \ - \ - - \ - \ - \ - \ \cup\cup \ - \ \times$$
sed fals(a) ad caelum mittunt insomnia Manes.

$$- \ \cup\cup \ - \ - \ \ - \ - - - - \ \cup \cup - \times$$
His ibi tum nat(um) Anchises unaque Sibyllam

$$- \cup \ \cup - \ - - \ - - \ \ - \ - \cup \cup - \ \times$$
prosequitur dictis portaqu(e) emittit eburna,

$$- \cup \cup- \ \cup \cup \ - \ \ - - \ \cup \cup - \ \ \cup \cup -\times$$
ille viam secat ad naves sociosque revisit.

(lines 896–899)

SIGHT PASSAGES WITH EXERCISES, MULTIPLE CHOICE QUESTIONS, AND ANSWERS

EXERCISE IN SIGHT READING AND SIGHT READING #1

You see a passage of poetry that includes the following words/phrases, some of which you may know and some you may not, and a vocabulary list beneath it. Write what you might expect the passage to be about—what it might mean, what its tone might be, what general ideas you might expect.

Multas per gentes et multa per aequora	heu
advenio	miser
miseras	parentum
frater	tradita sunt
mortis	in perpetuum
mutam cinerem	ave atque vale

Vocabulary Help

veho, -ere, vexi, vectum: to carry, convey
inferiae, -arum, f.: rites in honor of the dead; offerings to the dead
dono, -are: to honor
quandoquidem: since
tete = te
adimo, -ere, ademi, ademptum: to take, remove
priscus, -a, -um: old, ancient

I expect the following from the poem:

Student responses will, of course, vary. Among the expectations they anticipate might be the following:
- **death**
- **a family**
- **travel**
- **sorrow**
- **a 1st person speaker**

Sight Passage #1

Multas per gentes et multa per aequora vectus
    advenio has miseras, frater, ad inferias,
ut te postremo donarem munere mortis
    et mutam nequiquam alloquerer cinerem.
5   Quandoquidem fortuna mihi tete abstulit ipsum,
    heu miser indigne frater adempte mihi,
nunc tamen interea haec, prisco quae more parentum
    tradita sunt tristi munere ad inferias,
accipe fraterno multum manantia fletu,
10 atque in perpetuum, frater, ave atque vale.

Catullus 101

Vocabulary Help

veho, -ere, vexi, vectum: to carry, convey
inferiae, -arum, f.: rites in honor of the dead; offerings to the dead
dono, -are: to honor
quandoquidem: since
adimo, -ere, ademi, ademptum: to take, remove
priscus, -a, -um: old, ancient

1. Line 1 indicates that
   a. **the speaker has traveled far**
   b. the brother has been carried home
   c. many peoples have been carried across the seas
   d. many peoples and seas are carried

2. *vectus* (line 1) modifies
   a. *aequora* (line 1)
   b. *te* (line 3)
   c. **the subject of *advenio* (line 2)**
   d. *inferias* (line 2)

3. Line 4 is best translated
   a. and I will speak to your changed ash in vain
   b. and I never be addressed by [your] silent ash pointlessly
   c. and that I never address your changed ash
   d. **and that I address [your] silent ash in vain**

4. *mihi* (line 5) is best translated
   a. for me
   b. **from me**
   c. to me
   d. with me

164 • VERGIL

5. *indigne* (line 6) is
   a. an imperative with *frater* (line 6) as its subject
   b. a vocative adjective modifying *frater* (line 6)
   c. an adverb modifying *adempte* (line 6)
   d. an adjective modifying *mihi* (line 6)

7. *tristi* (line 8) modifies
   a. *more* (line 7)
   b. *quae* (line 7)
   c. *munere* (line 8)
   d. *fletu* (line 9)

8. *fraterno* (line 9) modifies
   a. *fletu* (line 9)
   b. *manantia* (line 9)
   c. *frater* (line 10)
   d. *ave* (line 10)

9. *manantia* (line 9) modifies
   a. *multum* (line 9)
   b. *fraterno* (line 9)
   c. *inferias* (line 8)
   d. *haec* (line 7)

10. In line 10,
    a. the speaker encourages his brother to stay well
    b. the two brothers say farewell to one another
    c. the speaker says his final farewell to his dead brother
    d. the speaker's brother hopes the speaker will remain healthy forever

Notes

EXERCISE IN SIGHT READING AND SIGHT PASSAGE #2

An introduction to a sight passage reads, *"Hannibal tries to convince the king to make him commander against the Romans by recalling a tale from his youth."*

List everything you might expect in such a passage:

Student responses will, of course, vary. Among the expectations they anticipate might be the following:
- **both direct and indirect discourse**
- **information about Carthage**
- **an appeal to the king**
- **reasons for Hannibal to hate the Romans**

The following words/phrases occur in the passage in this order (go down the columns, not across); other vocabulary words are given below. From them, construct a set of expectations about the passage.

pater meus	in castra	iurare iussit
Hamilcar	proficisci	numquam
in Hispaniam	ab eo petere	in amicitia cum Romanis
Karthagine	ne dubitaret	nemini dubium esse
Iovi Optimo Maximo	fidem	de Romanis cogitabis
divina res	sacrificare instituerat	bellum parabis

Student responses will, of course, vary. Among the expectations, based on these vocabulary entries, they anticipate might be the following:
- **Hannibal is speaking, and says that his father Hamilcar went from Carthage to Spain.**
- **He proceeded to the camp, where he prayed to Jupiter.**
- **So that someone would trust him, someone instituted the performance of a sacrifice.**
- **He swore never to be friends with the Romans.**
- **Hannibal asks the king to declare war on the Romans.**

Sight Passage #2

Hannibal tries to convince the king to make him commander against the Romans by recalling a tale from his youth.

'Pater meus,' inquit, 'Hamilcar puerulo me, utpote non amplius
novem annos nato, in Hispaniam imperator proficiscens, Karthagine
Iovi Optimo Maximo hostias immolavit. Quae divina res dum
conficiebatur, quaesivit a me vellemne secum in castra proficisci. Id
5   cum libenter accepissem atque ab eo petere coepissem ne dubitaret
ducere, tum ille, 'Faciam,' inquit, 'si mihi fidem quam postulo dederis.'
Simul me ad aram adduxit apud quam sacrificare instituerat eamque
ceteris remotis tenentem iurare iussit numquam me in amicitia cum
Romanis fore. Id ego iusiurandum patri datum usque ad hanc aetatem
10 ita conservavi, ut nemini dubium esse debeat quin reliquo tempore
eadem mente sim futurus. Quare, si quid amice de Romanis cogitabis,
non imprudenter feceris, si me celaris; cum quidem bellum parabis,
te ipsum frustraberis, si non me in eo principem posueris.'

                                        Cornelius Nepos *Life of Hannibal* 2

Vocabulary Help

utpote: seeing as
iusiurandum, -i, n.: oath (sometimes written as two words, ius iurandum)
cogito, -are: to think
celaris = celaveris: to refrain from informing, keep in ignorance
frustror, frustrari, frustratus sum: to fail, frustrate, disappoint

1. In lines 1–2 (*Pater . . . proficiscens*), Hannibal says that
   a. his father was setting out to Spain to fight Hamilcar
   b. he set out to Hamilcar as a young boy
   c. his father Hamilcar was heading to Spain as general
   d. his father had set out to Spain no more than nine years earlier

2. *me* (line 1) is
   a. accusative subject of infinitive
   b. accusative direct object
   c. ablative with special verb
   d. ablative in ablative absolute

3. *Karthagine* (line 2) is ablative of
   a. means
   b. separation
   c. place where
   d. absolute

4. *divina res* (line 3) is
   - **a. the subject of *conficiebatur* (line 4) and refers to the sacrifices**
   - b. the subject of *quaesivit* (line 4) and refers to Jupiter
   - c. the object of *quaesivit* (line 4) and refers to Jupiter
   - d. accusative of specification and refers to the sacrifices

5. *dum* (line 3) is best translated
   - a. as long as
   - b. when
   - c. until
   - **d. while**

6. *vellem* (line 4) is
   - a. subjunctive in a contrary to fact condition
   - **b. subjunctive in an indirect question**
   - c. subjunctive in a result clause
   - d. subjunctive in a purpose clause

7. The pronoun *se* in *secum* (line 4) refers to
   - a. Hannibal
   - **b. Hamilcar**
   - c. Jupiter
   - d. the subject of *conficiebatur* (line 4)

8. Lines 4–6 (*Id . . . ducere*) tell us that Hannibal
   - a. asks his father to take him along
   - **b. encourages his interlocutor to become a leader**
   - c. gladly accepted the god's request
   - d. never hesitated to lead

9. The speaker of line 6 (*Faciam . . . dederis*) says that
   - a. he would act if his promise should be given
   - b. he will give a promise upon its demand
   - c. he will complete the command given
   - **d. he will fulfill the request if a vow is taken**

10. *eam* (line 7) refers to the Latin word
    - a. *me* (line 7)
    - b. *fidem* (line 6)
    - **c. *aram* (line 7)**
    - d. *amicitia* (line 8)

11. *ceteris remotis* (line 8) is best translated
    - a. by moving others
    - b. after the other people had been removed
    - c. for others having been removed
    - **d. since the other objects had been removed**

12. *fore* (line 9) is
    - **a. infinitive in indirect statement**
    - b. subjunctive in indirect command
    - c. participle in ablative absolute
    - d. imperative

13. Lines 9–10 (*Id . . . conservavi*) tells us
    a. Hannibal saved his father through his oath
    b. Hannibal kept his oath while a young man
    c. Hannibal protected his father throughout his life
    d. Hannibal always kept his oath

14. *ut* (line 10) is best translated
    a. with the result that
    b. in order that
    c. how
    d. as

15. *reliquo tempore* (line 10) is best translated
    a. at the moment left
    b. in the time relinquished
    c. in the rest of my life
    d. for the period just passed

16. In lines 11–12 (*Quare . . . celaris*), Hannibal says
    a. if you are considering friendship with the Romans, conceal it from me
    b. you wouldn't be considering friendship with the Romans if you had acted as I suggested
    c. you weren't unwise to conceal your friendship with the Romans
    d. because you were friendly with the Romans, you concealed it from me

17. Lines 12–13 (*cum . . . posueris*) are best translated
    a. since you will prepare a certain war, you will be frustrated if you haven't been able to make me leader over him
    b. even though you are preparing war, you will fail yourself unless you have put me in possession of it as chief
    c. although you prepare war, you will disappoint yourself if you will not have established me as leader in it
    d. since indeed you will prepare war, you will frustrate yourself if you have not been able to make me chief in it

SIGHT READING EXERCISE #3

For the following introduction and Latin passage,
1. predict from the introduction all that you can
2. highlight all the Latin words that you recognize and try to predict what the passage might be about

Dion, once a hero, has had his rival assassinated and must now bear the consequences.

> Nemo enim illo interfecto se tutum putabat. Ille autem adversario
> remoto licentius eorum bona, quos sciebat adversus se sensisse,
> militibus dispertivit. Quibus divisis, cum cotidiani maximi fierent
> sumptus, celeriter pecunia deesse coepit; neque, quo manus porrigeret,
> 5   suppetebat nisi in amicorum possessiones. Id eius modi erat, ut, cum
> milites reconciliasset, amitteret optimates. Quarum rerum cura
> frangebatur et insuetus male audiendi non animo aequo ferebat de
> se ab iis male existimari, quorum paulo ante in caelum fuerat elatus
> laudibus. Vulgus autem offensa in eum militum voluntate liberius
> 10 loquebatur et tyrannum non ferendum dictitabat.
>   Cornelius Nepos *Life of Dion* 7

Student responses will, of course, vary. Among the predictions they make might be the following:

1. From the Introduction it appears that there will be a change of feelings and Dion will no longer be considered a hero, at least by some people.

2. From the familiar Latin words it appears that Dion divided up the rival's property, but soon needed money, so he took even his friends' possessions. He did not like being thought badly of by people who had praised him to the heavens before. The common people spoke against him and said that a tyrant should not be borne.

Exercise in Sight Reading and Sight Passage #3

Dion, once a hero, has had his rival assassinated and must now bear the consequences.

Nemo enim illo interfecto se tutum putabat. Ille autem adversario remoto licentius eorum bona, quos sciebat adversus se sensisse, militibus dispertivit. Quibus divisis, cum cotidiani maximi fierent sumptus, celeriter pecunia deesse coepit; neque, quo manus porrigeret,
5   suppetebat nisi in amicorum possessiones. Id eius modi erat, ut, cum milites reconciliasset, amitteret optimates. Quarum rerum cura frangebatur et insuetus male audiendi non animo aequo ferebat de se ab iis male existimari, quorum paulo ante in caelum fuerat elatus laudibus. Vulgus autem offensa in eum militum voluntate liberius
10   loquebatur et tyrannum non ferendum dictitabat.

Vocabulary Help

licenter: freely, without restraint
bonum, -i, n.: good, property
dispertio, -ire, -ivi, -itum: to divide, distribute
sumptus, -us, m.: expense, cost
porrigo, -ere: to reach out, hold forth
suppeto, -ere: to be at hand
insuetus, -a, -um: unaccustomed
offendo, -ere, -i, offensum: to damage, break
liber, libera, liberum: free

1. Line 1 (*Nemo . . . putabat*) tells us that
    a. because a man had been killed, Dion did not feel safe
    b. after he killed his rival, Dion no longer thought that he was safe
    c. because Dion had killed the man, no one thought that he was safe
    d. once the rival had been killed, no one felt safe

2. The form of *licentius* (line 2) is a
    a. nominative masculine adjective
    b. comparative adverb
    c. nominative neuter adjective
    d. accusative neuter adjective

3. The case and number of *bona* (line 2) is
    a. accusative plural
    b. nominative plural
    c. nominative singular
    d. ablative singular

4. The antecedent for *quos* (line 2) is
    a. *militibus* (line 3)
    b. *bona* (line 2)
    c. *eorum* (line 2)
    d. *se* (line 2)

5. Lines 2–3 (*licentius . . . dispertivit*) tell us that
   a. Dion's adversary had distributed to the soldiers the property of those who disagreed with Dion
   b. the soldiers felt that they rightly should receive the distribution of property of those with whom they had disagreed
   c. the goods of those who had known the adversary were distributed to the soldiers
   d. Dion divided among the soldiers the goods of those who had opposed him

6. *Quibus* (line 3) refers to
   a. *eorum* (line 2)
   b. *bona* (line 2)
   c. *militibus* (line 3)
   d. *sumptus* (line 4)

7. Lines 3–5 (*Quibus . . . possessiones*) tell us that
   a. because Dion's expenses were great, he was broke and had to take hold of his friends' possessions
   b. although the expenses were great, money was supplied to Dion by his friends in the form of possessions
   c. each day expenses became greater, but Dion was able to find money simply by asking for it
   d. Dion became wealthier day by day, both by quickly acquiring money and by reaching out his hands to his friends for their possessions

8. *ut* (line 5) is best translated
   a. as
   b. in order to
   c. with the result that
   d. how

9. In lines 5–6 (*cum . . . optimates*), Dion
   a. won back the support of the soldiers but lost that of the optimates
   b. reconciled the soldiers to one another and sent away the optimates
   c. won over the soldiers in order to send the optimates away
   d. lost the support of the optimates because they had won over the soldiers

10. Lines 6–9 (*Quarum . . . laudibus*) demonstrate that
    a. Dion destroyed those who thought badly about him
    b. in the end, the soldiers praised Dion
    c. the soldiers didn't care about Dion
    d. Dion cared about his reputation

11. *audiendi* (line 7) is a
    a. gerundive dependent on *insuetus* (line 7)
    b. gerund dependent on *insuetus* (line 7)
    c. gerundive showing purpose
    d. gerund showing purpose

12. The antecedent of *quorum* (line 8) is
    a. *se* (line 8)
    b. *laudibus* (line 9)
    c. *iis* (line 8)
    d. *audiendi* (line 7)

13. The subject of *loquebatur* (line 10) is
    a. *militum* (line 9)
    b. *tyrannum* (line 10)
    c. *liberius* (line 9)
    d. *vulgus* (line 9)

SIGHT PASSAGE #4

Ariadne addresses her lover, Theseus.

      Sicine me patriis avectam, perfide, ab aris,
      perfide, deserto liquisti in litore, Theseu?
      Sicine discedens neglecto numine divum
      immemor a, devota domum periuria portas?
5   Nullane res potuit crudelis flectere mentis
      consilium? Tibi nulla fuit clementia praesto,
      immite ut nostri vellet miserescere pectus?
      At non haec quondam blanda promissa dedisti
      voce mihi; non haec miseram sperare iubebas,
10   sed conubia laeta, sed optatos hymenaeos:
      quae cuncta aerii discerpunt irrita venti.
      nunc iam nulla viro iuranti femina credat,
      nulla viri speret sermones esse fideles.

                                                    Catullus 64

Vocabulary Help

Sicine = sic + -ne
periurium, -i, n.: false oath, perjury
praesto: at hand, ready, present
immitis, -e: harsh, severe, fierce
irritus, -a, -um: useless, without effect, vain

1. In lines 1–2, the speaker addresses her lover, who
   - a. is swearing an oath
   - **c. has left her behind**
   - b. is departing his father's altars
   - d. is embracing her on the shore

2. *divum* (line 3) is
   - **a. genitive plural**
   - b. accusative singular
   - c. nominative singular
   - d. vocative singular

3. In lines 5–6 (*Nullane . . . consilium*),
   - a. Ariadne wonders why such a cruel situation changed his plan
   - b. the poet poses a rhetorical question about the nature of love
   - **c. Ariadne asks if anything could change her lover's mind**
   - d. the poet asks how a cruel circumstance makes people change their minds

4. The metrical pattern of the first four feet of line 7 is
   a. dactyl-spondee-spondee-spondee
   b. spondee-spondee-spondee-dactyl
   c. spondee-dactyl-spondee-dactyl
   d. dactyl-spondee-spondee-dactyl

5. *ut* (line 7) is best translated
   a. in order to
   b. as
   c. how
   d. with the result that

6. *blanda* (line 8) modifies
   a. *haec* (line 8)
   b. *quondam* (line 8)
   c. *promissa* (line 8)
   d. *voce* (line 9)

7. *miseram* (line 9) describes
   a. the promises
   b. Ariadne
   c. the wedding
   d. his heart

8. *optatos hymenaeos* (line 10) is in contrast to
   a. *haec* (line 9)
   b. *miseram* (line 9)
   c. *conubia laeta* (line 10)
   d. *venti* (line 11)

9. A poetic device that occurs in line 12 is
   a. anastrophe
   b. synchysis
   c. hendiadys
   d. chiasmus

10. In lines 12–13, the speaker says that
    a. a man swearing an oath should not believe a woman's words are trustworthy
    b. no woman any longer makes speeches that are faithful
    c. she will never swear an oath to any other man
    d. women should not trust what men say

11. In this passage, Ariadne expresses feelings of
    a. affection
    b. betrayal
    c. piety
    d. contentment

SIGHT PASSAGE #5

Roman forces face the Carthaginians on land and at sea.

Eodem anno classis Romana cum M. Valerio Laevino proconsule ex
Sicilia in Africam transmissa in Uticensi Carthaginiensique agro late
populationes fecit. Extremis finibus Carthaginiensium circa ipsa
moenia Uticae praedae actae sunt. Repetentibus Siciliam classis
5   Punica—septuaginta erant longae naves—occurrit; septemdecim naves
ex iis captae sunt, quattuor in alto mersae, cetera fusa ac fugata classis.
Terra marique victor Romanus cum magna omnis generis praeda
Lilybaeum repetit. Tuto inde mari pulsis hostium navibus magni
commeatus frumenti Romam subvecti.

Livy *Ab urbe condita* 28.4.5–7

Vocabulary Help

populatio, populationis, f.: plundering, spoiling, devastation
praeda, -ae, f.: spoil, plunder, pillage
Uticensis, -e: of or belonging to Utica (a city in North Africa)
Carthaginiensis, -e: of or belonging to Carthage (in North Africa)
Punicus, -a, -um = Carthaginiensis
Lilybaeum, -i, n.: Lilybaeum (a city in Sicily)
commeatus, -us, m.: provisions, supplies

1. *Eodem anno* (line 1) is best translated
   a. for a certain year
   b. for the same year
   c. in the same year
   d. in a certain year

2. In lines 1–3 (*Eodem . . . fecit*), the Roman fleet was
   a. in Sicily
   b. on its way from Sicily
   c. on its way to Africa
   d. in Africa

3. *transmissa* (line 2) modifies
   a. *classis* (line 1)
   b. *Sicilia* (line 2)
   c. *Uticensi* (line 2)
   d. *late* (line 2)

4. In lines 1–3 (*Eodem . . . fecit*), we learn that
   a. Africans were plundering Utica and Carthage
   b. Romans were plundering African territory
   c. Sicilians had been plundered
   d. Sicilian plunder had been sent to Africa

5. The best translation of *Extremis finibus Carthaginiensium* (line 3) is
   a. for the extreme edge of the Carthaginians
   b. with the borders of the furthest Carthaginians
   c. at the very edge of the Carthaginians' territory
   d. from the very end of the Carthaginians

6. *moenia* (line 4) is
   a. nominative singular
   b. ablative singular
   c. nominative plural
   d. accusative plural

7. *Repetentibus* (line 4) describes the
   a. Romans
   b. Sicilians
   c. Carthaginians
   d. plunder

8. From lines 5–6 (*septemdecim . . . classis*) we learn that
   a. after capturing 17 ships, the Carthaginian fleet fled
   b. after capturing 17 ships, the Roman fleet fled
   c. many Carthaginian ships were captured or sunk
   d. many Roman ships were captured or sunk

9. *-que* (line 7) connects
   a. *Terra* and *mari* (line 7)
   b. *mari* and *victor* (line 7)
   c. *Terra* and *Romanus* (line 7)
   d. *Terra* and *magna* (line 7)

10. The best translation of lines 7–8 (*victor Romanus . . . repetit*) is
    a. when the Roman conqueror attacks Lilybaeum again because of all the great spoils
    b. the entire Roman group again attacks Lilybaeum for its great spoils
    c. the whole victorious Roman fleet returns to Lilybaeum for its great booty of every sort
    d. the Roman conqueror returns to Lilybaeum with great booty of every sort

11. The case, number, and gender of *subvecti* (line 9) is determined by
    a. *mari* (line 8)
    b. *commeatus* (line 9)
    c. *navibus* (line 8)
    d. *frumenti* (line 9)

12. From lines 8–9 (*tuto . . . subvecti*) we learn that
    a. supplies of grain were transported to Rome
    b. grain was carried to Rome by means of large ships
    c. provisions were transported by means of the enemy ships
    d. enemy ships intercepted the grain being carried to Rome

SIGHT PASSAGE #6

Polyxena, daughter of Priam and Hecuba, has just been sacrificed by Agamemnon at the behest of Achilles's ghost.

```
    quae corpus complexa animae tam fortis inane,
    quas totiens patriae dederat natisque viroque,
    huic quoque dat lacrimas; lacrimas in vulnera fundit
    osculaque ore tegit consuetaque pectora plangit
5   canitiemque suam concretam sanguine vellens
    plura quidem, sed et haec laniato pectore, dixit:
    'nata, tuae—quid enim superest?—dolor ultime matris,
    nata, iaces, videoque tuum, mea vulnera, vulnus:
    en, ne perdiderim quemquam sine caede meorum,
10  tu quoque vulnus habes; at te, quia femina, rebar
    a ferro tutam: cecidisti et femina ferro,
    totque tuos idem fratres, te perdidit idem,
    exitium Troiae nostrique orbator, Achilles.'
                            Ovid Metamorphoses 13.488–500
```

Vocabulary Help

plango, -ere: to beat, strike
lanio (1): to tear, rend
en: lo! behold!
orbator, orbatoris, m.: one who deprives others of children or parents

1. In line 1, Hecuba (*quae*)
   a. considers her daughter's heroic actions in vain
   b. realizes her life has been pointless
   c. is described as a brave soul
   d. embraces her dead daughter

2. The antecedent of *quas* (line 2) is
   a. *quae* (line 1)
   b. *animae* (line 1)
   c. *lacrimas* (line 3)
   d. *oscula* (line 4)

3. In line 2 (*quas . . . viroque*), we learn that Hecuba
   a. had given much to her country and family
   b. had wept for her country and the men in her family
   c. had been given much by her country and family
   d. had sons and a husband who had given much to their country

4. *huic* (line 3) refers to
   a. ***corpus* (line 1)**
   b. *quas* (line 2)
   c. *viro* (line 2)
   d. *ore* (line 4)

5. From line 4 (*osculaque . . . plangit*), we know that
   a. **Hecuba is in a state of grief for her daughter**
   b. the wounds which cover Polyxena's body make even the enemy weep
   c. Hecuba is enraged at Achilles and tries to harm his ghost
   d. the enemy continues to wound Polyxena despite Hecuba's pleas

6. *vellens* (line 5) describes
   a. *pectora* (line 4)
   b. *canitiem* (line 5)
   c. *plura* (line 6)
   d. **the subject of *dixit* (line 6)**

7. In line 6 (*plura . . . dixit*) we learn that
   a. Hecuba spoke only briefly because she was brokenhearted
   b. Polyxena's wounds expressed more than her words
   c. Polyxena's ghost spoke despite her wounds
   d. **Hecuba said more than the poet quotes here**

8. *nata* (line 7) is
   a. nominative
   b. ablative
   c. **vocative**
   d. accusative

9. *tuae* (line 7) modifies
   a. *nata* (line 7)
   b. *quid* (line 7)
   c. *dolor* (line 7)
   d. ***matris* (line 7)**

10. *-que* (line 8) connects
    a. ***iaces* and *video* (line 8)**
    b. *video* and *tuum* (line 8)
    c. *nata* and *vulnus* (line 8)
    d. *nata* and *vulnera* (line 8)

11. The best translation of lines 9–10 (*ne . . . habes*) is
    a. lest I will have lost anyone without the murder of my children, you have a sure wound
    b. **that I not lose any of my children without carnage, you also have a wound**
    c. may I not lose any of my enemies without slaughter, since you have a wound
    d. unless I will not have lost each of my enemies without slaughter, you have each wound

12. In lines 10–11 (*at te . . . tutam*) the speaker says
    a. she herself had been safe because she was a woman
    b. that no woman is safe from weapons in a war
    c. she thought her daughter safe because she was a woman
    d. every woman who thought she was safe was killed by a weapon

13. *idem* (line 12) refers to
    a. *femina* (line 11)
    b. *ferro* (line 11)
    c. *fratres* (line 12)
    d. *Achilles* (line 13)

14. The metrical pattern of the first four feet of line 13 is
    a. dactyl-spondee-spondee-spondee
    b. dactyl-spondee-dactyl-spondee
    c. spondee-dactyl-dactyl-spondee
    d. spondee-dactyl-spondee-dactyl

Notes

SIGHT PASSAGE #7

Pliny writes a letter about a mutual friend.

        C. Plinius Gemino Suo S.
        Grave vulnus Macrinus noster accepit. Amisit uxorem singularis
        exempli, etiamsi olim fuisset. Vixit cum hac triginta novem annis sine
        iurgio, sine offensa. Quam illa reverentiam marito suo praestitit, cum
        ipsa summam mereretur! Quot quantasque virtutes ex diversis
5   aetatibus sumptas collegit et miscuit!

        Habet quidem Macrinus grande solacium, quod tantum bonum tam
        diu tenuit; sed hoc magis exacerbatur, quod amisit. Nam fruendis
        voluptatibus crescit carendi dolor. Ero ergo suspensus pro homine
        amicissimo, dum admittere avocamenta et cicatricem pati possit, quam
10   nihil aeque ac necessitas ipsa et dies longa et satietas doloris inducit. Vale.
                                                      Pliny *Epistulae* 8.5

Vocabulary Help

uxor, uxoris, f.: wife
iurgium, -i, n.: strife, dispute
praesto, -are, praestiti, praestatum: to show, exhibit
aetas, aetatis, f.: era, generation
exacerbo (I): to grieve, afflict
suspensus: anxious
avocamentum, -i, n.: diversion, distraction
cicatrix, cicatricis, f.: scar, healing wound

1. From *Amisit . . . fuisset* (lines 1–2), we learn that
    a. Macrinus had been married only once
    b. Macrinus set a good example for his wife
    c. Macrinus's wife has died
    d. Macrinus's wife lost what she had once had

2. *hac* (line 2) refers to
    a. *vulnus* (line 1)
    b. *Macrinus* (line 1)
    c. *uxorem* (line 1)
    d. *offensa* (line 3)

3. *Quam . . . praestitit* (line 3) is best translated
    a. What respect she showed her husband
    b. Whom she showed respect on behalf of her husband
    c. She to whom respect was shown by her husband
    d. How much respect her husband showed her

4. *summam* (line 4) describes
   a. *quam* (line 3)
   b. *marito* (line 3)
   c. *illa* (line 3)
   d. *reverentiam* (line 3)

5. In lines 4–5 (*Quot . . . miscuit!*) Pliny says that
   a. Different eras value different virtues
   b. Macrinus's wife had virtues from different eras
   c. Macrinus gathered his courage from previous experiences in his life
   d. Each generation mixes many and great merits

6. In lines 6–7 (*Habet . . . tenuit*), Pliny says that
   a. because Macrinus had such a good, long life, he finds great consolation
   b. a certain solace for Macrinus is that he has held onto the good for a long time
   c. the only great thing Macrinus has left is his good character
   d. Macrinus has the great consolation that he had such a good, long marriage

7. With *Nam . . . dolor* (lines 7–8) Pliny explains that
   a. grief for the loss of something is in proportion to how much it has been enjoyed
   b. by enjoying what life has to offer, grief can be diminished
   c. the pain of caring for someone is offset by the pleasure it brings
   d. offering enjoyments to a person in grief only increases the sense of loss

8. *dum* (line 9) is best translated
   a. while
   b. until
   c. when
   d. provided that

9. The form of *pati* (line 9) is
   a. present imperative
   b. perfect participle
   c. perfect indicative
   d. present infinitive

10. The antecedent of *quam* (line 9) is
    a. the subject of *ero* (line 8)
    b. *avocamenta* (line 9)
    c. *cicatricem* (line 9)
    d. *necessitas* (line 10)

11. In lines 9–10 (*quam . . . inducit*), Pliny observes that
    a. necessity, time, and a sufficiency of grief will heal Macrinus
    b. Macrinus's wife herself led a long life with little need or grief
    c. nothing takes away the sense of need or the slow passage of time for a grieving person
    d. as soon as the days become long again, Macrinus will feel less grief

SIGHT PASSAGE #8

Turnus has just killed Pallas.

        Nescia mens hominum fati sortisque futurae
        et servare modum rebus sublata secundis!
        Turno tempus erit magno cum optaverit emptum
        intactum Pallanta, et cum spolia ista diemque
5   oderit. At socii multo gemitu lacrimisque
        impositum scuto referunt Pallanta frequentes.
        O dolor atque decus magnum rediture parenti,
        haec te prima dies bello dedit, haec eadem aufert,
        cum tamen ingentes Rutulorum linquis acervos!

                                  Vergil *Aeneid* 10.501–509

Vocabulary Help
emo, -ere, emi, emptum: to buy, ransom
Pallanta: Greek acc. of Pallas
decus, decoris, n.: honor
Rutuli, Rutulorum, m.: Rutulians

1. In line 1, the poet comments that
   a. the fates control people's minds
   b. all people fall to the same lot
   c. the fate of people is in the future
   d. people cannot tell the future

2. *servare* (line 2) is
   a. imperative
   b. indicative
   c. infinitive
   d. participle

3. *magno* (line 3) modifies
   a. *fati* (line 1)
   b. *Turno* (line 3)
   c. *Pallanta* (line 4)
   d. *spolia* (line 4)

4. The tense and mood of *optaverit* (line 3) are
   a. imperfect subjunctive
   b. future perfect indicative
   c. perfect subjunctive
   d. future indicative

5. The subject of *oderit* (line 5) is
   a. the same as the subject of *erit* (line 3)
   b. Turnus
   c. Pallas
   d. *spolia* (line 4)

6. In lines 3–5 (*Turno . . . oderit*), the poet comments that
   a. **Turnus will wish that he hadn't killed Pallas**
   b. time will heal all wounds
   c. Pallas wished for another chance to combat Turnus
   d. the chance for spoils motivated Turnus

7. In lines 5–6 (*At . . . frequentes*),
   a. the lamentation of the allies fills even their shields
   b. the Rutulian women weep for Pallas
   c. the allies speak frequently about Pallas
   d. **Pallas is carried off on his shield**

8. Line 7 contains an example of
   a. chiasmus
   b. hendiadys
   c. **apostrophe**
   d. litotes

9. *rediture* (line 7) is a(n)
   a. second person indicative
   b. ablative noun
   c. imperative
   d. **vocative participle**

10. The metrical pattern of the first four feet of line 8 is
    a. **spondee-dactyl-spondee-dactyl**
    b. dactyl-spondee-dactyl-spondee
    c. spondee-spondee-dactyl-dactyl
    d. spondee-dactyl-dactyl-spondee

11. From line 8 we learn that
    a. the first day of war has ended
    b. **Pallas died on his first day at war**
    c. those who come to war first, die first
    d. the same motive which makes people go to war makes them want to leave it

12. *cum* (line 9) is best translated
    a. since
    b. with
    c. **although**
    d. while

13. From line 9 we learn that
    a. **Pallas had slaughtered many Rutulians**
    b. Turnus had slaughtered many Rutulians
    c. the Rutulians had slaughtered huge numbers
    d. the allies had slaughtered huge numbers

SIGHT PASSAGE #9

The author introduces the Carthaginian general Hannibal.

Hannibal, Hamilcaris filius, Carthaginiensis. Si verum est,
quod nemo dubitat, ut populus Romanus omnes gentes virtute
superarit, non est infitiandum Hannibalem tanto praestitisse
ceteros imperatores prudentia, quanto populus Romanus
5   antecedat fortitudine cunctas nationes. Nam quotienscumque
cum eo congressus est in Italia, semper discessit superior.
Quod nisi domi civium suorum invidia debilitatus esset,
Romanos videtur superare potuisse. Sed multorum obtrectatio
devicit unius virtutem. Hic autem velut hereditate relictum
10 odium paternum erga Romanos sic conservavit, ut prius animam
quam id deposuerit, qui quidem, cum patria pulsus esset et
alienarum opum indigeret, numquam destiterit animo bellare
cum Romanis.

Cornelius Nepos *Life of Hannibal* 1–3

Vocabulary Help

infitior, -ari: deny
debilito (1): weaken
obtrectatio, -onis, f.: disparagement, belittling
erga (+ acc.): towards

1. In lines 1–3, the author says that
    a. Hannibal must not deny how much he surpassed the other generals
    b. in order to conquer the other nations, the Romans used their great bravery
    c. it was true that that the Roman people and Hannibal surpassed the other nations
    d. Hannibal's self-restraint was as great as the Romans' bravery

2. We learn from lines 5–6 (*Nam . . . superior*) that
    a. Hannibal departed as victor whenever he came to Italy
    b. However often there was a gathering, in Italy, he had a higher purpose
    c. Whenever someone encountered Hannibal in Italy, he departed by the higher route
    d. Everyone who met with Hannibal in Italy left as a victor

3. *Quod* (line 7) is best translated
    a. because
    b. which
    c. what
    d. but

4. *domi* (line 7) is best translated
   a. of home
   b. to home
   c. at home
   d. the homes

5. From lines 7–8 (*Quod . . . potuisse*) we learn that
   a. Hannibal hated the citizens
   b. the Romans were seen to be victorious
   c. the Roman citizens were weakened by jealousy at home
   d. Hannibal was weakened the citizens' jealousy

6. The subject of *videtur* (line 8) is
   a. *quod* (line 7)
   b. *invidia* (line 7)
   c. Hannibal (understood)
   d. Italy (understood)

7. Lines 8–9 (*Sed . . . virtutem*) contain an example of
   a. chiasmus
   b. metonymy
   c. synchysis
   d. hendiadys

8. *ut* (line 10) introduces a(n)
   a. purpose clause
   b. result clause
   c. indirect command
   d. indirect question

9. *patria* (line 11) is a(n)
   a. nominative singular noun
   b. ablative singular noun
   c. nominative plural adjective
   d. accusative plural adjective

10. In lines 9–11, the author claims that Hannibal
    a. inherited the remains of his father's estate
    b. would rather have died than stop hating the Romans
    c. saved the Romans
    d. never stopped using his mind when he fought with the Romans

SIGHT PASSAGE #10

The speaker addresses his girlfriend as he thinks about death.

      Non ego nunc tristis vereor, mea Cynthia, Manes,
         nec moror extremo debita fata rogo;
      sed ne forte tuo careat mihi funus amore,
         hic timor est ipsis durior exsequiis.
5   non adeo leviter nostris puer haesit ocellis,
         ut meus oblito pulvis amore vacet.
      illic Phylacides iucundae coniugis heros
         non potuit caecis immemor esse locis,
      sed cupidus falsis attingere gaudia palmis
10   Thessalis antiquam venerat umbra domum.
      illic quidquid ero, semper tua dicar imago:
         traicit et fati litora magnus amor.

                                            Propertius 1.19.1–12

Vocabulary Help

rogus, -i, m.: funeral pyre, grave
exsequiae, -arum, f. pl.: funeral procession, funeral obsequies
Phylacides, -ae, m.: Protesilaus, husband of Laodamia
Thessalis, -idis (adjective): Thessalian

1. In line 1, the poet says he
   a. does not now fear sadness
   c. does not fear death
   b. no longer honors her
   d. fears she will not be sad about his death

2. *fata* (line 2) is the object of
   a. *vereor* (line 1)
   b. *moror* (line 2)
   c. *extremo* (line 2)
   d. *rogo* (line 2)

3. In lines 3–4, the poet says that
   a. he is afraid that the funeral for him will be without his girlfriend's love
   b. his girlfriend is afraid that when he dies, so will his love
   c. love is longer lasting than funeral speeches suggest
   d. fear is enduring in funeral speeches, but they are not without love

4. Line 5 contains an example of
   a. metonymy
   b. litotes
   c. chiasmus
   d. anaphora

5. *nostris ocellis* (line 5) is best translated
   a. with my eyes
   b. by my eyes
   c. from my eyes
   d. to my eyes

6. *pulvis* (line 6) refers to
   a. the grains of sand in his eyes
   b. the sand on which a funeral pyre is built
   c. the poet's ashes
   d. the poet's girlfriend's ashes

7. The subject of *potuit* (line 8) is
   a. *pulvis* (line 6)
   b. *coniugis* (line 7)
   c. *heros* (line 7)
   d. *gaudia* (line 9)

8. *caecis* (line 8) describes
   a. *coniugis* (line 7)
   b. *heros* (line 7)
   c. *immemor* (line 8)
   d. *locis* (line 8)

9. In line 9,
   a. the dead Protesilaus is eager to embrace his wife
   b. the Thessalian grasps his delights with his unfaithful hands
   c. a greedy person is unable to have happiness
   d. joys touched by hands make the Thessalian desirous

10. *umbra* (line 10) is
    a. nominative, in apposition with *gaudia* (line 9)
    b. nominative, subject of venerat (line 10)
    c. ablative of separation
    d. ablative of means

11. *quidquid ero* (line 11) is best translated
    a. whatever I will be
    b. whatever [belongs] to the master
    c. although I will be
    d. although [it belongs] to the master

12. The metrical pattern of the first four feet of line 11 is
    a. spondee-spondee-dactyl-dactyl
    b. dactyl-spondee-dactyl-spondee
    c. spondee-dactyl-spondee-dactyl
    d. dactyl-spondee-spondee-dactyl

13. In line 12 the poet concludes
    a. great love is the result of fate
    b. the image of fate surpasses the shores of love
    c. great love continues beyond life
    d. the fates send great love to the shores

SIGHT PASSAGE #11

Pliny writes to the Emperor Trajan for advice about a temple in the province.

> Ante adventum meum, domine, Nicomedenses priori foro novum
> adicere coeperunt, cuius in angulo est aedes vetustissima Matris
> Magnae aut reficienda aut transferenda, ob hoc praecipue quod est
> multo depressior opere eo quod cum maxime surgit. Ego cum
> 5 quaererem, num esset aliqua lex dicta templo, cognovi alium hic,
> alium apud nos esse morem dedicationis. Dispice ergo, domine, an
> putes aedem, cui nulla lex dicta est, salva religione posse transferri;
> alioqui commodissimum est, si religio non impedit.
>
> Pliny *Epistulae* 10.49

Vocabulary Help

Nicomedenses: from Nicomedia, Nicomedian
depressus, -a, -um: low
cum maxime: now, at this time
lex dicta: regulation
dispicio, -ere, dispexi, dispectus: consider
alioqui: otherwise

1. In lines 1–2, Pliny says that
   a. the earlier Nicomedians began a new practice in their forum
   b. the Nicomedians began to worship a new master in their forum
   c. his arrival helped spur the Nicomedians to finish their new forum
   d. the Nicomedians were building a new forum next to the old one

2. *vetustissima* (line 2) indicates that
   a. the temple is very old
   b. the goddess Magna Mater is very revered
   c. the most ancient part of the city is affected
   d. the Nicomedians revere the goddess Magna Mater the most

3. The Nicomedians have determined that
   a. rebuilding or moving the temple will dishonor it
   b. the antiquity of the building makes it impossible to rebuild or move
   c. the temple must be rebuilt or moved
   d. the goddess Magna Mater is too important for her temple to be moved

4. The antecedent of *quod* (line 4) is
   a. *angulo* (line 2)
   b. *hoc* (line 3)
   c. *multo* (line 4)
   d. *opere* (line 4)

5. The reason for the situation is that
   a. the building began to sink because of its weight
   b. the building is rising higher than the depressed area around it
   c. the building is too low compared to the new ones
   d. because of all the digging in the area, the building seems to rise too high

6. *opere* (line 4) is a(n)
   a. present infinitive
   b. adverb
   c. ablative noun
   d. adjective

7. *esset* (line 5) is in a(n)
   a. purpose clause
   b. result clause
   c. indirect question
   d. clause of doubting

8. *hic* (line 5) contrasts with
   a. *ego* (line 4)
   b. *aliqua* (line 5)
   c. *lex* (line 5)
   d. *apud nos* (line 6)

9. *posse* (line 7) is a(n)
   a. infinitive in indirect statement
   b. complementary infinitive
   c. gerund
   d. infinitive showing purpose

10. Pliny explains in lines 4–6 that
    a. the Nicomedians and the Romans have different religious practices
    b. laws were established according to the custom of dedication
    c. although he searched, he was able to learn only two different customs
    d. the dedication of the temple was not made according to regulation

11. In lines 6–7, Pliny asks Trajan to consider
    a. whether the religion is able to be saved
    b. why there is no law
    c. how the shrine can be safe
    d. whether the temple can be moved

SIGHT PASSAGE #12

The poet makes a request of Maecenas.

> quandocumque igitur vitam mea fata reposcent,
> et breve in exiguo marmore nomen ero,
> Maecenas, nostrae spes invidiosa iuventae,
> et vitae et morti gloria iusta meae,
> 5   si te forte meo ducet via proxima busto,
> esseda caelatis siste Britanna iugis,
> taliaque illacrimans mutae iace verba favillae:
> 'Huic misero fatum dura puella fuit.'
>
>   Propertius 2.1.71–78

Vocabulary Help

bustum, -i, n.: funeral pyre, mound
esseda, -orum, n.: chariot
caelatus, -a, -um: carved, engraved
Brittanus, -a, -um: British, from England
favilla, -ae, f.: ash, ashes

1. *quandocumque* (line 1) means
   a. even so
   b. although
   c. since
   d. whenever

2. *fata* (line 1) is
   a. nominative, subject of *reposcent* (line 1)
   b. accusative, direct object of *reposcent* (line 1)
   c. participle modifying *mea* (line 1)
   d. ablative of means

3. *breve* (line 2) modifies
   a. *exiguo* (line 2)
   b. *marmore* (line 2)
   c. *nomen* (line 2)
   d. *ero* (line 2)

4. Lines 1–2 refer to a time when
   a. Maecenas is famous
   b. the poet is famous
   c. the poet is dead
   d. Maecenas is dead

5. *Vitae* (line 4) is what case and number?
   a. genitive singular
   b. dative singular
   c. nominative plural
   d. vocative plural

6. In lines 3–4, the poet
   a. **expresses praise for Maecenas**
   b. hopes that he will have glory in death
   c. is envious of Maecenas's youth
   d. says that hope is for the young, but glory lasts longer

7. *forte* (line 5) modifies
   a. *gloria* (line 4)
   b. *via* (line 5)
   c. *busto* (line 5)
   d. ***ducet* (line 5)**

8. The subject of *ducet* (line 5) is
   a. *gloria* (line 4)
   b. *via* (line 5)
   c. *esseda* (line 6)
   d. ***Britanna* (line 6)**

9. Line 6 contains an example of
   a. hyperbole
   b. **synchysis**
   c. chiasmus
   d. hyperbaton

10. *-que* (line 7) joins
    a. ***siste* (line 6) and *iace* (line 7)**
    b. *esseda* (line 6) and *verba* (line 7)
    c. *talia* (line 7) and *illacrimans* (line 7)
    d. *talia* (line 7) and *favillae* (line 7)

11. In lines 6–7, the poet asks Maecenas to
    a. stand on his chariot and weep silently
    b. depart from Britain on his chariot and weep for the poet's ashes
    c. **stop his chariot and address the poet's ashes**
    d. hold back the harness on his chariot and speak silently to the ashes

12. *illacrimans* (line 7) describes
    a. ***esseda* (line 6)**
    b. the subject of *iace* (line 7)
    c. *talia* (line 7)
    d. *verba* (line 7)

13. *huic misero* (line 8) refers to
    a. Maecenas
    b. **the poet**
    c. the girl
    d. the funeral pyre/grave

14. In line 8,
    a. **a girl was harsh because of fate**
    b. the fate of the miserable man was harsh to the girl
    c. because of a miserable man, the girl was harsh
    d. a harsh girl was the cause of death

VOCABULARY

The following signs and abbreviations are used in this glossary.

abl. = ablative
acc. = accusative
adj. = adjective
adv. = adverb
compar. = comparative
conj. = conjunction
dat. = dative
etc. = *et cētera* (i.e., and so on)
f. = feminine
gen. = genitive
i.e., *id est* (i.e., that is)
indecl. = indeclinable

indef. = indefinite
interrog. = interrogative
lit = literally
m. = masculine
n. = neuter
n. subst. = noun substantive
nom. = nominative
pass. = passive
pers. = person
pl. = plural
pron. = pronoun
superl. = superlative

A

a(d)spectō (1) *see* **aspectō**
a(d)spectus, ūs *m. see* **aspectus**
a(d)spiciō, ere, spexī, spectus *see* **aspiciō**
a(d)stō, āre, stitī *see* **astō**
ā, ab, abs (away) from, by (*abl.*)
Abās, antis *m.* a Trojan leader
abdō, ere, didī, ditus hide, put away, bury
abeō, īre, iī (īvī), itus depart
abluō, ere, uī, ūtus wash (off)
abripiō, ere, uī, reptus carry off, snatch away
abscondō, ere, (di)dī, ditus hide
absistō, ere, stitī cease, stop
absum, esse, āfuī be away, be distant, be lacking
absūmō, ere, sūmpsī, sūmptus take away, diminish, use up, consume
ac, atque and, also; as, than

accēdō, ere, cessī, cessus approach, reach
accendō, ere, ī, ēnsus inflame, kindle, enrage, burn
accingō, ere, cīnxī, cīnctus gird (on), equip
accipiō, ere, cēpī, ceptus receive, accept; learn, hear, conceive
accumbō, ere, cubuī, cubitus recline (at) (+ *dat.*)
āccumulō (1) heap up; pile up; honor
Acestēs, ae *m.* king in Sicily
Achātēs, ae *m.* faithful comrade of Aeneas
Achillēs, is (eī, ī) *m.* central character of Homer's *Iliad*, first among the Greek chieftains in the Trojan War
Achīvus, a, um Achaean, Greek
aciēs, ēī *f.* edge; eye(sight); battle line, army
āctus, a, um *see* **agō**
acūtus, a, um sharp, pointed, keen
ad to, toward, at, near, about (*acc.*)
addō, ere, didī, ditus add

The Latin to English vocabulary is taken with permission from Barbara Weiden Boyd's *Vergil's Aeneid: Selected Readings from Books 1, 2, 4, and 6* (Bolchazy-Carducci Publishers, 2012).

adeō *adv.* to such an extent, so (much)
adeō, īre, iī (īvī), itus approach, encounter
adfātus, ūs *m.* address, speech
adfor, fārī, fātus address, accost, speak to
adfore; adforem, ēs, et *see* **adsum**
adgredior, ī, gressus attack, address, approach
adhūc *adv.* to this point, till now
aditus, ūs *m.* approach, entrance, access
adloquor, ī, locūtus address, accost
admīror, ārī, ātus wonder (at), admire
admittō, ere, mīsī, missus admit
admoneō, ēre, uī, itus advise, warn
adnītor, ī, sus (nixus) lean (against, on), struggle, strive
adnō (1) swim, to, swim up to
adorior, īrī, ortus attempt, attack
adōrō (1) worship, adore, honor
adquīrō, ere, quīsīvī, sītus acquire, gain
adsum, esse, fuī be present, assist (*dat.*)
adsurgō, ere, surrēxī, surrēctus rise
adultus, a, um grown, adult
adveniō, īre, vēnī, ventus arrive, reach
adversus, a, um opposite, facing
advertō, ere, ī, rsus turn to, heed
adytum, ī *n.* inner shrine, sanctuary
Aeacidēs, ae *m.* descendant of Aeacus, Achilles, Greek chieftain
aeger, gra, grum sick, weary, wretched
Aeneadae, (ār)um *m.* descendants (followers) of Aeneas
Aenēās, ae, *acc.* **ān,** *m.* Trojan prince, son of Venus and Anchises, hero of the *Aeneid*
Aeolia, ae *f.* one of the Liparian Islands near Sicily
Aeolus, ī *m.* god of the winds
aequaevus, a, um of equal age
aequō (1) (make) equal(ize), match, level, even
aequor, oris *n.* sea, waves; (level) plain
āēr, āeris, *acc.* **āera,** *m.* air, mist, fog
aes, aeris *n.* bronze (implement), trumpet
aestās, ātis *f.* summer
aestus, ūs *m.* flood, tide, boiling, surge; heat
aetās, ātis *f.* age, time
aeternus, a, um eternal, everlasting
aethēr, eris, *acc.* **era** *m.* upper air, sky, ether, heaven

aetherius, a, um of the upper air, high in the air, airy, ethereal
Āfricus, ī *m.* (southwest) wind
age, agite (agō) up! come! lead on!
ager, agrī *m.* field, territory, land
agger, eris *m.* mound, heap, dike, dam, bank
aggerō (1) heap up, pile up, increase
agmen, inis *n.* army, line, troop; course
agnōscō, ere, nōvī, nitus recognize
agō, ere, ēgī, āctus lead, drive, do, treat, pass, conduct
Aiāx, ācis *m.* Greek leader, who in the sack of Troy had taken Priam's daughter, Cassandra, by force from the sanctuary of Minerva
aiō, ais, ait; aiunt say, speak, assert
āla, ae *f.* wing, (group of) hunters
ālātus, a, um winged, furnished with wings
Albānus, a, um Alban, of Alba Longa in central Italy, mother city of Rome
Alcīdēs, ae *m.* patronymic (meaning "descendant of Alceus") for Hercules, son of Jupiter and Alcmena
Alētēs, ae *m.* Trojan leader
aliēnus, a, um belonging to another, other's, alien, foreign
aliquis (quī), qua, quid (quod) some(one), any(one)
aliquis, quid some(one), any(one)
aliter *adv.* otherwise, differently
alius, a, ud other, another, else
alligō (1) bind, hold (to)
almus, a, um nourishing, kind(ly)
alter, era, erum one (of two), other (of two), second
alternō (1) change, alternate, waver
altum, ī *n.* the deep (sea); heaven
altus, a, um (on) high, lofty, deep
alumnus, ī *m.* nursling, (foster) child
alveus, ī *m.* hollow; boat; trough
alvus, ī *f.* belly, body
amāns, antis *m. (f.)* lover
amārus, a, um bitter, unpleasant
ambiō, īre, īvī (iī), itus go around; conciliate
ambō, ae, ō both
āmēns, entis mad, crazy, frenzied, insane, distracted
amictus, ūs *m.* cloak, robe
amnis, is *m.* river, stream, torrent

amor, ōris *m.* love, desire, passion
Amphrȳsius, a, um Amphrysian, of Amphrysus, a river in Thessaly frequented by Apollo
amplector, ī, plexus embrace, encompass, enfold
an *interrog.* or, whether
an(ne) *interrog.* whether, or
Anchīsēs, ae, *acc.* **ēn,** *m.* Trojan prince, father of Aeneas
ancora, ae *f.* anchor
anguis, is *m. (f.)* snake, serpent
anima, ae *f.* air, breath, life, soul, shade
animus, ī *m.* soul, spirit, breath, courage; anger, pride; purpose, thought
annus, ī *m.* year, season
ante before (*acc.*); sooner, previously
Antheus, eī, *acc.* **ea,** *m.* Trojan leader, comrade of Aeneas
antīquus, a, um ancient, old, aged, former, of olden times, time-honored
antrum, ī *n.* cave, cavern, grotto
aperiō, īre, uī, ertus open, disclose, reveal
apertus, a, um open, clear
apis, is *f.* bee
Apollō, inis *m.* god of light, music, and prophecy
appāreō, ēre, uī, itus appear
aprīcus, a, um sunny, sun-loving
aptō (1) equip, make ready, furnish
aqua, ae *f.* water
Aquilō, ōnis *m.* (north) wind
āra, ae *f.* altar
Ārae, ārum *f.* the Altars, a ledge of rocks between Sicily and Africa
arboreus, a, um branching, tree-like
arceō, ēre, uī keep off, defend, restrain
arcus, ūs *m.* bow
ardeō, ēre, arsī, arsus burn, be eager
Argī, ōrum *m.* Argos, city of southern Greece, home of Diomedes, a Greek chieftain against Troy; center of the worship of Juno
Argīvus, a, um Argive, Greek
Argolicus, a, um Argive, Greek
āridus, a, um dry
arma, ōrum *n.* arms, equipment, tools
armentum, ī *n.* herd, flock, drove, cattle
armō (1) arm, equip, furnish

armus, ī *m.* shoulder, flank, side
arō (1) plow, till, furrow
arrigō, ere, rēxī, rēctus erect, raise, prick up, stand on end, rear
ars, artis *f.* skill
artus, ūs *m.* joint, limb, member, body
arvum, ī *n.* plowed land, field, region
arx, arcis *f.* citadel, fort; height, hill
Ascanius, (i)ī *m.* son of Aeneas
ascendō, ere, ī, ēnsus ascend, mount
aspectō (1) look at, see, face, behold
aspectus, ūs *m.* sight, appearance, vision, aspect
asper, era, erum rough, harsh, fierce
aspiciō, ere, spexī, spectus see, behold, look (at)
ast *conj.* (= **at**) but
astō, āre, stitī stand (on, at, near, by) (+ *dat.*)
astrum, ī *n.* star, constellation
at, ast but, yet, however, at least
āter, tra, trum black, gloomy, deadly
atque, ac and, also; as, than
ātrium, ī *n.* hall, court, atrium
attollō, ere lift, rear, raise
attonitus, a, um thunderstruck, astounded
audeō, ēre, ausus sum dare, venture
audiō, īre, īvī (iī),ītus hear (of), hearken
auferō, auferre, abstulī, ablātus carry away, remove, take off, take away
aula, ae *f.* hall, palace, court
aura, ae *f.* breeze, air; favor; light
auris, is *f.* ear
aurum, ī *n.* gold (object, equipment)
Ausonius, a, um Ausonian, Italian
auspicium, (i)ī *n.* auspices, authority
Auster, trī *m.* (south) wind
aut or, either; **aut . . . aut** either . . . or
autem *adv.* but, however, moreover
autumnus, ī *m.* autumn, fall
auxilium, (i)ī *n.* aid, help, assistance
āvehō, ere, vēxī, vectus carry, convey (away)
āvellō, ere, āvellī or **āvulsī, āvulsus** tear (off, from)
āvertō, ere, ī, rsus keep off, turn aside, turn away, avert
avis, is *f.* bird, fowl
avus, ī *m.* grandfather; ancestor

B

bacchor, ārī, ātus rush wildly, rave, rage
Bacchus, ī *m.* (god of) wine
barba, ae *f.* beard, whiskers
barbarus, a, um foreign, strange, barbarous, uncivilized
beātus, a, um happy, blessed, fortunate
bellum, ī *n.* war(fare), combat, fight
bene *adv.* well, rightly, securely, fully
bīgae, ārum *f.* two-horse chariot
birēmis, is *f.* bireme, galley (with two banks of oars)
bis twice
bonus, a, um good, kind(ly), useful
brevis, e short, shallow
breviter *adv.* shortly, briefly, concisely

C

cadō, ere, cecidī, cāsus fall, fail, sink, die, subside
cadus, ī *m.* jar, urn
caecus, a, um blind, dark, hidden
caelestis, e divine, heavenly
caelicola, ae *m./f.* divinity, deity
caelum, ī *n.* sky, heaven; weather
caeruleus, a, um dark (blue)
Caīcus, ī *m.* comrade of Aeneas
calcar, āris *n.* spur, goad
cālīgō, āre, āvī be dark, darken
calor, ōris *m.* heat, warmth, glow
campus, ī *m.* plain, field, level surface
candēns, entis shining, white, gleaming
canō, ere, cecinī, cantus sing (of), chant, prophesy, proclaim
capessō, ere, īvī, ītus (under)take, perform, (try to) seize, reach
capiō, ere, cēpī, captus take, seize, catch; captivate; deceive; occupy
caput, itis *n.* head; summit; life, person
Capys, yos, *acc.* **Capyn,** *m.* comrade of Aeneas
carcer, eris *m.* prison, enclosure
careō, ēre, uī, itus be free from, lack (+ *abl.*)
carīna, ae *f.* keel; ship, boat
carus, a, um dear, beloved, fond
Cassandra, ae *f.* Trojan prophetess, punished by Apollo and so never believed

castus, a, um pure, holy, chaste
cāsus, ūs *m.* chance, (mis)fortune; fall
caterva, ae *f.* band, troop, crowd
causa, ae *f.* cause, reason, occasion, case (at law)
cautēs, is *f.* rock, cliff, crag
caverna, ae *f.* hollow, cavity, cave
cavus, a, um hollow, vaulted
cēdō, ere, cessī, cessus yield, depart
celer, eris, ere swift, speedy, quick
cella, ae *f.* cell, storeroom
celsus, a, um high, lofty, towering
centum *indecl.* hundred
Cerberus, ī *m.* monstrous three-headed dog in Hades
Cereālis, e of Ceres, (goddess of) grain
Cerēs, eris *f.* (goddess of) grain
cernō, ere, crēvi, crētus discern, perceive, understand, decide; fight
certō (1) strive, fight, vie, contend
certus, a, um fixed, sure, certain, reliable
cervīx, īcis *f.* neck
cervus, ī *m.* stag, deer
Charōn, ontis *m.* ferryman of souls of the dead across the river Styx
cieō, ēre, cīvī, citus (a)rouse, stir (up)
cingō, ere, cīnxī, cīnctus encircle, surround, gird
cinis, eris *m.* ashes (of the dead), embers
circā *adv.* around, about
circum around, about, at, near (*acc.*)
circumstō, āre, stetī surround, stand around
circumvolō (1) fly around, fly about
Cithaerōn, ōnis *m.* Greek mountain near Thebes, on which the rites of Bacchus were celebrated
citō *adv.* quickly, soon
cīvis, is *m.* (*f.*) citizen, compatriot
clāmō (1) shriek, cry (out), call (on)
clāmor, ōris *m.* shout, roar, applause
clārus, a, um clear, bright, illustrious
classis, is *f.* fleet, army, ship
claudō, ere, sī, sus (en)close, shut (in)
claustrum, ī *n.* bolt, fastening, barrier
clipeus, ī *m.* (or **clipeum, ī** *n.*) round shield, buckler
Cōcȳtus, ī *m.* river of Hades
coepī, isse, ptus begin, commence
Coeus, ī *m.* one of the Titans, a giant, son of Earth

cognōmen, inis *n.* (sur)name, cognomen, nickname
cōgō, ere, coēgī, coāctus bring together, force, muster, compel
colligō, ere, lēgī, lēctus collect, gather
collis, is *m.* hill
collum, ī *n.* neck
colō, ere, uī, cultus cultivate, dwell (in), cherish, honor
colōnus, ī *m.* colonist, settler
color, ōris *m.* color
coluber, brī *m.* snake, serpent
columna, ae *f.* column, pillar
cōma, ae *f.* hair, locks, tresses
comes, itis *m.* (*f.*) comrade, follower
comitātus, ūs *m.* retinue, train, company
comitō (1) accompany, attend, escort, follow
comitor, ārī, ātus accompany, attend, escort, follow
commendō (1) entrust, commit
commisceō, ēre, uī, mixtus mix, mingle
commissum, ī *n.* fault, crime
commoveō, ēre, mōvī, mōtus move, stir, shake, agitate, disturb
commūnis, e (in) common, joint, mutual
compāgēs, is *f.* joint, seam, fastening
compellō (1) address, accost, speak to
compellō, ere, pulī, pulsus drive, compel, force
compōnō, ere, posuī, pos(i)tus compose, construct, calm, quiet, put together, settle
comprimō, ere, pressī, pressus (re)press
conciliō (1) win over, unite
conclāmō (1) cry, shout, exclaim
conclūdō, ere, sī, sus (en)close
concrētus, a, um grown together, hardened, matted
concursus, ūs *m.* throng, crowd
concutiō, ere, cussī, cussus shake, shatter, agitate
condō, ere, didī, ditus found, establish; hide, bury
cōnfiteor, ērī, fessus confess, reveal
coniugium, (i)ī *n.* wedlock; husband, wife, marriage
coniūnx, iugis *m.* (*f.*) husband, wife
conlābor, ī, lāpsus fall in a heap, faint, collapse
cōnor, ārī, ātus attempt, try, endeavor
cōnscendō, ere, ī, ēnsus mount, climb, ascend, embark
cōnscius, a, um aware; privy to
cōnsīdō, ere, sēdī, sessus sit (down), settle
cōnsistō, ere, stitī, stitus stand (fast), rest, stop, settle
cōnspectus, ūs *m.* sight, view
cōnspiciō, ere, spexī, spectus see, look at, behold
contendō, ere, ī, ntus strive, contend; bend, draw tight; shoot, aim, hasten
contineō, ēre, uī, tentus hold together, restrain, check
contingō, ere, tigī, tāctus touch, befall
continuō *adv.* immediately, at once
contorqueō, ēre, rsī, rtus hurl, twirl
contra opposite, facing , against, in reply (+ *acc.*); *adv.* opposite, facing, in reply
contus, ī *m.* pole, pike
cōnūbium, (i)ī *n.* right of intermarriage, marriage
convertō, ere, ī, rsus turn (around), reverse
coōrior, īrī, ortus (a)rise
cōpia, ae *f.* abundance, plenty, forces
cor, cordis *n.* heart, spirit, feelings
cōram *adv.* before the face, face to face, openly
corneus, a, um of horn
cornū, ūs *n.* horn, tip, end
corpus, oris *n.* body, corpse, form
corripiō, ere, uī, reptus seize, snatch up
corrumpō, ere, rūpī, ruptus spoil, ruin
coruscus, a, um waving, quivering, flashing
crēber, bra, brum frequent, repeated, crowded
crēdō, ere, didī, ditus believe, (en)trust (+ *dat.*), suppose
crētus, a, um grown, sprung
Creūsa, ae *f.* wife of Aeneas, lost during the sack of Troy
crīnis, is *m.* hair, locks, tresses
croceus, a, um yellow, saffron, ruddy
crūdēlis, e cruel, bloody, bitter, harsh
crūdus, a, um raw, fresh; bloody
cruentus, a, um bloody, cruel
cruor, ōris *m.* blood, gore
cubitum, ī *n.* elbow, arm
culmen, inis *n.* roof, peak, summit, top
culpa, ae *f.* fault, blame, weakness, guilt, offense
culpō (1) blame, censure, reprove
cum (*conj.*) when, while, since, although
cum (*prep.*) with (*abl.*)
cumba, ae *f.* skiff, boat
cumulus, ī *m.* heap, mass, pile

cūnctus, a, um all, whole, entire
cupīdō, inis *f.* love, desire, longing
cūr why? for what reason?
cūra, ae *f.* care, anxiety, grief; love
currus, ūs *m.* chariot, car
cursus, ūs *m.* course, running; haste
curvus, a, um curved, winding, bent
cuspis, pidis *f.* point, spear, lance
custōs, ōdis *m. (f.)* guard(ian), keeper, sentinel
Cyclōpius, a, um Cyclopean, of the Cyclopes, huge one-eyed giants of Sicily
Cyllēnius, (i)ī *m.* the Cyllenean, i.e., Mercury, born on Mt. Cyllene in Arcadia; *adj.*, Cyllēnius, a, um Cyllenean, of Mt. Cyllene in Arcadia, birthplace of Mercury
Cȳmothoē, ēs *f.* a sea nymph

D

damnō (1) condemn, sentence, doom, devote
Danaus, a, um Danaan, Greek
Dardan(i)us, a, um Trojan, Dardanian
Dardania, ae *f.* Troy, citadel of Dardanus
Dardanidēs, ae *m.* Dardanian, Trojan
dē (down, away) from, of, concerning, according to (*abl.*)
dea, ae *f.* goddess
dēbellō (1) exhaust through war, crush
dēbeō, ēre, uī, itus owe, be due, be destined
dēcēdō, ere, cessī, cessus depart
dēclīnō (1) turn aside, bend down, droop
dēcurrō, ere, (cu)currī, cursus run (down), hasten
decus, oris *n.* ornament, glory, dignity, beauty
dēdūcō, ere, dūxī, ductus lead forth, lead down, launch, lead off, abduct
dēfendō, ere, ī, fēnsus ward off, protect
dēferō, ferre, tulī, lātus carry (down), report
dēfessus, a, um weary, tired, worn
dēficiō, ere, fēcī, fectus fail, faint, be lacking
dēfungor, ī, fūnctus perform, finish (+ *abl.*)
dehinc *adv.* then, thereupon
dehīscō, ere, hīvī yawn, gape, open (up), split
dēiciō, ere, iēcī, iectus throw (down), cast down, dislodge
deinde *adv.* thence, next, thereupon

Dēiopēa, ae *f.* a nymph
dēlūbrum, ī *n.* shrine, temple, sanctuary
dēmittō, ere, mīsī, missus send down, let down, drop, lower, derive
dēmum *adv.* at length, finally
dēnique *adv.* finally, at last (esp. at the end of a list), in short, in a word
dēpascor, ī, pāstus feed on, devour
dēpendeō, ēre hang (down), depend
dēscendō, ere, ī, ēnsus descend
dēscrībō, ere, psī, ptus mark out, map
dēserō, ere, uī, rtus desert, forsake
dēsinō, ere, sīvī (iī), situs cease, desist (+ *dat.*)
dēsistō, ere, stitī, stitus cease (from), desist
dēstruō, ere, strūxī, strūctus destroy
dēsuper *adv.* from above
dētineō, ēre, uī, tentus detain, hold back
dētorqueō, ēre, rsī, rtus turn (away)
dētrūdō, ere, sī, sus push off, dislodge
dēturbō (1) drive off, dislodge
deus, ī *m.* god, divinity, deity
dēveniō, īre, vēnī, ventus come (down), arrive (at)
dēvolō (1) fly down
dexter, (e)ra, (e)rum right (hand); favorable; *f. subst.* right hand
dī(ve)s, dī(vi)tis rich, wealthy (+ *gen.*)
dicō (1) consecrate, assign, proclaim, dedicate
dīcō, ere, dīxī, dictus say, speak, tell, call, name, describe, chant
dictum, ī *n.* word, speech, command
Dīdō, ōnis *f.* legendary founder and queen of Carthage
diēs, diēī *m. (f.)* day, time, season
difficilis, e difficult, hard, painful
diffugiō, ere, fūgī flee apart, scatter
diffundō, ere, fūdī, fūsus scatter, spread
dignor, ārī, ātus deem worthy, deign (+ *abl.*)
dīlābor, ī, lāpsus glide away, depart
dīmittō, ere, mīsī, mīssus send out, scatter, dismiss
dīripiō, ere, uī, reptus plunder, ravage, tear from
dis(s)iciō, ere, iēcī, iectus scatter, disperse
Dīs, Dītis *m.* Pluto, god of Hades
discernō, ere, crēvī, crētus divide, separate; dissolve (a dispute)
discessus, ūs *m.* departure, separation

discrīmen, inis *n.* crisis, danger
dispellō, ere, pulī, pulsus drive apart, disperse, scatter
dissimulō (1) conceal, dissimulate, pretend otherwise, hide, disguise
distendō, ere, ī, ntus distend, stretch
dīvellō, ere, ī (or **vulsī**), **vulsus** tear apart
dīversus, a, um scattered, various, separated, different, diverse
dīvidō, ere, vīsī, vīsus divide, separate, distribute
dīvus, a, um divine, heavenly, deified; *subst.* divinity, god, goddess
dō, dare, dedī, datus give (forth), grant, allow, bestow; put, place, make
doceō, ēre, uī, ctus teach (about), tell
doleō, ēre, uī, itus suffer, grieve (at), be angry (at, with), resent
dolor, ōris *m.* grief, pain, passion, anger, suffering
dolus, ī *m.* deceit, wiles, trick, fraud, scheme, stratagem
domina, ae *f.* mistress, queen
dominus, ī *m.* master, lord, ruler
domus, ūs *f.* house(hold), home, abode; family, race, line
dōnum, ī *n.* gift, offering, prize, reward
dorsum, ī *n.* back, ridge, reef
dracō, ōnis *m.* dragon, serpent
dūcō, ere, dūxī, ductus lead, draw (out), protract; produce; think
ductor, ōris *m.* leader, chieftain, guide
dulcis, e sweet, dear, fond, pleasant, delightful
dum while, as long as, until, provided
duo, ae, o two
duplex, icis double, both
dūrō (1) harden, endure
dūrus, a, um hard(y), harsh, rough, stern
dux, ducis *m./f.* leader, conductor, guide, chief

E

ē, ex out of, from, according to (*abl.*)
eburnus, a, um (of) ivory
ecce see! look! behold!
ēdūcō, ere, dūxī, ductus lead out, raise, lead forth
efferō, ferre, extulī, ēlātus carry (out), raise, lift up, carry forth

efficiō, ere, fēcī, fectus make, form
effodiō, ere, fōdī, fossus dig out, excavate
effugiō, ere, fūgī flee (from), escape
effulgeō, ēre, lsī flash, glitter, gleam
effundō, ere, fūdī, fūsus pour out
ēgī *see* **agō**
ego, meī (*pl.* **nōs, nostrum**) I
ēgredior, ī, gressus go out, disembark
ēgregius, a, um extraordinary, distinguished
ei alas! ah!
ēiciō, ere, iēcī, iectus cast out, eject
elephantus, ī *m.* elephant, ivory
Elissa, ae *f.* Dido
ēmittō, ere, mīsī, missus send forth, shoot, hurl
ēmoveō, ēre, mōvī, mōtus move from
Enceladus, ī *m.* one of the Titans, a giant, son of Earth
enim *adv.* for, indeed, truly, surely
ēnsis, is *m.* sword, knife
ēnumerō (1) recount, enumerate
eō, īre, īvī (iī), itus go, proceed, come
epulae, ārum *f.* banquet, feast
epulor, ārī, ātus feast, banquet (+ *abl.*)
eques, itis *m.* cavalryman, knight, man of equestrian rank
equidem *adv.* indeed, truly, surely
equus, ī *m.* horse, steed, charger
Erebus, ī *m.* underworld, Hades
ergō *adv.* therefore, then, consequently
Erīnys, yos *f.* Fury, Curse (personified)
ēripiō, ere, uī, reptus snatch (from), tear away; rescue; hasten
errō (1) stray, wander, err; linger
error, ōris *m.* error, wandering, deceit, trick
ēruō, ere, uī, utus overthrow, tear up
Eryx, ycis *m.* Eryx, a mountain in western Sicily named after a son of Venus (and half-brother of Aeneas) who settled there
et and, also, even, too; **et . . . et** both . . . and
etiam *adv.* also, even, besides, yet, still
etsī although, even if
euntis, ī, em, e, ēs, ium, ibus *see* **eo**
Eurus, ī *m.* (east) wind
ēvādō, ere, sī, sus go forth (from), escape, pass over, traverse

ēvānēscō, ere, nuī vanish, disappear
ēvertō, ere, ī, rsus overturn, destroy
ex, ē out of, from, according to (*abl.*)
exanimis, e breathless, lifeless; also, exanimus, a, um breathless, lifeless
exardēscō, ere, arsī, arsus blaze (up)
excidium, (i)ī *n.* destruction, overthrow
excīdō, ere, ī, sus cut out, destroy; fall from, perish
exciō, īre, īvī, itus arouse, excite, stir
excipiō, ere, cēpī, ceptus catch, receive, take (up)
excitō (1) arouse, stir up, excite
excubiae, ārum *f.* watch(fire), sentinel
excūdō, ere, ī, sus hammer out, fashion
excutiō, ere, cussī, cussus cast out, shake off
exerceō, ēre, uī, itus drive, exercise, perform, be busy, train
exhālō (1) breathe out, exhale
exigō, ere, ēgī, āctus drive out, complete, pass; determine, discover
exiguus, a, um small, scanty, petty
exim, exin(de) *adv.* from there, next, thereupon
exitus, ūs *m.* exit, issue, end
exoptō (1) choose, desire, hope (for)
exordium, (i)ī *n.* beginning, commencement
expediō, īre, īvī (iī), ītus bring out, prepare
expendō, ere, ī, pēnsus expiate, pay (for)
experior, īrī, pertus try, experience
expleō, ēre, ēvī, ētus fill (out), fulfil
explōrō (1) explore, search (out), examine
expōnō, ere place out, (cause to) disembark
exprōmō, ere, mpsī, mptus express, bring forth
exsanguis, e bloodless, lifeless, pale
exspectō (1) await (eagerly), expect
exspīrō (1) breathe out, exhale
exsting(u)ō, ere, īnxī, īnctus extinguish, blot out, destroy, ruin
exstruō, ere, strūxī, strūctus build (up), rear
extemplō *adv.* immediately, at once, suddenly, straightaway
extendō, ere, extendī, extensus (or extentus) stretch out, extend, increase
exterreō, ēre, uī, itus terrify, frighten
exterus, a, um outside, foreign
extrēma, ōrum *n.* end, death, funeral
extrēmus, a, um final, last, furthest, farthest

exuō, ere, uī, ūtus bare, doff, discard
exūrō, ere, ussī, ustus burn (up)
exuviae, ārum *f.* spoils, booty, relics, mementos; slough

F

fabricō (1) fashion, make
facessō, ere, (īv)ī, ītus do, make, fulfill
faciēs, ēī *f.* appearance, face, aspect
facilis, e easy, favorable, ready
faciō, ere, fēcī, factus do, make, perform; grant, offer; suppose
factum, ī *n.* deed, act, exploit
fallō, ere, fefellī, falsus deceive, cheat, mock, beguile, escape the notice (of)
falsus, a, um false, deceitful, mock
fāma, ae *f.* fame, report, reputation
famēs, is *f.* hunger
fandus, a, um to be uttered, right, just
fāre, fārī; fātur; fātus, a, um *see* for
fās *n. indecl.* right, justice, divine will, divine law
fastīgium, (i)ī *n.* top, roof, summit
fātālis, e fatal, deadly, fated, fateful
fatīscō, ere split, open, gape
fātum, ī *n.* fate, destiny, doom; oracle
faux, faucis *f.* jaws, throat; gulf
fax, facis *f.* firebrand, torch
fēmina, ae *f.* woman, female
fēmineus, a, um feminine, of women
feriō, īre strike, smite, beat, kill
ferō, ferre, tulī, lātus bear, endure; wear; report, say; carry (off), plunder; extol; tend; grant, offer
ferrūgineus, a, um rusty (in color), dusky
ferrum, ī *n.* iron; sword, weapon, tool
ferus, ī *m.* beast, monster
ferv(e)ō, ēre, (ferbu)ī glow, boil; be busy
fessus, a, um tired, weary, feeble, worn
fēstus, a, um festal, festival, pertaining to a holiday
fētus, a, um teeming, pregnant, filled
fētus, ūs *m.* offspring, brood, shoot
fictum, ī *n.* falsehood, fiction
fidēs, eī *f.* faith, belief, trust(worthiness), honor, pledge, fidelity; Fidēs, eī *f.* Faith, Honor (personified)

fīdūcia, ae *f.* confidence, trust
fīdus, a, um faithful, trustworthy, safe
fīgō, ere, fīxī, fīxus fix, fasten, pierce
fīlius, (i)ī *m.* son
fingō, ere, fīnxī, fictus fashion, pretend, imagine, form, mold, shape
fīnis, is *m.* (*f.*) end, limit, border; country; goal; starting-place
fīō, fierī, factus become, be made, arise
flamma, ae *f.* flame, fire, torch; love
flammō (1) inflame, burn, fire, kindle
flāvus, a, um yellow, tawny, blond
flectō, ere, flexī, flexus bend, move, turn, guide
fleō, ēre, ēvī, ētus weep, lament, mourn
flētus, ūs *m.* weeping, tears, lament
flōreō, ēre, uī bloom, flourish, blossom
flōreus, a, um flowery
flōs, ōris *m.* flower, blossom, bloom
flūctus, ūs *m.* wave, tide, flood, sea
fluentum, ī *n.* stream, flood
flūmen, inis *n.* river, stream, flood
fluvius, (i)ī *m.* river, stream
fodiō, ere, fōdī, fossus dig, pierce, spur
foedō (1) befoul, defile, pollute; mar, mangle, disfigure
foedus, a, um foul, loathsome, filthy
foedus, eris *n.* treaty, agreement, pact
folium, (i)ī *n.* leaf, foliage
fōmes, itis *m.* tinder, fuel, shaving
for, fārī, fātus speak, say, tell, utter
fore; forem, ēs, et *see* **sum**
forma, ae *f.* form, beauty, shape
fors(it)an *adv.* perhaps, possibly, perchance
fors, fortis *f.* chance, fortune, hap
fortis, e strong, brave, valiant
fortūna ae *f.* fortune, chance, luck
fortūnātus, a, um fortunate, blessed
forus, ī *m.* gangway, deck (of a boat)
foveō, ēre, fōvī, fōtus cherish, fondle
fraglāns, antis fragrant, sweet-smelling
fragor, ōris *m.* crash, uproar
frangō, ere, frēgī, frāctus break, crush, shatter
frāter, tris *m.* brother
fraudō (1) defraud, deprive, cheat
fraus, fraudis *f.* deceit, guile, fraud

fremō, ere, uī, itus murmur, lament, groan, roar, rage
frēnō (1) curb, check, restrain
fretum, ī *n.* strait, sound, channel, narrow sea
frīgidus, a, um cold, chill, frigid
frīgus, oris *n.* cold, frost, chill
frondeus, a, um leafy
frōns, frontis *f.* front, forehead, brow, face
frūx, frūgis *f.* fruit, grain
fūcus, ī *n.* drone
fuga, ae *f.* flight, haste, exile, speed
fugiō, ere, fūgī flee (from), escape, shun
fugō (1) put to flight, rout
fulg(e)ō, ēre (or ere), lsī shine, flash, gleam, glitter
fulmen, inis *n.* thunderbolt, lightning
fulvus, a, um tawny, yellow, blond
fūmus, ī *m.* smoke, vapor, fog, fume
fundāmentum, ī *n.* foundation, base
fundō (1) found, establish, make fast
fundō, ere, fūdī, fūsus pour (out), shed; lay low, slay, rout; extend
fungor, ī, fūnctus perform, fulfil (+ *abl.*)
fūnis, is *m.* rope, cable
fūnus, eris *n.* funeral, death, disaster
furiae, ārum *f.* furies, madness, frenzy
furiō (1) madden, frenzy, infuriate
furō, ere, uī rage, rave, be frantic
furor, ōris *m.* madness, frenzy, rage, passion, fury; **Furor, ōris** *m.* Madness, Rage, Frenzy (personified)
fūrtīvus, a, um secret, stolen
fūrtum, ī *n.* stealth, theft, trick
futūrus, a, um future, destined (to be), impending, about to be; *see* **sum**

G

Gaetūlus, a, um of the Gaetuli, a tribe of North Africa
galea, ae *f.* helmet
Gallus, a, um Gallic, Gaul
Ganymēdēs, is *m.* son of Laōmedon, first king of Troy; carried off by Jupiter's eagle and made cupbearer to the gods
Garamantis, idis of the Garamantes, an African tribe

gaudeō, ēre, gāvisus sum (semideponent) rejoice, exult
gaza, ae *f.* wealth, treasure
geminus, a, um twin, double, two
gemitus, ūs *m.* groan(ing), wail(ing), lament, moan
gemō, ere, uī, itus groan (for), lament
generō (1) beget, bear
genitor, ōris *m.* begetter, father, sire
gēns, gentis *f.* clan, race, nation, herd
genua, eris *n.* birth, origin, race; descendant; kind, family
germāna, ae *f.* sister
gerō, ere, gessī, gestus bear, carry (on), wage
gestō (1) bear, wear, carry
gignō, ere, genuī, genitus bear, produce, beget
glaeba, ae *f.* a lump of earth, clod
glaucus, a, um gray, grayish-green, gleaming
glomerō (1) roll together, gather, collect
glōria, ae *f.* renown, glory, fame, pride
Gorgō, onis *f.* Gorgon
gradus, ūs *m.* step, gait, pace, stride
Graius, a, um Greek
grandaevus, a, um aged, old
grandō, inis *f.* hail(storm, stones)
grātus, a, um welcome, pleasing, grateful
gravis, e heavy, weighty, serious; venerable; pregnant
graviter *adv.* heavily, violently, greatly
gressus, ūs *m.* step, walk, course, gait
Grȳnēus, a, um of Grynium, a town in Asia Minor, with an oracle of Apollo
gurges, itis *m.* whirlpool, abyss, gulf
guttur, uris *n.* throat, gullet

H

habēna, ae *f.* rein, curb, check
habeō, ēre, uī, itus have, hold; consider
haereō, ēre, haesī, haesus stick (to), cling (to) (+ *dat.*)
hālitus, ūs *m.* breath, exhalation
Hammōn, ōnis *m.* Hammon (or Ammon), god of North Africa, famous for his oracle and identified by the Romans with Jupiter
harēna, ae *f.* sand, beach
hasta, ae *f.* spear, lance, dart
haud not, by no means, not at all
hauriō, īre, hausī, haustus drain, drink (in)
hebetō (1) blunt, dull, dim, weaken
Hector, oris, *acc.* **ora** *m.* Trojan leader, son of Priam and Hecuba
hērēs, ēdis *m.* heir, successor
hērōs, ōis *m.* hero, mighty warrior
Hesperia, ae *f.* Hesperia, Italy; *lit.*, the western place
heu alas! ah! ah me!
hībernus, a, um wintry, of the winter, stormy
hīc (*adv.*) here, there, hereupon
hic, haec, hoc this, that; he, she, it
hiems, emis *f.* winter, storm
hinc from this place, hence, thence
homō, inis *m.* (*f.*) man, mortal, human
honōs (or), ōris *m.* honor, glory, reward; offering, sacrifice; charm, grace
hōra, ae *f.* hour, season, time
horrendus, a, um horrifying, dire, awesome
horreō, ēre, uī bristle, shudder, tremble, quake
horrēscō, ere, horruī shudder, tremble
horror, ōris *m.* horror, terror, shudder(ing)
hospes, itis *m.* (*f.*) guest, host, stranger
hospitium, (i)ī *n.* hospitality, welcome
hostis, is *m.* (*f.*) enemy, foe, stranger
hūc to this place, hither, here
hūmānus, a, um of man, human
humus, ī *f.* ground, soil, earth
hymenaeus, ī *m.* wedding (hymn), so called after Hymen, god of marriage

I

ī, ībam, ībō, īre, it, īte *see* **eō**
iaceō, ēre, uī, itus lie (low, outspread)
iactō (1) toss, buffet, vaunt, boast, utter
iaculor, ārī, ātus hurl, throw, fling
iam now, already, finally, at once
iānitor, ōris *m.* doorkeeper
Iarbās, ae *m.* African chieftain, one of Dido's suitors
iaspis, idis *f.* jasper, a semiprecious stone
ibi *adv.* there, then
ibīdem in the same place
īdem, eadem, idem same, the same
ignārus, a, um ignorant, unaware, inexperienced; unknown, strange

ignāvus, a, um lazy, idle
igneus, a, um fiery, flaming
ignis, is *m.* fire, flame, light, lightning, star; passion, love, fury, wrath
ignōbilis, e inglorious, common, lowly
ignōtus, a, um unknown, strange
Īliacus, a, um Trojan, Ilian
Īlias, adis *f.* Trojan woman
Īlioneus, eī *m.* Trojan leader
Īlium, (i)ī *n.* Troy, Ilium, a city of Asia Minor
ille, la, lud that (famous); he, she, it
illīc *adv.* there, at that place
illūc *adv.* there, thither, to that place
imāgō, inis *f.* likeness, image, ghost, soul, form, picture
imber, bris *m.* rain, flood, storm, water
immānis, e huge, monstrous, enormous, mighty, dreadful, cruel, atrocious
immemor, oris unmindful, heedless, forgetful
immēnsus, a, um boundless, measureless, immense, immeasurable
immineō, ēre menace (+ *dat.*), hang over, threaten
immītis, e fierce, cruel
immittō, ere, mīsī, missus let in, send in (to), loose(n), give freely (+ *dat.*)
immōtus, a, um unmoved, immovable, unshaken
impellō, ere, pulī, pulsus strike (against), drive, force, impel
imperium, (i)ī *n.* command, power, dominion, rule, sway, mastery, realm(s)
impius, a, um unholy, impious, disloyal, wicked, accursed
implicō, āre, āvī (uī), ātus (itus) entwine
impōnō, ere, posuī, positus place upon, set to, impose (+ *dat.*), establish
imprimō, ere, pressī, pressus press (upon), imprint
impūne *adv.* unpunished, with impunity
īmus, a, um *superl. of* **īnferus**
in in, on, in the case of, among (*abl.*); into, against, until, toward (*acc.*)
inānis, e empty, idle, useless, vain
incēdō, ere, cessī, cessus walk (proudly), stride, march, go (majestically)
incendium, (i)ī *n.* a burning, fire, blaze, conflagration
incendō, ere, ī, ēnsus inflame, kindle, burn

inceptum, ī *n.* beginning, undertaking, purpose
incertus, a, um uncertain, doubtful, wavering
incipiō, ere, cēpī, ceptus begin, undertake
inclēmentia, ae *f.* cruelty, harshness
inclūdō, ere, sī, sus (en)close, confine
inclutus, a, um famous, renowned
incolumis, e safe, unharmed, intact
increpō, āre, uī, itus reprove, chide
incubō, āre, uī (āvī), itus (ātus) recline, lie upon, brood over (+ *dat.*)
incumbō, ere, cubuī, cubitus lean upon, urge on, brood over, lower (over), lie upon, hang over (+ *dat.*)
incutiō, ere, cussī, cussus strike (into) (+ *dat.*)
inde *adv.* thence, afterward, thereupon
indignor, ārī, ātus be angry, chafe; deem unworthy, despise
indignus, a, um undeserved, unworthy
indomitus, a, um uncontrolled, ungoverned
induō, ere, uī, ūtus don, clothe, put on
īnfandus, a, um unspeakable, accursed
īnfectus, a, um not done, false
īnfēlīx, īcis unfortunate, accursed, unhappy, ill-omened, unlucky, wretched
īnfēnsus, a, um hostile, bitter
īnferō, ferre, tulī, lātus bear (in, into), bring (to), present
īnferus, a, um low, below, underneath
īnfēstus, a, um hostile, threatening
īnfīgō, ere, xī, xus fix, pierce, fasten (on), impale
informis, e shapeless, hideous
ingemō, ere, uī groan, roar, lament
ingēns, entis enormous, mighty, huge
ingredior, ī, gressus advance, enter, proceed, step, stride
inhumātus, a, um unburied
inimīcus, a, um hostile, enemy, unfriendly
inīquus, a, um unfair, unjust, hostile
iniūria, ae *f.* wrong, insult, injustice, injury
inlābor, ī, lāpsus glide in(to) (+ *dat.*)
inlīdō, ere, sī, sus dash against (into) (+ *dat.*)
innūptus, a, um unmarried, virgin
inops, opis needy, destitute, bereft (of)
inremeābilis, e from which there is no return, irretraceable

inrītō (1) vex, enrage, provoke
īnsānia, ae *f.* madness, frenzy, folly
īnsequor, ī, secūtus follow, pursue
īnsidiae, ārum *f.* snare, ambush, treachery
īnsīdō, ere, sēdī, sessus sit in (on), occupy
īnsignis, e distinguished, marked, splendid
īnsinuō (1) wind, creep, coil
īnsomnium, (i)ī *n.* dream, vision in sleep
īnsonō, āre, uī (re)sound, roar, echo
īnspiciō, ere, spexī, spectus look into
īnstar *n. indecl.* likeness, dignity, image (+ *gen.*)
īnstō, āre, stitī urge on, press on (+ *dat.*)
īnsula, ae *f.* island
īnsuper *adv.* above, besides
intentō (1) threaten, aim, stretch, extend
inter between, among, during (*acc.*)
intereā *adv.* meanwhile, (in the) meantime
interpres, etis *m. (f.)* interpreter, agent
intorqueō, ēre, rsī, rtus hurl (against) (+ *dat.*)
intrō (1) enter, penetrate
intrōgredior, ī, gressus to step in, enter
intus *adv.* within, inside
inultus, a, um unavenged, unpunished
invādō, ere, sī, sus attack, address
invehō, ere, ēxī, ectus carry in, convey
invictus, a, um unconquered, invincible
invidia, ae *f.* grudge, envy, jealousy
invīsus, a, um hateful, hated, odious
invius, a, um pathless, trackless
iovis, ī, em, e *see* Iuppiter
ipse, sa, sum (him, her, it) self; very
īra, ae *f.* wrath, rage, anger, passion
īre *see* eō
Īris, (id)is *f.* goddess of the rainbow, messenger of Juno
is, ea, id this, that; he, she, it
iste, ta, tud that (of yours)
istinc from there (where you are)
it, īte *see* eō
ita *adv.* thus, so
Ītalia, ae *f.* Italy
Italus, a, um Italian, of Italy
iter, itineris *n.* way, road, journey, route
iuba, ae *f.* mane, crest

iubeō, ere, iussī, iussus command, order, bid, enjoin (upon), urge
iūdicium, (i)ī *n.* decision, judgment
iugum, ī *n.* yoke, (mountain) ridge
Iūlus, ī *m.* Ascanius, son of Aeneas
iungō, ere, iūnxī, iūnctus join, unite, yoke
iūnō, ōnis *f.* queen of the gods
Iuppiter, Iovis *m.* king of the gods
iūrō (1) take oath, swear, conspire
iūs, iūris *n.* right, law, decree, justice
iussī; iussus, a, um *see* iubeo
iussum, ī *n.* order, command, behest
iussus, ūs *m.* command, order, behest
iūstitia, ae *f.* justice, equity, righteousness, uprightness
iūstus, a, um just, fair, right(eous)
iuvenis, is *m. (f.)* youth, young (man or woman)
iuventūs, ūtis *f.* youth, (group of) young men
iuvō, āre, iūvī, iūtus help, please
iuxtā *adv.* close; (+ *acc.*) close to, next to

K

Karthāgō, inis *f.* Carthage, great commercial city in North Africa, rival of Rome

L

lābor, ī, psus slip (by), slide, glide (by), descend; fail; faint, fall, perish; flow
labōs (or), ōris *m.* labor, hardship, task
Lacaenus, a, um Spartan, Lacedaemonian
lacrima, ae *f.* tear, compassion
lacus, ūs *m.* lake, marsh
laedō, ere, sī, sus strike, hurt, offend, thwart
laena, ae *f.* (woolen) mantle, cloak
laetor, ārī, ātus rejoice, exult
laetus, a, um happy; fertile; fat, sleek
laevus, a, um left, foolish, unlucky
lambō, ere lick, lap
lāmenta, ōrum *n.* lamentation, shriek
Lāocoōn, ontis *m.* Trojan priest of Neptune
lāpsus, ūs *m.* gliding, rolling, sinking
largus, a, um abundant, copious
lātē *adv.* widely, far and wide
latebra, ae *f.* hiding place, cavern, lair

lateō, ēre, uī lie hidden, hide, lurk, escape the notice (of)
Latīnus, a, um Latin, of Latium
Latīnus, ī *m.* early king of Italy whose daughter, Lavinia, married Aeneas
Latium, (i)ī *n.* Latium, district of central Italy around Rome
lātrātus, ūs *m.* bark(ing), howl(ing)
latrō (1) bark, howl, bay
lātus, a, um broad, wide, spacious
latus, eris *n.* side, flank
laudō (1) praise
Laurēns, entis of Laurentum, a city near Rome
laus, laudis *f.* glory, praise, merit
Lāvīn(i)us, a, um Lavinian, of Lavinium, an early Italian city
laxō (1) loosen, free, open, release
laxus, a, um loose, open, lax, free
legō, ere, lēgī, lēctus choose, collect, select, gather
Lēnaeus, a, um Lenaean, Bacchic, of Bacchus, god of wine
lēniō, īre, īvī (iī), ītus soothe, calm, soften
lētum, ī *n.* death, destruction, ruin
levis, e light, unsubstantial, slight, swift
levō (1) lift, lighten, raise, relieve
lēx, lēgis *f.* law, jurisdiction, regulation, decree
lībō (1) pour (as a libation), offer
Libya, ae *f.* region of North Africa
Libycus, a, um Libyan, of Libya, a region of North Africa
licet, ēre, uit, itum it is permitted
lignum, ī *n.* wood, timber
ligō (1) bind, tie, fasten
līlium, (i)ī *n.* lily
līmen, inis *n.* threshold, doorway, entrance; abode; shrine; palace
limus, ī *m.* slime, mud, mire
lingua, ae *f.* tongue, language
linquō, ere, līquī, lictus leave, desert
līquēns, entis liquid, flowing
lītus, oris *n.* shore, strand, coast, beach
līvidus, a, um blue, dark, livid
locō (1) place, locate, establish, lay
locus, ī *m.* (*pl.* **locī, loca**) place, region; condition, situation; opportunity

longaevus, a, um aged, very old
longē *adv.* far (off, from), at a distance, (from) afar
longus, a, um long, wide, distant
loquor, ī, locūtus speak, say, tell, talk
lōrum, ī *n.* thong, leather strap, rein
luctor, ārī, ātus struggle, wrestle
lūctus, ūs *m.* grief, mourning, sorrow
lūdō, ere, sī, sus play with, deceive, mock
lūmen, inis *n.* light, lamp; eye; life *f.* light, sun, day; life; glory
lūna, ae *f.* moon, moonlight
luō, ere, ī atone for
lūstrō (1) purify, survey, traverse
luxus, ūs *m.* luxury, splendor, excess
Lycia, ae *f.* country of Asia Minor
Lycius, a, um Lycian, of Lycia, a country of Asia Minor
lympha, ae *f.* water

M

māchina, ae *f.* machine, engine, device
mactō (1) sacrifice, slaughter, kill; honor through sacrifice
madeō, ēre, uī drip, be wet, reek
Maeonius, a, um Maeonian, Lydian, Asiatic
maereō, ēre mourn, grieve, pine (for)
maestus, a, um sad, mournful, gloomy
māgālia, ium *n.* huts, hovels
magis *adv.* more, rather
magister, trī *m.* master, pilot
magistrātus, ūs *m.* magistrate, officer
magnanimus, a, um great-souled
magnus, a, um great, large, huge, vast; noble, illustrious, mighty, important
maior, maius *compar. of* **magnus**
malum, ī *n.* evil thing, misfortune, disaster, trouble
mandātum, ī *n.* command, mandate, charge, behest, order
maneō, ere, mānsī, mānsus remain, abide, linger, stay, (a)wait
Mānēs (or **mānēs**), **ium** *m.* (souls of) the dead, Hades
manifestus, a, um clear, manifest
manus, ūs *f.* hand; band, troop; deed

Mārcellus, ī *m.* 1. Marcus Claudius Marcellus, d. 208 BCE; famous Roman consul, served in both 1st and 2nd Punic Wars; 2. Marcus Claudius Marcellus, 42–23 BCE; son of Octavia (sister of Augustus) and first husband of Augustus' daughter Julia

mare, is *n.* sea

marmor, oris *n.* marble

Marpēs(s)ius, a, um of Marpe(s)sus, a mountain on the island of Paros famous for its white marble

māter, tris *f.* mother, dam; matron

mātūrō (1) hasten, speed; ripen

Maurūsius, a, um Moorish

maximus *superl. of* **magnus**

meātus, ūs *m.* course, path, motion

medicō (1) drug, medicate

meditor, ārī, ātus meditate, design, consider, think over, practice

medium, (i)ī *n.* middle, midst, center

medius, a, um mid(dle), intermediate

mel, mellis *n.* honey

melior, ius better, superior, preferable

membrum, ī *n.* member, limb, (part of) body, part

meminī, isse remember, recall (+ *gen.*)

memor, oris remembering, mindful, unforgetting (+ *gen.*)

memorābilis, e memorable, glorious

memorō (1) (re)call, recount, relate

mēns, mentis *f.* mind, feeling, intention

mēnsis, is *m.* month

mentum, ī *n.* chin, beard

mereō, ēre, uī, itus deserve, earn, merit

meritum, ī *n.* reward, service, merit

metuō, ere, uī fear, dread

metus, ūs *m.* fear, anxiety, dread, fright

meus, a, um my (own), mine

micō, āre, uī quiver, flash, dart

mīlle; *pl.* **mīlia, ium** *n.* thousand

minister, trī *m.* attendant, servant

ministrō (1) tend, serve, supply

minor, ārī, ātus tower (over); threaten (+ *dat.*)

minōrēs, um *m.* descendants; *lit.,* smaller or younger ones (*compar.* of **parvus**)

minus *adv.* less

mīrābilis, e wonderful, marvelous

mīror, ārī, ātus wonder (at), admire

misceō, ēre, uī, mixtus confuse, mix, mingle, stir (up)

miser, era, erum miserable, unhappy, wretched, unfortunate, pitiable

miserābilis, e miserable, wretched, pitiable

misereor, ērī, itus pity, commiserate (+ *gen.*)

mitra, ae *f.* mitre, cap, turban

mittō, ere, mīsī, missus send, hurl, dismiss, let go; end, finish; offer, pay

Mnēstheus, eī (eos), *acc.* **ea** *m.* Trojan leader

mōbilitās, ātis *f.* activity, motion, speed

modus, ī *m.* manner, measure, limit, method

moenia, ium *n.* walls; city; structures

mōlēs, is *f.* mass, burden, heap, structure; difficulty

mōlior, īrī, ītus undertake, (strive to) accomplish, do, work, effect, make, prepare, attempt

molliō, īre, īvī (iī), ītus soothe, tame

mollis, e soft, yielding, easy, mild, tender

molliter *adv.* softly, gently, gracefully

monitum, ī *n.* advice, warning

monitus, ūs *m.* advice, warning

mōns, montis *m.* mountain, height

mōnstrō (1) point out, show, teach

mōnstrum, ī *n.* prodigy, portent, monster

mora, ae *f.* delay, hesitation, hindrance

moribundus, a, um dying, about to die

morior, ī, mortuus die, perish

moror, ārī, ātus delay, tarry, hinder, hesitate

mors, rtis *f.* death, destruction, ruin

morsus, ūs *m.* bite, biting, jaws, fangs

mortālis, is *m.* mortal, man, human, earthly

mōs, mōris *m.* custom, ritual, manner, usage

mōtus, ūs *m.* movement, emotion

moveō, ēre, mōvī, mōtus move; ponder

mox *adv.* soon, presently

mūgītus, ūs *m.* bellow(ing), roar

mulceō, ēre, lsī, lsus calm, soothe

multiplex, icis manifold, multiple

multus, a, um much, many, abundant

mūnus, eris *n.* function, duty; gift

mūrex, icis *m.* purple (dye), crimson, scarlet

murmur, uris *n.* murmur, roar, rumble

mūrus, ī *m.* (city) wall, battlement, rampart

Mūsa, ae *f.* Muse, patron goddess of the liberal arts

mūtō (1) (ex)change, transform, alter
Mycēnae, ārum *f.* city of central Greece, home of Agamemnon, leader of the Greek expedition against Troy

N

nam, namque for; indeed, truly
nātus, ī *m.* son, child, young
nāvigō (1) (set) sail, navigate
nāvis, is *f.* ship, boat, vessel, galley
nāvita, ae *m.* sailor, boatman
nē lest, that not, no, not
-ne *sign of a question;* whether, or
nebula, ae *f.* cloud, mist, fog
necdum *adv.* not yet, nor yet
nectar, aris *n.* nectar
nectō, ere, nex(u)ī, nexus bind, fasten, weave
nefandus, a, um unspeakable, unutterable
nefās *n. indecl.* impiety, unspeakable thing, crime
negō (1) deny, refuse, say no (not)
nemus, oris *n.* grove, wood, forest
nepōs, ōtis *m.* grandson; descendant
Neptūnus, ī *m.* Neptune, god of the sea
neque, nec nor, neither, and not; **neque . . . neque** neither . . . nor
nēquīquam *adv.* in vain, uselessly, idly
nesciō, īre, īvī (iī) not know, know not, be ignorant
neu, nēve and (that) not, and lest
nī, nisi if not, unless, except
nihil, nīl nothing, not at all
nimbōsus, a, um stormy, rainy
nimbus, ī *m.* rainstorm, (storm)cloud
nimium *adv.* too (much), too great(ly), excessively
nitēns, entis gleaming, bright, shining
nō (1) swim, float
nocturnus, a, um of the night, nocturnal
nōdus, ī *m.* knot, node; fold, coil
Nomas, adis *m.* tribe of North Africa
nōmen, inis *n.* name, fame, renown
nōn not, no
nōndum *adv.* not yet
noster, tra, trum our (own), ours
nōtus, a, um (well) known, familiar
Notus, ī *m.* (south) wind

novitās, ātis *f.* newness, novelty
novō (1) renew, make (new), build, alter
novus, a, um new, young, strange, late
nox, noctis *f.* night, darkness; sleep
noxa, ae *f.* crime, fault, hurt, harm
nūbēs, is *f.* cloud, fog, mist
nūbila, ōrum *n.* clouds, cloudiness
nūbilum, ī *n.* cloud, cloudiness
nūllus, a, um none, no, no one
nūmen, inis *n.* divinity, divine power (will, favor, purpose, presence)
numerus, ī *m.* number, multitude
numquam *adv.* never, at no time
nunc (but) now, soon, as it is
nuntia, ae *f.* messenger
nuntius, (i)ī *m.* messenger, message
nūsquam *adv.* nowhere, never
nūtrīmentum, ī *n.* food, fuel, nourishment
Nympha (or **nympha**), **ae** *f.* nymph, a minor divinity of the forests, waters, etc., appearing to humans as a beautiful maiden

O

Ō O! Oh! Ah!
ob on account of (+ *acc.*)
obdūcō, ere, dūxī, ductus draw over
obiciō, ere, iēcī, iectus present, place before
obiectus, ūs *m.* projection, hang, overhang
obitus, ūs *m.* death, downfall, ruin
oblīviscor, ī, lītus forget (+ *gen.*)
obmūtēscō, ere, tuī be dumb, stand speechless
obnītor, ī, sus (nixus) push against, strive, struggle
oborior, īrī, ortus (a)rise, spring up
obruō, ere, uī, utus overwhelm, crush
obscūrus, a, um dark, shadowy, gloomy, dim, obscure
obstipēscō, ere, stipuī be dazed, stand agape
obtundō, ere, tudī, tūsus (tūnsus) blunt, weaken, exhaust, make dull
obvius, a, um in the way, meeting, to meet (+ *dat.*)
occidō, ere, occidī, occāsus fall, perish, end, die
occubō, āre lie prostrate, lie dead
occultō (1) hide, conceal, secrete
occumbō, ere, cubuī, cubitus fall (in death)

occupō (1) seize (beforehand), occupy
ōcior, ius swifter, quicker; very swift
oculus, ī *m.* eye
ōdī, isse hate, detest, loathe
Oenōtrus, a, um Oenotrian, from Oenotria in southern Italy
offa, ae *f.* morsel, cake
offerō, ferre, obtulī, oblātus present
officium, ī *n.* service, kindness, favor, courtesy
Oīleus, eī *m.* Greek king, father of Ajax
ōlim *adv.* (at) some time, once
olle *etc., old forms of* **ille**
Olympus, ī *m.* high Greek mountain, home of the gods; heaven
ōmen, inis *n.* portent, omen, sign
omnīnō *adv.* altogether, completely, utterly
omnipotēns, entis almighty, all-powerful, omnipotent
omnis, e all, every, whole, universal
onerō (1) load, burden
onus, eris *n.* burden, load
operiō, īre, uī, rtus cover, hide
opīmus, a, um rich, splendid, sumptuous; **spolia opīma** "spoils of honor," won when a Roman general with his own hand slew the general of the enemy
oppetō, ere, īvī (iī), ītus encounter, meet (death)
opprimō, ere, pressī, pressus overwhelm, crush
ops, opis *f.* help, resources, power, wealth
optimus, a, um best, finest (superl. of **bonus, a, um**)
optō (1) choose, desire, hope (for)
opus, eris *n.* work, task, toil, deed
ōra, ae *f.* shore, coast, region, border
orbis, is *m.* circle, fold, coil, orb, revolution, earth
Orcus, ī *m.* Hades, (god of) the lower world
orgia, ōrum *n.* mystic rites, rituals
Ōriōn, ōnis *m.* the storm-bringing constellation, named for a famous hunter transported to heaven
ōrō (1) beseech, pray (for), entreat, plead, argue
Orontēs, is (**ī**) *m.* comrade of Aeneas
ōs, ōris *n.* mouth, face; speech
os, ossis *n.* bone
ostendō, ere, ī, ntus show, display, promise
ōstium, (i)ī *n.* mouth, entrance; harbor
ōtium, (i)ī *n.* leisure, idleness, quiet

P

paeniteō, ēre, uī repent, be sorry
Pallas, adis *f.* Minerva, goddess of wisdom and the arts
palma, ae *f.* palm, hand
palūs, ūdis *f.* swamp, marsh
pandō, ere, ī, passus spread, open, loosen
Parcae, ārum *f.* the Fates
parcō, ere, pepercī (parsī), parsus spare (+ *dat.*)
parēns, entis *m.* (*f.*) parent, ancestor, father, mother
pāreō, ēre, uī, itus obey, yield (+ *dat.*)
pariō, ere, peperī, partus (re)produce, gain, acquire, give birth to
Paris, idis *m.* Trojan prince, son of Priam, took Helen from her husband Menelaus and thus caused the Trojan War
pariter *adv.* equally, side by side, alike
parō (1) prepare, make (ready)
pars, rtis *f.* part, portion, share, side
partior, īrī, ītus distribute, divide
parum *adv.* slightly, too little, not
parvulus, a, um tiny, very small, little
parvus, a, um small, little
pascor, ī, pāstus feed, graze
passim *adv.* everywhere, all about
pater, tris *m.* father, ancestor, sire
patior, ī, passus suffer, endure, allow
patria, ae *f.* homeland, country
patrius, a, um paternal, ancestral, native
patruus, ī *m.* paternal uncle
paucus, a, um little, few, light, scanty
pavor, ōris *m.* terror, shuddering, alarm
pāx, pācis *f.* peace, favor, grace, repose, quiet
pectus, oris *n.* breast, heart., soul
pecus, oris *n.* flock, herd, swarm
pecus, udis *f.* animal (of the flock)
pedes, itis *m.* foot soldier, infantry; foot-traveller; (person) on foot
pelagus, ī *n.* sea, flood, waves
penātēs, ium *m.* household gods
pendeō, ēre, pependī hang, depend
penetrālis, e inmost, interior
penitus *adv.* deep within, deeply, wholly
penna, ae *f.* wing, feather

per through, by (means of), over among, because of, during (*acc.*)
peragō, ere, ēgī, āctus accomplish, finish, traverse
pereō, īre, iī (īvī), itus perish, die
pererrō (1) wander through, traverse
perficiō, ere, fēcī, fectus finish, make
perfidus, a, um treacherous, perfidious
perflō (1) blow (over, through)
perfundō, ere, fūdī, fūsus soak, drench
Pergama, ōrum *n.* (citadel of) Troy
perhibeō, ēre, uī, itus present, say
perlābor, ī, lāpsus glide over
permittō, ere, mīsī, missus entrust, allow
pernīx, īcis active, nimble, swift
personō, āre, uī, itus sound through, make (re)sound
pēs, pedis *m.* foot; sheet-rope, sheet
petō, ere, īvī (iī), ītus seek, attack, aim (at), ask; scan
Phoenissa, ae *f.* Phoenician (woman), Dido
Phrygius, a, um Phrygian, Trojan
pietās, ātis *f.* loyalty, devotion, (sense of) duty, righteousness
piget, ēre, uit it displeases
pingō, ere, pīnxī, pictus paint, embroider
pinguis, e fat, fertile, rich
Pīrithoüs, ī *m.* Greek hero who descended to Hades with his friend Theseus to carry off Proserpina
pius, a, um devoted, loyal, righteous
placidus, a, um peaceful, calm, quiet
plācō (1) calm, quiet
plangor, ōris *m.* clamor, wailing, beating (of the breast), shriek
planta, ae *f.* heel; sole of foot
plēnus, a, um full, complete, swelling, filled
plūma, ae *f.* feather, plume
plūrēs *compar. of* **multus**
plūrimus *superl. of* **multus**
plūs *compar. of* **multus**
poena, ae *f.* punishment, penalty, satisfaction, revenge, vengeance
Poenus, a, um Phoenician, Carthaginian
polus, ī *m.* pole, sky, heaven
pondus, eris *n.* weight, burden
pōne *adv.* behind, after
pōnō, ere, posui, pos(i)tus put, place (aside); found, establish; bury

pontus, ī *m.* sea, waves
populō (1) devastate, plunder, ravage
populus, ī *m.* people, nation, crowd
porta, ae *f.* door, gate, entrance, exit, opening
portitor, ōris *m.* ferryman
portō (1) carry, bear, take, convey, bring
portus, ūs *m.* port, harbor, haven
possum, posse, potuī be able, can, avail
post after, behind (+ *acc.*); *adv.* afterward, next
posthabeō, ēre, uī, itus place after, esteem less
postquam after (that), when
potēns, entis powerful, ruling (+ *gen.*), mighty
potior, īrī, ītus possess, gain (+ *abl.*)
potior, ius preferable, better
praeceptum, ī *n.* advice, instruction
praeda, ae *f.* booty, spoils, prey
praemetuō, ere fear beforehand
praeruptus, a, um steep, towering
praesēns, entis present, instant
praesentiō, īre, sēnsī, sēnsus perceive first, suspect
praesēpe, is *n.* stall, hive
praestāns, antis excellent, superior, surpassing
praestō, āre, stitī, status (stitus) excel, be better, surpass
praetendō, ere, ī, ntus hold before, use as screen; stretch before, extend
praetereā *adv.* besides, also, furthermore, hereafter
praeterlābor, ī, lāpsus glide by
praetexō, ere, uī, xtus fringe, cloak
prāvum, ī *n.* wrong, perverse act
pre(he)ndō, ere, ī, nsus seize, grasp
premō, ere, pressī, pressus (re)press, control, overwhelm, crush
pretium, (i)ī *n.* price, reward, value
prex, precis *f.* (usually in pl.) prayer, entreaty, vow
Priamus, ī *m.* Priam, king of Troy
prīmō *adv.* at first, in the beginning
prīmus, a, um first, foremost, chief
prior, ius soon, former, first, prior
prīscus, a, um ancient, primitive
prīstinus, a, um ancient, former
prius *adv.* former(ly), sooner, first, before
prō instead of, on behalf of, for, before (+ *abl.*)
procāx, procācis bold, insolent, wanton

procella, ae *f.* blast, gale, gust
procul far, at a distance, (from) afar
profor, ārī, ātus speak (out), say
profugus, a, um exiled, fugitive
profundus, a, um deep, profound, vast
prōgeniēs, ēī *f.* offspring, progeny
prōgignō, ere, genuī, genitus bring forth, bear
prohibeō, ēre, uī, itus keep away, prevent, prohibit
prōlēs, is *f.* progeny, offspring
prōmereor, ērī, itus deserve, render service, merit, earn
prōnuba, ae *f.* matron of honor, bride's attendant
prōnus, a, um leaning forward, headlong
propāgō, inis *f.* offshoot, offspring, descendant, posterity
properō (1) hasten, hurry, speed
propinquō (1) approach, draw near (+ *dat.*)
propior, ius nearer, closer
proprius, a, um one's own, permanent, special
propter on account of, near (+ *acc.*)
prōra, ae *f.* prow (of a ship)
prōsequor, ī, secūtus follow, attend, escort
Prōserpina, ae *f.* wife of Pluto and queen of the underworld
prōspectus, ūs *m.* view
prōspiciō, ere, spexī, spectus look out on, see
prōtinus *adv.* continuously, at once, immediately
pudor, ōris *m.* shame, modesty, honor
puella, ae *f.* girl
puer, ī *m.* boy, child; slave
pugnus, ī *m.* fist
pulcher, chra, chrum beautiful, handsome, splendid, illustrious, noble
pulvis, pulveris *m.* dust
puppis, is *f.* stern; ship, vessel, galley
purpureus, a, um purple, crimson
pūrus, a, um pure, bright, clean, clear
putō (1) think, suppose, consider
Pygmaliōn, ōnis *m.* brother of Dido

Q

quā *adv.* where(by), wherever, in any (some) way
quaerō, ere, quaesīvī, quaesītus seek (in vain), miss, inquire, ask, try
quālis, e (such) as, of what sort
quam *adv.* how, than, as
quamquam although, and yet, however
quandō when, since, if ever, because
quantus, a, um how great, how much, how many, as much (as)
quassō (1) shake, shatter, toss
quater four times
quatiō, ere, quassus shake, shatter
-que and, also, even; **-que . . . -que** both . . . and
queō, quīre, īvī (iī), ītus be able, can
querēla, ae *f.* complaint, lament
queror, ī, questus complain, (be)wail
quī, quae, quod who, which, what, that
quia because, since
quīcumque, quaecumque, quodcumque whoever, whatever
quiēs, ētis *f.* quiet, rest, sleep, peace
quiēscō, ere, ēvī, ētus rest, calm, cease
quiētus, a, um quiet, serene, calm, peaceful
quīn that not, but that, why not, in fact
quippe *adv.* to be sure, surely, indeed, truly
Quirīnus, ī *m.* the deified Romulus, legendary founder of Rome, represented as god of war
quis (qua), quid, (quī, quae, quod) who? which? what? why? any, some(one)
quisquam, quaequam, quicquam any(one), any(thing)
quisquam, quicquam anyone, anything
quisquis, quidquid (quicquid) *indef. pron.*; **quisquis, quodquod** *indef. adj.* whoever, whatever
quō whither, where(fore), whereby
quōnam *adv.* whither, (to) where on earth
quondam (at) some time, formerly, ever
quoniam since, because
quoque *adv.* also, furthermore, even, too, likewise
quot as many as
quotiēns how often, as often as

R

rabidus, a, um raving, mad, frenzied
rabiēs, ēī *f.* rage, fury, frenzy, madness
radius, (i)ī *m.* rod. spoke, ray, compass
rāmus, ī *m.* branch, bough, limb

rapidus, a, um swift, snatching, whirling, consuming
rapiō, ere, uī, ptus snatch (up, away), seize, ravish; whirl
raptō (1) snatch, drag, carry off
raptum, ī *n.* plunder, prey, booty
rārus, a, um scattered, wide-meshed, far apart
ratis, is *f.* raft, ship, boat
raucus, a, um hoarse, sounding, clanging
re(l)liquiae, ārum *f.* remnants, relics, leavings, rest
rebellis, e rebellious, insurgent
recēdō, ere, cessī, cessus depart, withdraw
recēns, entis recent, fresh, new
recidīvus, a, um revived, renewed
recipiō, ere, cēpī, ceptus receive, accept, take back, recover
recubō (1) recline, lie
recūsō (1) refuse, decline, object
recutiō, ere, cussī, cussus strike (back), shake
redeō, īre, iī (īvī) itus return
redoleō, ēre, uī be fragrant, smell (of)
redūcō, ere, dūxī, ductus bring back, lead back
referō, ferre, tulī, lātus bear back, restore, carry off; reproduce, renew, re- call; relate, say (re)pay
refugiō, ere, fūgī flee, retreat, recoil, shun
refulgeō, ēre, lsī gleam, shine, glitter
refundō, ere, fūdī, fūsus pour (back, out)
rēgīna, ae *f.* queen; *adj.* royal
regiō, ōnis *f.* district, region, quarter
rēgnātor, ōris *m.* ruler, lord, director
rēgnō (1) rule, reign
rēgnum, ī *n.* royal power, kingdom, realm, rule, sway, sovereignty
regō, ere, rēxī, rēctus rule, guide, direct, control
relinquō, ere, līquī, lictus leave, desert, surrender, abandon, relinquish
rēmus, ī *m.* oar
repellō, ere, reppulī, repulsus drive back, repel, reject
reperiō, īre, repperī, repertus find (out)
repleō, ēre, ēvī, ētus fill, stuff
repōnō, ere, posuī, pos(i)tus replace, lay away, store (up), deposit, put (back, away)
rēs, reī *f.* thing, affair, matter, deed, fact, fortune; state, commonwealth

resīdō, ere, sēdī sit down
resistō, ere, stitī stop, resist (+ *dat.*)
resolvō, ere, ī, solūtus loose(n), free, pay, unravel
resonō (1) (re)sound, roar
respiciō, ere, spexī, spectus look (back) at, regard
respondeō, ēre, ī, ōnsus answer; sympathize with
restō, āre, stitī remain, be left
resurgō, ere, surrēxī, surrēctus rise again
revīsō, ere revisit, see again, return to
revocō (1) recall, call back, retrace, restore
revolvō, ere, ī, volūtus roll over, revolve
rēx, rēgis *m.* king; *adj.* ruling, royal
rīma, ae *f.* crack, fissure
rīmōsus, a, um leaky, full of cracks
rīpa, ae *f.* bank, shore
rōbur, oris *n.* oak; strength
rogus, ī *m.* (or **rogum, ī** *n.*) funeral pyre
Rōma, ae *f.* Rome, a city and empire
Rōmānus, a, um Roman, of Rome
Rōmulus, a, um of Romulus, Roman
rōscidus, a, um dewy
roseus, a, um rosy, pink
rota, ae *f.* wheel; chariot
rudēns, entis *m.* rope, cable
ruīna, ae *f.* downfall, ruin
rūmor, ōris *m.* rumor, report, gossip
rumpō, ere, rūpī, ruptus break, burst (forth), utter
ruō, ere, ī, ru(i)tus fall; rush; sink; plow
rūpēs, is *f.* rock, cliff, crag
rūrsus, um *adv.* again, anew, back(ward)
rūs, rūris *n.* country (district)

S

sacer, era, crum sacred, holy, consecrated; accursed; *n. subst.* sacrifice, holy implement (object); mystery
sacerdōs, dōtis *m. (f.)* priest(ess)
sacrō (1) hallow, consecrate, dedicate
saepe *adv.* often, frequently, again and again
saepiō, īre, psī, ptus hedge in, enclose
saeviō, īre, īvī (iī), ītus rage, storm, be fierce
saevus, a, um fierce, harsh, stern, cruel
sagitta, ae *f.* arrow
sal, salis *n. (m.)* salt (water), sea

saltem *adv.* at least, at any rate
saltus, ūs *m.* forest, glade, pasture; leap, bound, dancing
salum, ī *n.* sea, swell (of the sea)
salūs, ūtis *f.* safety, salvation, health
Samos, ī *f.* island of the Aegean, center of the worship of Juno
sānctus, a, um sacred, holy, revered
sanguineus, a, um bloody, blood-red
sanguis, inis *m.* blood; race, descendant
saniēs, ēī *f.* blood, gore
Sarpēdōn, onis *m.* Sarpedon, Lycian son of Jupiter and ally of the Trojans
sat(is) *adv.* enough, sufficient(ly)
satiō (1) satisfy, sate, satiate, glut
Sāturnia, ae *f.* Juno, daughter of Saturn, father of the gods
Sāturnius, a, um (born) of Saturn, father of Jupiter and Juno
saucius, a, um wounded, hurt
saxum, ī *n.* stone, rock, reef, cliff, crag
scaena, ae *f.* stage, background
Scaeus, a, um Scaean (referring to the name of a gate at Troy)
scandō, ere, ī, scānsus mount, climb
scelerātus, a, um criminal, wicked
scelus, eris *n.* crime, impiety
scēptrum, ī *n.* staff, scepter, power
scīlicet *adv.* of course, to be sure, doubtless
scindō, ere, scidī, scissus split, divide
scintilla, ae *f.* spark
sciō, īre, īvī (iī), ītus know (how), understand
scopulus, ī *m.* rock, cliff, crag
scūtum, ī *n.* shield
Scyllaeus, a, um of Scylla, a ravenous sea-monster, part woman and part sea creature, girdled with fierce dogs and destructive to mariners who attempted to sail past her cave situated on a narrow strait opposite the great whirlpool Charybdis
sēcessus, ūs *m.* inlet, recess
sēclūdō, ere, sī, sus shut off, seclude, part
secō, āre, uī, sectus cut, slice, cleave
sēcrētus, a, um remote, hidden, secret
secundus, a, um following, favorable, obedient
secūris, is *f.* axe

sed but, moreover, however
sedeō, ēre, sēdī, sessus sit (down), settle
sēdēs, is *f.* seat; abode, habitation; bottom; tomb, shrine; place, region
sedīle, is *n.* seat, bench
sēmianimis, e half-dead, dying
sēmita, ae *f.* path
sēmivir, virī half-man, effeminate
senātus, ūs *m.* senate, council of elders
senectūs, ūtis *f.* old age
senior, ōris *m.* old (aged) man, sire
sententia, ae *f.* opinion, purpose, view, resolve
sentiō, īre, sēnsī, sēnsus feel, perceive
sentus, a, um rough, thorny
sepeliō, īre, īvī (iī), pultus bury, inter
septem seven
sequor, ī, secūtus follow, attend, pursue, accompany, seek
serēnus, a, um serene, calm, fair, clear
Serestus, ī *m.* Trojan leader
Sergestus, ī *m.* Trojan leader
sermō, ōnis *m.* conversation, speech
serō, ere, sēvī, satus sow, beget
serpēns, entis *m.* (*f.*) serpent, snake
serpō, ere, psī, pstus creep (on), crawl
sertum, ī *n.* wreath, garland
servō (1) observe, watch; preserve, save, guard, keep, rescue; nurse
sī whether, if (only), in case that
sībilus, a, um hissing, whirring
Sibylla, ae *f.* the Sibyl, an ancient Italian prophetess
sīc thus, so, in this manner
Sīcania, ae *f.* Sicily, a large island south of Italy
siccō (1) dry, stanch
Siculus, a, um Sicilian, of Sicily, a large island south of Italy
Sīdonius, a, um of Sidon, a famous city of Phoenicia
sīdus, eris *n.* star, constellation, meteor; season, weather; heaven
signum, ī *n.* sign, signal, token, mark
sileō, ēre, uī be silent, be still
silex, icis *m.* (*f.*) flint, rock, crag
silva, ae *f.* forest, wood(s), tree(s)
similis, e like, similar (+ *dat.* or *gen.*)
Simoīs, entis *m.* river near Troy

simul at the same time, together; **simul (ac, atque)** as soon as
simulācrum, ī *n.* image, phantom, likeness, statue
simulō (1) pretend, imitate, feign
sīn if however, if on the contrary, but if
sine without (+ *abl.*)
singulī, ae, a each, one by one
sinō, ere, sīvī, situs permit, allow; desert
sinuō (1) fold, curve, twist, wind
sinus, ūs *m.* fold, bosom, bay, hollow, gulf
sistō, ere, stetī, status stand, stop, stay
situs, ūs *m.* position; neglect; decay
sīve, seu whether, or, either if, or if
socius, (i)ī *m.* ally, comrade, follower
socius, a, um allied, associated, friendly
sōl, sōlis *m.* sun; day; personified as **Sōl, Sōlis** *m.* sun-god
soleō, ēre, itus sum be accustomed
solium, (i)ī *n.* throne, seat
solum, ī *n.* ground, soil, earth
sōlus, a, um alone, only, lonely, sole
solvō, ere, ī, solūtus loose(n), release, break down, free, pay
Somnus, ī *m.* Sleep, Slumber personified as a divinity
sonitus, ūs *m.* sound, roar, crash, noise
sonmus, ī *m.* sleep, slumber, dream
sonō, āre, uī, itus (re)sound, roar
sonōrus, a, um roaring, howling
sopōrō (1) make drowsy, drug
sopōrus, a, um sleepy, causing slumber
soror, ōris *f.* sister
sors, rtis *f.* lot, destiny, portion, oracle, fate
spargō, ere, rsī, rsus scatter, sprinkle
Sparta, ae *f.* region of Greece, home of Helen and Menelaus
speciēs, ēī *f.* appearance, sight, aspect
spēlunca, ae *f.* cave, cavern, grotto
spernō, ere, sprēvī, sprētus scorn, reject, despise
spērō (1) hope (for, to), expect, suppose
spēs, eī *f.* hope, expectation
spīra, ae *f.* fold, coil, spire
spīritus, ūs *m.* breath, spirit, life, soul
spīrō (1) breathe (forth), blow, quiver (i.e., with signs of life), live

spolium, (i)ī *n.* hide (of an animal); commonly, in the *n. pl.*, spoils, arms stripped from an enemy, plunder
spōns, spontis *f.* wish, will, desire
spūma, ae *f.* foam, froth, spray
spūmō (1) foam, froth, spray
squāleō, ēre, uī be rough, be filthy
squāmeus, a, um scaly
stabilis, e firm, stable, lasting
stāgnum, ī *n.* still waters, depth
statuō, ere, uī, ūtus set (up), found, establish
stēllātus, a, um starred, star-spangled
sternō, ere, strāvī, strātus lay low, spread, strew
Sthenelus, ī *m.* Greek leader
stimulō (1) spur, goad, prick, incite
stīpō (1) stuff, crowd, throng, stow
stirps, pis *f.* stock, lineage, race
stō, āre, stetī, status stand (fast, up); halt; endure; stick (to), remain
strātum, ī *n.* bed, couch; pavement
strepitus, ūs *m.* uproar, noise
strīd(e)ō, ere (*or* **ēre**), **dī** grate, creak, whir, hiss, rustle, roar
strīdor, ōris *m.* noise, creaking, roar, grating, whirring
stringō, ere, strinxī, strictus graze
struō, ere, strūxī, strūctus build, plan, contrive
studium, (i)ī *n.* eagerness, desire, zeal, pursuit
stuppeus, a, um (of) flax or hemp (used in the production of rope)
Stygius, a, um Stygian, of the Styx, a river in Hades
sub (from) under, close (to), beneath, (deep) in, after (*acc., abl.*)
subdūcō, ere, dūxī, ductus take away, remove, beach, bring out of water
subeō, īre, īvī (iī), itus go under, bear; approach, enter; arise (*dat.*)
subiciō, ere, iēcī, iectus place under (+ *dat.*), vanquish
subigō, ere, ēgī, āctus push, force; subdue
subitō *adv.* suddenly
subitus, a, um sudden, unexpected
sublātus, a, um *see* **tollō**
subnectō, ere, nex(u)ī, nexus tie (beneath), fasten
subolēs, is *f.* offspring, progeny, child

subrigō, ere, surrēxī, rēctus raise, rise
subsistō, ere, stitī halt, stop, withstand, resist
subter beneath, below
subtrahō, ere, trāxī, tractus withdraw
subvectō (1) bear, convey, transport
subvolvō, ere, ī, volūtus roll up
sūdō (1) sweat, perspire
suetulī *see* **tollō**
sufficiō, ere, fēcī, fectus supply, suffuse; be sufficient
suī (of) himself, herself, itself, themselves; him, her, it, them
sulcus, ī *m.* furrow, trench, ditch
sum, esse, fuī, futūrus be, exist
summergō (subm–), ere, rsī, rsus sink, drown
summoveō, ēre, mōvī, mōtus remove
summus *superl. of* **superus**
sūmō, ere, mpsī, mptus take, assume; (+ **poenam**) exact (a penalty)
super above, beyond, left, in addition, upon, concerning, about (*acc., abl.*)
superbia, ae *f.* loftiness, haughtiness, pride, arrogance
superbus, a, um proud, haughty
superēmineō, ēre tower above
superō (1) surmount, surpass, overcome, survive
superus, a, um upper, higher, above; *subst.* god, divinity
supīnus, a, um flat, upturned
supplex, icis *m. (f.)* suppliant; *adj.* suppliant, humble
suprā above, over (+ *acc.*)
suprēmus, a, um *superl. of* **superus**
surgō, ere, surrēxī, surrēctus raise, (a)rise, spring up, surge
suscipiō, ere, cēpī, ceptus take up, beget, bear, receive, catch (up)
suscitō (1) arouse, stir up, excite
suspendō, ere, ī, ēnsus suspend, hang (up)
suspiciō, ere, spexī, spectus look from beneath, suspect, look up at
sūtilis, e sewn, with seams
suus, a, um his, her, its, their (own)
Sȳchaeus, ī *m.* deceased husband of Dido
Syrtis (or **syrtis**), **is** *f.* region of quicksand on the northern coast of Africa; sand bar, reef

T

tābeō, ēre drip, soak, melt, waste
tabula, ae *f.* plank, board
tacitus, a, um silent, noiseless, secret, still
taeda, ae *f.* (bridal) torch, pinewood torch
tālis, e such, of such sort, the following
tam *adv.* so (much), such, as
tamen *adv.* nevertheless, however, but
tandem at length, finally; pray
tangō, ere, tetigī, tāctus touch, reach
tantum *adv.* so much, so great(ly), only
tantus, a, um so great, so much, so far
Tartareus, a, um of or concerning Tartarus, abode of the wicked and impious in Hades
taurus, ī *m.* bull, ox, bullock
tēctum, ī *n.* roof; house, home, abode
tegō, ere, tēxī, tēctus cover, hide, protect
tēla, ae *f.* web, textile
tellūs, ūris *f.* earth, land, country
tēlum, ī *n.* weapon; wound, blow
temnō, ere scorn, disdain, despise
temperō (1) control, restrain, refrain, calm
tempestās, ātis *f.* tempest, storm; time
templum, ī *n.* temple, sanctuary, sacred space, shrine
temptō (1) try, test, seek, examine, attempt
tempus, oris *n.* time; occasion, crisis
tenāx, ācis tenacious, holding (to)
tendō, ere, tetendī, tentus stretch; hasten, strive, (ex) tend, aim; tent
Tenedos, ī *f.* small island near Troy
teneō, ēre, uī, tus have, hold, restrain
tenuis, e slight, thin, fine, delicate
ter three times
tergum, ī *n.* back, body, rear, hide (of an animal)
terō, ere, trīvī, trītus rub, wear, waste
terra, ae *f.* earth, land, country, soil
terreō, ēre, uī, itus frighten, terrify
terrificō (1) frighten, terrify, alarm
territō (1) frighten, terrify, alarm
tertius, a, um third
testor, ārī, ātus call to witness, swear by, testify
Teucrus, a, um Teucrian, Trojan
thalamus, ī *m.* marriage chamber, bedroom

theātrum, ī *n.* theater

Thēseus, eī (eos), *acc.* **ea** *m.* mythical king of Athens, who, among his other exploits, descended to Hades with his friend Pirithoüs to carry off Proserpina.

Thyias, adis *f.* Bacchant, a woman devotee of the worship of Bacchus

thymum, ī *n.* thyme, a flowering plant

Tiberīnus, a, um of the Tiber, an Italian river on which Rome is situated

Tiberīnus, ī *m.* (god of) the Tiber, river on which Rome is situated

timeō, ēre, uī fear, dread, be anxious

timor, ōris *m.* fear, anxiety, dread

tollō, ere, sustulī, sublātus lift, raise, upheave, stir up; remove, destroy

torqueō, ēre, rsī, rtus twist, sway, hurl, turn

torreō, ēre, uī, tostus parch, roast

torus, ī *m.* (banqueting, funeral) couch, bed

torvus, a, um fierce, grim, lowering

tot so many, as many

totidem as many, so many

totiēns so often, so many times

tōtus, a, um all, every, whole, full

trabs (trabēs), trabis *f.* beam, timber, tree

trahō, ere, trāxī, tractus drag (out), draw (in), lead, protract, spend

trāiciō, ere, iēcī, iectus throw across, pierce

tranquillus, a, um tranquil, calm

trāns across, beyond (+ *acc.*)

trānsfīgō, ere, xī, xus pierce, transfix

trānsmittō, ere, mīsī, missus cross, send across

trānsportō (1) carry across, transport

tremefaciō, ere, fēcī, factus make tremble, appall, alarm

tremō, ere, uī tremble, quiver, shake

trepidus, a, um trembling, excited

trēs, tria three

tridēns, entis *m.* trident, symbol of Neptune as god of the sea

trietēricus, a, um triennial

trifaux, faucis three-throated

Trīnacrius, a, um Trinacrian, Sicilian

trīstis, e sad, unhappy, dreary, fatal

Trītōn, ōnis *m.* a minor sea-god known for his skill in blowing a conch (sea shell) as a trumpet

Trītōnis, idis *f.* Minerva, goddess of wisdom and the arts

Trītōnius, a, um Tritonian (an epithet of Minerva)

triumphus, ī *m.* triumph, victory

Troia, ae *f.* Troy, a city of Asia Minor

Troiānus, a, um Trojan, of Troy

Trōius, a, um Trojan, of Troy

Trōs, Trōis *m.* Trojan

tū, tuī (*pl.* **vōs, vestrum**) you

tueor, ērī, itus (tūtus) watch, look at, protect, eye

tulī *see* **ferō**

tum, tunc then, at that time; further

tumeō, ēre, uī swell, be swollen

tumidus, a, um swollen, swelling

tumultus, ūs *m.* tumult, uprising, clamor

tumulus, ī *m.* hill, mound, tomb

turba, ae *f.* mob, crowd

turbidus, a, um troubled, agitated

turbō (1) throw into confusion, agitate, confuse, shake, disturb

turbō, inis *m.* whirl(wind, pool), storm

turpis, e shameful, disgraceful

turris, is *f.* tower, turret

tūtus, a, um protected, safe, secure

tuus, a, um your(s), your own

Tȳdīdēs, ae *m.* son of Tydeus, Diomedes, who fought against Aeneas in single combat before Troy and would have killed him had Venus not spirited her son away

Tyndaris, idis *f.* daughter of Tyndarus, Helen

tyrannus, ī *m.* ruler, chieftain, tyrant

Tyrius, a, um Tyrian, Carthaginian

Tyrrhēnus, a, um Tyrrhenian, of Etruria, a district of northwestern Italy

Tyrus (os), ī *f.* city of Phoenicia, birthplace of Dido

U

ūber, eris *n.* udder, breast; (symbol of) fertility

ubi where, when, as soon as

ulcīscor, ī, ultus avenge, punish

Ulixēs, is (eī, ī) *m.* Odysseus, the wily Greek leader who is the central character in Homer's *Odyssey* (his name in Latin is **Ulixes**, or Ulysses)

ūllus, a, um any, any one

ulterior, ius farther, further, beyond

ultimus, a, um last, final, farthest
ultrā more than (+ *acc.*); *adv.* beyond, farther
ultrīx, īcis avenging, vengeful
ultrō *adv.* further, voluntarily
ululātus, ūs *m.* wail, shriek, howl, shout
ululō (1) howl, wail, shout, shriek
ulva, ae *f.* sedge, marsh grass
umbra, ae *f.* shade, shadow, ghost
umbrifer, era, erum shady
ūmēns, entis moist, dewy, damp
umerus, ī *m.* shoulder
ūmidus, a, um moist, damp, dewy
umquam *adv.* ever, at any time
ūnā *adv.* together, at the same time
uncus, a, um curved, bent, hooked
unda, ae *f.* wave, billow, water, sea
unde from where, from which source
undique *adv.* everywhere, from all sides
undo (1) swell, roll, wave
undōsus, a, um billowing, wavy
unguis, is *m.* nail, claw
ūnus, a, um one, only, alone, single
urbs, urbis *f.* city, town
urgeō, ēre, ursī drive, force, press
ut(ī) as, when; that, so that; how
uterque, utraque, utrumque each (of two), both
uterus, ī *m.* belly, womb
utinam *adv.* oh that!, I wish that!
ūtor, ī, ūsus use, employ (+ *abl.*)
uxōrius, a, um wife-ruled, uxorious

V

vadum, ī *n.* shallow(s), shoal, depth(s)
vagor, ārī, ātus wander, roam, rove
valeō, ēre, uī be strong, avail, be able, fare well
validus, a, um strong, mighty, sturdy
vallis, is *f.* valley, vale, dale
vānus, a, um vain, idle, empty, useless, false
varius, a, um varied, different, diverse, manifold
vastus, a, um desolate, vast, enormous
vatēs, is *m.* (*f.*) prophet, seer, bard
-ve, vel or, either, even; **vel . . . vel** either . . . or
vectō (1) convey, carry, bear
vehō, ere, vēxī, vectus carry, convey
velim, velle, vellem *see* **volo**
vēlō (1) veil, cover, deck, clothe
vēlōx, ōcis swift, quick, rapid, fleet
vēlum, ī *n.* cloth, canvas, sail
velut(ī) (even) as, just as
venēnum, ī *n.* poison, venom, drug
venerābilis, e venerable, causing awe
veniō, īre, vēnī, ventus come, go
ventus, ī *m.* wind, breeze, blast, air
Venus, eris *f.* goddess of love and beauty, love
vērō *adv.* truly, indeed, but
verrō, ere, ī, versus sweep (over)
versō (1) keep turning, roll, revolve
vertex, icis *m.* peak, summit, head, top; whirlpool
vertō, ere, ī, rsus (over)turn, (ex)change
vērum, ī *n.* truth, right, reality; *adv.* but
vērus, a, um true, real, genuine, honest
vēscor, ī use as food, feed upon, eat (+ *abl.*)
Vesta, ae *f.* goddess of the hearth
vester, tra, trum your(s), your own
vestīgium, (i)ī *n.* track, footprint, step, trace
vestis, is *f.* garment, cloth(ing), robe
vetō, āre, uī, itus forbid, prevent
vetus, eris old, aged, ancient, former
via, ae *f.* way, road, journey, street
vibrō (1) quiver, vibrate, dart
victor, ōris *m.* victor; *adj.* victorious
victōria, ae *f.* victory, conquest, triumph
videō, ēre, vīdī, vīsus see, perceive; *pass.* be seen, appear, seem (best)
vigeō, ēre, uī flourish, be strong, thrive
vigil, īlis *m.* (*f.*) guard, watchman, sentinel; *adj.* wakeful, watchful, sleepless
vinc(u)lum, ī *n.* chain, bond, cable
vincō, ere, vīcī, victus conquer, surpass
vīnum, ī *n.* wine
vir, ī *m.* (real) man; hero; husband
vīrēs *pl. of* **vīs**
virga, ae *f.* staff, wand, twig
virgō, inis *f.* girl, maid(en)
viridis, e green, fresh, vigorous
virtūs, ūtis *f.* manliness, excellence in battle, valor
vīs, vīs *f.* force, violence, energy

vīsus, ūs *m.* sight, view, vision, aspect
vīta, ae *f.* life, soul, spirit
vitta, ae *f.* fillet, garland, band
vīvus, a, um living, natural, alive
vix scarcely, feebly, with difficulty
vocō (1) call, name, address, convoke, invoke, invite, challenge
volitō (1) fly, speed, flit, flutter
volō (1) fly, move with speed
volō, velle, voluī will, wish, be willing
volūmen, inis *n.* fold, coil, roll
volūtō (1) revolve, turn (over), roll, ponder
volvō, ere, ī, volūtus revolve, (un)roll roll (round, through); undergo
vorō (1) swallow (up)
vōx, cis *f.* voice, word, speech, sound
vulgus, ī *n. (m.)* crowd, throng, herd
vulnus, eris *n.* wound, deadly blow
vultus, ūs *m.* countenance, face, aspect

Z
Zephyrus, ī *m.* (west) wind

ERRATA

The following errata pertain to the 2012 printing of *A Vergil Workbook, Second Edition* student version.

Page		For	Read
x	III	Questions	Exercises
x	VIb	Figures . . . Devices	Literary Style
68	#2	*exhalentem*	*exhalantem*
82	#29	no line refs	(line 198) for both choices
85	#4	cāē	cāē
	#5	Māē	Māē
105	#2	Troy	Carthage
114	#24 c	Charon	*Charon*
130	2nd citation	Book 4.450–455	Book 6.450–455
	Essay 2 prompt	*Aeneid.*	*Aeneid* and is emotionally moved.
172	#2	no line refs	(line 1) for choices a, b, c
173	#8 d	*Brittana*	*Britanna*
Vocabulary		Please note that the vocabulary is missing some entries and has other entries that are not needed for the Latin in the workbook. The more complete vocabulary is posted online at http://www.bolchazy.com/pdf/vergilworkbookvocab.pdf